DEBATING GOD'S ECONOMY

DEBATING GOD'S ECONOMY

Social Justice in America on the Eve of Vatican II

CRAIG R. PRENTISS

THE PENNSYLVANIA STATE UNIVERSITY PRESS
UNIVERSITY PARK, PENNSYLVANIA

Library of Congress
Cataloging-in-Publication Data

Prentiss, Craig R.
Debating God's economy : social justice in America
on the eve of Vatican II / Craig R. Prentiss.
    p.   cm.
Includes bibliographical references and index.
ISBN-13: 978-0-271-03341-9 (cloth : alk. paper)
1. Distributive justice—Religious aspects—Catholic Church.
2. Distributive justice—United States.
3. Labor economics—United States.
4. Social justice—Religious aspects—Catholic Church.
5. Catholic Church—Doctrines.
I. Title.

BX1795.D59P74 2007
261.80973—dc22
2007042088

Copyright © 2008
The Pennsylvania State University
All rights reserved
Printed in the United States of America
Published by The Pennsylvania State
University Press,
University Park, PA 16802-1003

The Pennsylvania State University Press
is a member of the Association of
American University Presses.

It is the policy of The Pennsylvania State University
Press to use acid-free paper. This book is printed on
Natures Natural, containing 50% post-consumer waste,
and meets the minimum requirements of American
National Standard for Information Sciences—
Permanence of Paper for Printed Library Material,
ANSI Z39.48–1992.

FOR SHANA

Contents

List of Acronyms ix

Acknowledgments xi

Introduction 1

1) The Encyclicals 17

2) Sanctifying Life on the Land 39

3) Sanctifying Industrial Labor 83

4) Sanctifying American Capitalism 143

5) Catholics and Right-to-Work Laws 175

6) Industry Councils 199

Conclusion 237

Bibliography 245

Index 261

Acronyms

ACTU	Association of Catholic Trade Unionists
ACUA	American Catholic History Research Center and University Archives
CBPM	Council of Business and Professional Men of the Catholic Faith
CW	Catholic Worker
FUA	Fordham University Archives
MUA	Marquette University Archives
NCRLC	National Catholic Rural Life Conference
NCWC	National Catholic Welfare Conference
RUA	Rockhurst University Archives
SAD	Social Action Department of the National Catholic Welfare Conference
UNDA	University of Notre Dame Archives
YCW	Young Christian Workers

Acknowledgments

This project has followed a long and winding path. It grew out of research initiated over a decade ago, but as with many long-term endeavors, my passion for the material waxed and waned. I was excited by other projects that have taken me in different directions, and it appeared for some time that I would leave this material behind. But as I became more engaged in assessing theoretical perspectives in religious studies—an interest that seemed to spring out of necessity while reflecting on what it means to teach religion in a college classroom—the characters and stories that had been so alive to me in my early research kept creeping back into my head. Only now I had new questions to ask about those characters and stories—questions about how arguments are made, how persuasion takes place, how communities are imagined, and how authority is generated and used. With a new perspective, I began the process of slowly revisiting my research with the hope that it might someday be a book. Plenty of things slowed me down, but I could not be more content with where the road has taken me.

In the course of working on this book for many years now, dozens of people have contributed to its publication. The seeds of this project were planted in conversations with Martin Marty, whose encouragement and wisdom have been a constant for well over a decade now. The advice and criticism of Bernard McGinn and Martin Riesebrodt were valuable, as was the time-saving advice of R. Scott Appleby. Were it not for Scott, I would never have completed this book.

Among the people whose help has stood out, I want to thank Joie Cowan, Patricia Beckman, Joann Maguire, Bill Stancil, Russell McCutcheon, Pete Bicak, Joann Spillman, Colleen McDannell, Dan Martin, Phillip M. Runkel of Marquette University Archives, the staffs at the Catholic

University of America Archives, University of Notre Dame Archives, and Fordham University Archives, as well as Ed Kos at the Rockhurst University Archives. Librarians are the researcher's best friends, and in my case this was no exception. The staff of the Rockhurst University Greenlease Library, especially Verna Rutz, Laurie Hathman, Jeanne Langdon, and Kim Cullinan, were instrumental to my completing this book. I would like to thank the librarians at the University of Chicago, the New York Public Library, Marquette University, Conception Seminary College, DePaul University, and Loyola University-Chicago, as well. Janet Kalven of Grailville was a big help with my chapter on rural life, as was Jeffrey Marlett. Msgr. George Higgins generously took the time to talk to me, and John Cort allowed me to pick through his memories over the phone. A summer research grant from Rockhurst University funded some valuable trips to archives in New York City and Washington, D.C. I am also very thankful for two excellent anonymous outside readers provided by Penn State University Press, and for all of the folks at the Press who worked so hard to finish this book.

In the summer of 2005, my most valuable critic and one of my dearest friends, Peter D'Agostino, was senselessly killed just blocks from his home in Chicago. Peter always managed to rip my work to shreds while still making me feel like I had accomplished something great. He was a natural teacher, and he was my mentor. Were it not for the countless hours spent talking to Peter about this project over the years, it simply would never have been finished.

My parents, Brett and Branca Prentiss, and my sister, Laura, have grown quite tired of hearing about this project. For their love and patience, I am forever grateful. My sons, Benjamin and Cole, made certain that every time I sat down to read or write for this book, I have been on the verge of falling asleep. But every moment of exhaustion has been worth it, and they continue to be the sun and the moon and all of the stars to me. Shana, the cosmos that houses these celestial beings, and houses my heart as well, deserves my greatest thanks. I dedicate this book to her.

Introduction

In March 1878, an eyewitness to the coronation of Pope Leo XIII provided this vivid description of the atmosphere that permeated the scene:

> The darkness of the place, the limited company, the air of effacement and almost mystery—everything led our thoughts back to the first enthronement of Popes in the Catacombs. Pius IX [Leo's predecessor] had left an abounding fame and a great void: the despoiled Papacy seemed to have engulfed with him. The heir without a heritage who was shown to us, had a look of weakness, and his title to renown was still discussed. His coronation seemed the *simulacrum* of vanished realities, the elevation of a phantom. And these were the years when the shadow of the cross on the world was growing less.[1]

The gloom characterizing this account of Leo XIII's enthronement reflected the state of the Roman Catholic Church during an age in which, as the historian Carleton J. H. Hayes once described, the Church was "losing [a] feud with the whole modern world, intellectually, politically, and morally."[2] But it was Leo XIII who began to turn around the fortunes of the Church, largely by engaging the great issues of his day, especially the industrial revolution, class conflict, and the rise of both Marxist and capitalist ideologies. His most significant contribution to this debate was the 1891 encyclical *Rerum Novarum*, a document that

---

1. Vicomte de Vogue, quoted in John Ireland's eulogy in "Leo XIII, His Work and Influence," *North American Review* 177 (September 1903): 325.
2. Carleton J. H. Hayes, *A Generation of Materialism, 1871–1900*, 2nd ed. (New York: Harper and Row, 1947), 141–42; cited in Lillian Parker Wallace, *Leo XIII and the Rise of Socialism* (Durham, N.C.: Duke University Press, 1966), 82.

set the stage for dozens of official pronouncements generated by the Vatican on the economy and society for over a century.

In the years following *Rerum Novarum,* the seemingly all-encompassing term "Catholic social thought" came into frequent use. The phrase served primarily as shorthand for Catholic commentary and action regarding economics, the social order, and the notion of "justice," particularly when applied to labor, property rights, commodity distribution, and tensions between the poor and the wealthy. Social thought was set in contrast to conceptions of justice relating strictly to the individual—individualism that appeared to be the focus of the ascendant liberal worldview.

Catholic social thought in America is the subject of this book. It describes Roman Catholics in the United States in the last generation before the Second Vatican Council who were bound by their self-conscious attempts to articulate and institute conceptions of a "just" and authentically Christian social order in the American context. These Catholics were in dialogue with theology generated by the magisterium of the Church and, in many cases, they were also in dialogue with one another. This time frame, between the Great Depression and 1962, encompassed a profound transition in the American economy as well as in the social status of Roman Catholics in the United States. Nearly all previous histories of Catholic engagement with economics in the United States have been directed primarily to either the pre–World War II years or the post–Vatican II years. The chronological gap may reflect a sense among historians that the Catholic mission to transform the American economic order lost considerable steam in these two intervening decades. It is precisely this transitional quality that interests me.[3]

I hope to accomplish three things. First, I want to tell a story about a collection of men and women who were passionately committed to improving their society by bringing the teachings of the Roman Catholic Church to bear on its economy. Like all stories about real people and real events, not everyone or every group is covered. But those that are covered go far toward illustrating both the intensity of activity among American Catholics engaged in economic debates, as well as the remarkable

---

3. Though this study makes no claim to being a comprehensive account of American Catholic economic thought during those decades, I believe that it is the most detailed study to date. "Taming Leviathan: The American Catholic Church and Economics, 1940–1960," 2 vols. (Ph.D. diss., University of Chicago, 1997), has been substantially revised in the making of this book.

range of perspectives reflected in their rendering of papal teaching. That their conclusions regarding those teachings often pitted them in rhetorical battle with one another should not detract from the fact that these were sincere people who in many cases devoted their lives to the pursuit of justice, however differently conceived. Armed with little more than their convictions and persuasive skills, their struggles played out in the pages of Catholic periodicals, on factory floors, in farming communities, in classrooms, in congressional hearing rooms, and at times behind the pulpit.

My second aim is methodological. When I began researching the interaction between Catholic thought and economic rhetoric, I was struck by how difficult it was to find secondary sources that did not privilege particular approaches to economics in their selection of data. These economic perspectives, moreover, appeared deeply interwoven with the religious values of the authors, values that were almost always implicit and often explicit in their writings. Scholarship on this topic has been the domain of those invested in promoting a normative Catholic perspective on justice.

This book suggests a way of redescribing the history of Catholic social thought that has its roots in the field of religious studies. I believe this approach helps avoid the trap of theologizing history by promoting particular readings of "true justice" or an "authentically Catholic" social order. Using a method of cultural analysis that takes *myth* as its central descriptive category, this study looks at how the two texts that dominated the framework of Catholic economic discourse before Vatican II, *Rerum Novarum* and *Quadragesimo Anno*, were received by Catholic activists and commentators. While I will say more about this method below, I believe this approach succeeds in steering clear of the sort of intra-Catholic polemics widespread within this field of study. Avoiding these polemics will give outsiders to Catholicism an easier entryway to both the primary sources of Catholic social thought as well as the secondary literature. More important, for Catholics and non-Catholics alike, it will clarify the dynamics of the pre–Vatican II American Catholic community with respect to these issues in a way that better enables connections to be drawn to other American subgroups tackling similar questions during this time. Perhaps it will even engender reflection among historians and religious studies scholars as to how they present the data of the Catholic world in their own work and the extent to which their histories replicate their theologies.

My last objective is to advance the cause of integrating the history of Catholicism in America with the larger body of work exploring American culture from both historical and religious studies perspectives. I believe that the kind of advocacy scholarship noted above can impede that goal. At times, "insider" histories employ categories and methods shaped by questions accessible only to participants in their distinctive theological universes. Even the best histories in this field have been engaged in advocating a preferred reading of Catholic economic teaching. Aaron I. Abell's 1963 study, *American Catholicism and Social Action: A Search for Social Justice, 1865–1950*, was not only the first survey of U.S. Catholic engagement in economic issues but also the source of the standard chronology for nearly every narrative of preconciliar American Catholic economic thought that followed. But Abell distinguished his work by claiming a "social justice approach" to history.[4] While depicting Catholic disagreements on how to attain "justice," justice itself appeared, for Abell, to correspond to a reality grounded in an almost self-evident natural order. On occasion, he would venture into the realm of theology when assessing policy positions "from a social justice point of view," and he did not hesitate to declare certain perspectives "wrongly" or "rightly" conceived.[5]

The heart of David O'Brien's thesis in *American Catholics and Social Reform: The New Deal Years* (1968) was that the social encyclicals were subject to multiple readings. But as nuanced and attentive to the

---

4. Aaron I. Abell, *American Catholicism and Social Action: A Search for Social Justice, 1865–1950* (Notre Dame, Ind.: University of Notre Dame Press, 1963), 7.

5. Like all abstract categories, the concept of justice, as Aristotle noted in *Nicomachean Ethics*, is ultimately ineffable. The contours of any individual's understanding of justice are shaped by the particularities of that person's sociohistorical position. Though most of us attempt to universalize individual applications of the concept in our daily lives, these attempts must be viewed as venturing into the metaphysical territory of philosophy or theology. David Mapel's account of debates between two philosophers of social justice, Ronald Dworkin and Michael Walzer, is instructive in the manner with which most who invoke justice "ignore the inevitable indeterminacy of their subject matter and deny the role of politics in providing answers where philosophy cannot." Although a skillful historian, Abell's usage of "justice" in his history rendered him a player in the intra-Catholic struggle to establish a normative reading of justice in the Catholic context. See *American Catholicism and Social Action*, 266; examples in Abell's writing include: "[Coughlin] *wrongly* restricted the vocational group plan or the guild system to labor unions and relied on compulsory arbitration to secure peace and justice in the industrial field" (240, emphasis added), and "Not all persons *recognized* that a *rightly* organized Industry Council involved more than a device for union-management co-operation" (268, emphasis added). On the contest over "justice," see David Mapel, *Social Justice Reconsidered: The Problem of Appropriate Precision in a Theory of Justice* (Urbana: University of Illinois Press, 1989), 152.

diversity of Catholic thinking as O'Brien managed to be, the book was still a celebration of post–Vatican II Catholicism. By arguing for fuller Catholic engagement in the economic and social issues of the American scene with a preference for government regulation and a security network for the working class, the book constituted a call for resistance to the perceived comfort and allure of the Catholic "ghetto."[6] In contrast, Kevin Schmiesing's *Within the Market Strife: American Catholic Economic Thought from "Rerum Novarum" to Vatican II* (2004) sought to be a corrective to the predominantly liberal/pro-labor perspective of most work in the field. Where O'Brien's depiction of a figure like Msgr. John Ryan tended toward the heroic, Schmiesing used Ryan as his foil in casting the "Right Reverend New Dealer"—as Father Charles Coughlin famously labeled him—to have been following his own reckless agenda and being too closely linked to party politics. Where O'Brien celebrates liberal Catholic activists, Schmiesing tells the story as if they were largely inconsequential to a Catholic social teaching more easily aligned with conservative economic views.[7] These observations are not meant to

---

6. For instance, O'Brien engages in his own theologizing when he writes, "When the Church is seen as the only link between spheres of nature and grace . . . when it is viewed as having a monopoly of the means of divine assistance, then Catholicism easily deteriorates into ideology, presenting a rationale for ecclesiastical interests." See *American Catholics and Social Reform: The New Deal Years* (New York: Oxford University Press, 1968), 4. Though O'Brien maintained that such "deteriorat[ion]" was common in the 1930s, his story pointed to "signs of a new maturity" that had begun to show themselves three decades later—a maturity that presumably came into fuller bloom with the postconciliar age. Though never succumbing to hagiography, his tale was still replete with heroes (John Ryan, Dorothy Day, George Shuster, Robert C. Pollock) and villains (Patrick Scanlan, Father Coughlin). These characters and others, while examined critically, were employed as representations of that latent "maturity" and stodgy parochialism pitted against one another in an evolutionary tale moving toward a "Catholic Church [that] could offer far more space, far more depth, and far more freedom than Americans, including Catholics, had suspected" (O'Brien, *American Catholics and Social Reform*, 226–27). O'Brien has never been shy about lending his politically and theologically progressive voice to internal Catholic dialogue. His 1972 treatise, *The Renewal of American Catholicism* (New York: Paulist Press), with its call for a more hands-off approach by the bishops toward the development of American Catholic culture and greater lay autonomy, signaled with flair O'Brien's location on the Catholic left.

7. Schmiesing's book covers much of the same time frame as this study, but with a different objective. Committed to exploring the diversity of Catholic economic thought with an awareness that "factors other than the authors' adherence to the authoritative social teaching of their Church" played a central role in their writings on economics, Schmiesing sets out to tell the story of these economic debates in a manner that, he admits, "does not aspire to be comprehensive." Schmiesing is, in a sense, opening space for marginalized perspectives within the "canon" of Catholic social thought, which is vital to a more comprehensive understanding of history. But a methodological problem arises when neither the title nor the introduction reveals that Schmiesing's survey is really a history of *conservative*

detract from the value of the work done by Abell, O'Brien, or Schmiesing; rather they are meant to indicate that even the best histories in the field have sought to advance a reading of Church teaching colored by their own theologies of social justice.

By far, the most common treatments of Catholic social thought have quite self-consciously advanced particular economic perspectives as more authentically Catholic. Here, history is openly brought to the service of promoting political agendas favorable to either free markets or more collectivist stances typical of liberation theologies. Michael Warner's *Changing Witness: Catholic Bishops and Public Policy, 1917–1994* (1995) is a call for restoring Thomism to its centrality in American Catholic thinking (a move Warner contends will engender greater sympathy to capitalism).[8] The scholarship of "neoconservative" Catholics like Michael Novak has tried to push "normative" Roman Catholic thought in the direction of embracing a "free market" as the surest means to social justice.[9] On the left wing, advocacy histories are just as common, though

---

Catholic thought on economics (though certainly a valuable one). For instance, the conservative Edward Keller is presented as the wise centrist. The Bishops' Program of 1919 (a set of policy recommendations typically lauded by those on the political left) is rendered ideologically and theologically suspect and not as reflective of the bishops' authentic voice as their more moderate pastoral letter of the same year. The labor movement is scarcely mentioned, and the work of the labor sympathizer Msgr. George Higgins—perhaps the most ubiquitous figure in these public debates by the 1950s—is reduced to one mention with no commentary. In shaping the intra-Catholic debate, Schmiesing is not interested in openly attacking liberal Catholic social activists. Instead, his rendering of history tells the story as if the liberals were minor players, with the occasional anomaly of a figure like John Ryan creeping into the picture. Kevin E. Schmiesing, *Within the Market Strife: American Catholic Economic Thought from "Rerum Novarum" to Vatican II* (Lanham, Md.: Lexington Books, 2004), esp. xiii, xv, 29–31, 41–46, 67–72, 85–94, 102–4, and 143.

8. *Changing Witness* aimed to illustrate the "failure" of the American Church to exert moral leadership on economic issues (and other topics of social import) as a result of its having largely abandoned Thomistic natural-law theology as its guiding principle. Instead, Warner saw the American hierarchy succumb to the pressures of liberation theologians and others on the left wing in presenting a vision of economic justice that was, in Warner's view, incoherent and unworkable. Warner accused the American bishops of failing to follow the guidance of Pope John Paul II, whose economic positions, according to Warner's reading, were friendlier to market-based solutions to social ills. See Michael Warner, *Changing Witness: Catholic Bishops and Public Policy, 1917–1994* (Washington, D.C.: Ethics and Public Policy Center; Grand Rapids, Mich.: William B. Eerdmans, 1995).

9. George Weigel has grouped Novak—along with Richard John Neuhaus and Weigel himself—as a "neoconservative." Weigel distinguishes them from the "Catholic right" by their openness to modernity and their embracing of Vatican II. See George Weigel, "The Neoconservative Difference: A Proposal for the Renewal of Church and Society," in *Being Right: Conservative Catholics in America*, ed. Mary Jo Weaver and R. Scott Appleby (Bloomington: Indiana University Press, 1995), 138–40. Michael Novak has made a career arguing

instead of promoting market-friendly interpretations of Church teachings, they critique them. Joseph Gremillion's *Gospel of Peace and Justice: Catholic Social Teaching Since Pope John* (1976) combined a collection of social justice documents with historical theology and a "call for deeper theological reflection." For Gremillion, this meant authorizing a view of economic justice that questioned capitalism and saw Western social systems as promoting inequality and oppression.[10] Marvin Krier Mich's *Catholic Social Teaching and Movements* (1998) combines historical overview with theological primer in sympathy with liberation theology, and yet another vision of an authentic reading of Catholic social teaching is born. Where John Paul II is the hero of Michael Warner's story, in Mich's, he is an inconsistent and troublesome barrier to the Church's living out its gospel mission.[11]

All of these studies and many others left unmentioned—whether by professional historians, social theorists, theologians, or ethicists—promote particular readings of Catholic thought and behavior as normative; they work under the assumption that the individuals they describe and the ideas they express can be and should be measured against a Catholic "ideal." Let me state clearly that there is nothing inherently *wrong* with this approach to history, as such treatments can be every bit as insightful, critical, and valuable as scholarship with no normative Catholic position. But inevitably these methods place subtle—and sometimes not-so-subtle—restrictions on those invited into the conversation.[12] These histories are written not only about the Church, but also *for* the Church. Some historians who might otherwise have much to contribute are left on the outside. I do not wish to participate in this intra-Catholic debate; instead, I wish to make this debate and its sources more accessible

---

for a reading of an authentic Catholic tradition that is favorable to "free market" economic policy formulations. When Novak narrates the history of Catholic social thinking, he typically engages in critical dialogue with the players of the past. In the end, Novak's history authorizes a pro-capitalist (with caveats) worldview. See Michael Novak, *The Catholic Ethic and the Spirit of Capitalism* (New York: The Free Press, 1993), especially his assessments of *Rerum Novarum* and *Quadragesimo Anno* in chaps. 1 and 2; see also Novak, *Freedom with Justice: Catholic Social Thought and Liberal Institutions* (San Francisco: Harper and Row, 1984).

10. Joseph Gremillion, *The Gospel of Peace and Justice: Catholic Social Teaching Since Pope John* (Maryknoll, N.Y.: Orbis Books, 1976), 21, 138, and esp. chaps. 3–5.

11. Marvin L. Krier Mich, *Catholic Social Teaching and Movements* (Mystic, Conn.: Twenty-third Publications, 1998), 391–94.

12. See Jonathan Z. Smith, "Sacred Persistence," in *Imagining Religion: From Jonestown to Babylon* (Chicago: University of Chicago Press, 1982), 43.

and intelligible to historians of American culture. This study places the data of Catholic social thought in shared space with material studied by other historians and scholars of religion by using more explicit theoretical models designed to demystify the theological language and presuppositions of the insider. In other words, I hope to push the study of the data we designate as "Catholic" further in the direction of second-order analysis.

Toward a Redescription of Catholic Social Thought

My model for making sense of what is "going on" among Catholics who are engaged in economic dialogue from a self-consciously Catholic perspective uses two terms that come to us with substantial baggage: *ideology* and *myth*. Though both terms have been used with varying levels of precision in academic contexts for some time, they are frequently invoked pejoratively in popular discourse. We often apply the term "ideology" to dismiss or trivialize the perspectives of *others* who see the world through lenses that make them blind to the "common sense" and "reason" of those who think like *we* do. Myth, in popular parlance, is contrasted to "truth" and invested with a fanciful and delusional quality. I am not using these terms in their popular senses in this book. My definitions do not require rendering ideology and myth as antithetical to knowledge or truth.

Historically, particularly in its Marxist context, ideology has been seen as something socially produced by a ruling class for control over the classes that serve them. This view obscures the complexity of human thought and intercourse, however, by presupposing not only that ideologies are produced by our alienation from a natural reality inherent to the human self, but also by failing to see that ideological production can generate from a potentially limitless number of social groupings. Ideologies can be produced (and reproduced) by any group of people interested in setting the terms for social order, knowledge, and the imputation of meaning to our world; ideology can come from all of us. Some ideologies dominate while others struggle to gain acceptance,[13] but positions

---

13. Bruce Lincoln describes this process as "one in which hegemonic ideology is challenged by one of the many counterhegemonies that exist within any society" in his *Discourse and the Construction of Society: Comparative Studies of Myth, Ritual, and Classification* (New York: Oxford University Press, 1989), 6.

of dominance are always vulnerable when faced with the changing particulars of sociohistorical circumstance (witness the downfall of Marxism in the former Soviet Union, replaced by a Western capitalist ideology, which itself continues to be transformed and challenged as its promises struggle to bear fruit).

My definition of ideology borrows from the literary theorist James Kavanagh, who characterizes it "as a system of representations, perceptions, and images that precisely encourages men and women to 'see' their specific place in a historically peculiar social formation as inevitable, natural, a necessary function of the real itself."[14] Though he applies this definition within a neo-Marxian textual analysis, Kavanagh's understanding of ideology remains useful for any number of contexts.[15] This book treats the "system of representations, perceptions, and images" produced by the Roman Catholic church as ideology—one that can be seen as standing alongside of, in dialogue with, and sometimes even reflective of an array of other ideological currents.

Ideology is reproduced in many ways, including ritual, art, and law. But among the most important and effective tools in the promotion of an ideology is myth. Dating back to Plato's pitting myth in opposition to "reasoned" discourse,[16] the term has been commonly used dismissively in order to invalidate strategies of persuasion. While scholars continue to argue about what the term should mean and how it is best applied, the popular understanding of myth meaning falsehood is today almost nonexistent in religious studies, and my own understanding of myth is not that it means falsehood. In fact, just as we all reproduce ideologies, I maintain that we all inhabit mythic worldviews that grow from and reconstitute those ideologies.

---

14. James H. Kavanagh, "Ideology," in *Critical Terms for Literary Study*, 2nd ed., ed. Frank Lentricchia and Thomas McLaughlin (Chicago: University of Chicago Press, 1995), 310.

15. Ibid., 319. The careful reader may note that my "naturalizing" of ideology, rendering it, in large measure, inescapable, may open me to the charge of subjecting the term "ideology" to an ideological definition. I respond by maintaining a distinction between, on the one hand, a transparent and explicit construction of an analytical rubric to be used in the heuristic analysis of data that is being willfully put forward for the purpose of scholarly evaluation and critique, and on the other hand, ideology that fails to present itself as ideology but rather as "objectivity," transcending the particularities of time and space.

16. This distinction is thoroughly problematized in Bruce Lincoln's *Theorizing Myth: Narrative, Ideology, and Scholarship* (Chicago: University of Chicago Press, 1999), 3–43, in which Lincoln resurrects the pre-Socratic use of *mythos* and argues for a politically grounded shift in the use of the term by Plato and his followers as they attempted to validate their own authority in ancient Athens.

The definition of myth I find most useful has been informed especially by the work of a historian of religion, Bruce Lincoln, who calls myth "ideology in narrative form."[17] Lincoln's definition was fleshed out in his 1989 book *Discourse and the Construction of Society: Comparative Studies of Myth, Ritual, and Classification,* when he described myth as a narrative that not only claims itself to be true but also achieves the status of both *credibility* and *authority* in a given community. The community understands myth as credible in the sense that it is believed to express truth. It understands myth as authoritative in the sense that it serves as a paradigm, a standard, or an example that communities (or more precisely, individuals attempting to speak for communities) use to authorize beliefs and practices.[18] This definition identifies discourse as myth, not because of its content (e.g., superhuman actors or miraculous occurrences), but because it functions as myth in the context of a community. Stories become myths by the way people use them.

It is important to remember that the relationship between myth and community is symbiotic. Narratives grow out of actual social contexts and are addressed to imagined communities like the Church, the Nation, or the People of God. Once that narrative, for whatever reasons, has been invested with the authority necessary to attain the status of myth, it can then be employed to recreate and redefine the community in which it is used. The community of origin is not always synonymous with the community of use. Furthermore, we can distinguish one social grouping from another by the myths that bind each.

Two characteristics common to myths are especially applicable to this book. First, myths often contain classificatory schemes. Categories are created and placed in relation to one another in a taxonomy, often arranged hierarchically.[19] Though this claim may not be sustainable for all myths, it is nonetheless a useful one—as we will see—for illustrating the mythic character of the Catholic teachings we explore, due to the large role played by social hierarchies.

---

17. Ibid., 147.
18. Lincoln, *Discourse and the Construction of Society,* 23–25.
19. Lincoln cited a sentence appearing in Emile Durkheim and Marcel Mauss's 1901 essay, *Primitive Classification,* which he describes as implying that "myth may be understood as taxonomy in narrative form." See *Theorizing Myth,* 147; the sentence Lincoln rephrases reads, "Every mythology is fundamentally a classification, but one which borrows its principles from religious beliefs, not scientific ideas." Taken from Emile Durkheim and Marcel Mauss, *Primitive Classification,* trans. Rodney Needham (Chicago: University of Chicago Press, 1963; French original published 1901–2), 77–78.

The second noteworthy characteristic of myth is the way that particular perspectives reflecting precise times and places in human history and culture are presented as self-evident.[20] Mythic narrative contributes to naturalizing ideology. It makes contesting mythic categories tantamount to the contesting of "reality" itself. Lincoln identified "this misrepresentation of culture as nature" to be a significant element of myth through "the projection of a narrator's ideals, desires, and favored ranking of categories" onto a supposedly preordained natural order that dictates "how things must be."[21] Rephrased in the words of Russell McCutcheon, "by means of a disguised or undetected ideological slippage, 'is' becomes 'ought,' the myth of presence and self-identity is established, and value-neutral 'change' is judged to be either good or bad, progressive or retrograde."[22] The naturalizing power of myth renders it effective in promoting ideology, which will prove especially important in the context of Catholic economic thought.

A familiar illustration of myth and its function may be helpful as a point of comparison for the material we will be exploring. Christians and Jews frequently invoke the stories of creation in the book of Genesis to give authority to a variety of beliefs about the way the world should be. For a large portion of American society, these stories are *credible* (sometimes even understood as literal truth). Genesis is also *authoritative* among many and provides parameters for a social order that God had originally intended. Creation is divided up into multiple classificatory schemes, sometimes hierarchically arranged: light/darkness, heavens/earth, animals of the sea/animals of the land, male/female, and so forth. And nature is defined, in this context, as the will of God.

There is, of course, no single way to read the creation account in Genesis, which brings up the point that myths are not static, eternal, and unchanging realities, but instead function like wellsprings into which we dip to authorize our own preferences.[23] For instance, we may selectively use passages relating to God's creation of man and woman as a means of generating support for competing perspectives on gender roles. A supporter of women's equality might invoke Genesis 1:27, in which

---

20. For more on this aspect of myth, see Russell T. McCutcheon, "Myth," in *Guide to the Study of Religion*, ed. Willi Braun and Russell T. McCutcheon (London: Cassell, 2000), 190–208, esp. 201–2.
21. Lincoln, *Theorizing Myth*, 149.
22. McCutcheon, "Myth," 204–5.
23. Ibid., 205.

"male and female, God created them," both at once and in God's image. On the other hand, a proponent of patriarchy might cite Eve's creation from Adam's rib in chapter 2 to argue for female submission to male authority. We must keep in mind that these arguments are only effective if the participants share the common binding myth. The exploits of the Hindu deity Kali, for example, are likely to have little effect on persuading a fundamentalist Southern Baptist from Oklahoma that men have no innate authority over women.

Finally, in keeping with Genesis as a point of reference, we have what I like to call an *umbrella myth* that exists alongside the text of Genesis itself and, in a real sense, is an axiom on which the authority of the Genesis myth depends. This is the umbrella myth that God reveals Godself to us through human beings who compose text, so that the text itself can be understood as being the Word of God. Of course, at no point in Genesis do words tell us that Genesis is the revealed word of God. While God is quoted, the nameless narrator does not claim divine inspiration. It is the umbrella myth, the *sacred tradition* in which Genesis is given authority, that enables people to infuse the text with the status of divine authority. As I will argue, the mythic character of Genesis and its role in contemporary society is comparable to the mythic quality of the papal encyclicals that shaped Catholic economic thinking in the pre–Vatican II years.

Setting the Stage

The following pages look at human beings engaged in the ordinary task of negotiating access to and control over material resources, and the concomitant levels of security, freedom, and social status that come with those resources. What distinguishes the characters in this book is their shared adherence to publicly articulating Catholic ideology as expressed in the papal encyclicals—*Rerum Novarum* and *Quadragesimo Anno*—two texts that may be profitably described as myths. Because adaptability is a quality of myth (a quality that may be a precondition for any narrative to achieve the status of myth), we will see American Catholics in the generation before Vatican II continuously refashioning those myths in ways that reflected their diverse social contexts.

Removed from both the time and the place of their composition, the encyclicals were appropriated in a rapidly changing American and

Catholic landscape. Thanks in large measure to the "GI Bill of Rights," Catholics by the 1950s were quickly moving from their working-class roots to the middle and upper-middle classes.[24] Many would argue that the apparent success of Roosevelt's New Deal had, ironically, laid the groundwork for a measure of confidence in the market system of economics by the 1950s, after two decades of post-Depression cynicism.[25] Catholics were not immune to the popularization of capitalism, and it affected their very understanding of "justice."

The role of the laity was also changing in the Church. Pius XI's initiation of the Catholic Action movement in the 1920s mobilized a once-passive laity into activists on behalf of Church interests in the social and economic sphere.[26] At times an empowered laity engendered tension with a clergy whose authority had rarely been challenged. Though still removed from the revolutionary changes that would come with Vatican II (1962–65), the altered climate enabled a generation of lay Catholics to feel secure in their own theological discourse.[27]

Finally, whereas American Catholics once saw themselves, with reason, as an embattled minority, by the 1950s the fortress mentality that had dominated the previous century—pitting Catholics against a hostile outside world—had begun to fade. Doubling in population from twenty-one million in 1940 to forty-two million in 1960 did much to encourage the flight from the Catholic "ghetto," as did increasing material prosperity.[28] At the same time, Catholicism's hostility toward communism inspired among American Protestants the sense that Catholics were full partners in the Cold War struggle. Jay Dolan has gone so far as to describe

---

24. See Charles R. Morris, *American Catholic: The Saints and Sinners Who Built America's Most Powerful Church* (New York: Vintage Books, 1997), 256; Jay P. Dolan, *The American Catholic Experience: A History from Colonial Times to the Present* (Notre Dame, Ind.: University of Notre Dame Press, 1992), 128–57; James Hennesey, S.J., *American Catholics: A History of the Roman Catholic Community in the United States* (New York: Oxford University Press, 1981), 283.

25. George E. Mowry and Blaine A. Brownell, *The Urban Nation, 1920–1980* (New York: Hill and Wang, 1981), 205–6.

26. For more on Catholic Action, see Peter D'Agostino, *Rome in America: Transnational Catholic Ideology from the Risorgimento to Fascism* (Chapel Hill: University of North Carolina Press, 2004), 169, 223–28.

27. See Hennesey, *American Catholics*, 228–29; J. Dolan, *American Catholic Experience*, 244–46.

28. Martin E. Marty, *Modern American Religion, Volume 3: Under God, Indivisible, 1941–1960* (Chicago: University of Chicago Press, 1996), 158–59, 417; William M. Halsey, *The Survival of American Innocence in an Era of Disillusionment, 1920–1940* (Notre Dame, Ind.: University of Notre Dame Press, 1980), esp. 169–71.

American Catholics has having "come of age" by the end of the 1950s, meaning, in this context, attaining the fullest benefits of citizenship.[29]

In theologically oriented narratives, American Catholic engagement with and promotion of *Rerum Novarum* and *Quadragesimo Anno* are commonly described as the story of Catholicism promoting justice. In my redescription I hope to dispense with the value-laden terminology of earlier studies and problematize the narrative. Rather than the promotion of justice (which, no doubt, was the intention of those involved in this dialogue), this is a tale of competing attempts to define justice itself and invest that definition with the voice of *authentic* Roman Catholicism. The politics of authenticity is played on a rhetorical field where phrases like "true meaning," "deeper understanding," "a more sophisticated view," "when seen in the full context," "at its essence," and the term "authentic" itself encode positions of authority and interpretive license that have shown themselves to be vital in shaping, preserving, and contesting ideological status in the world. Invoking *Rerum Novarum* and *Quadragesimo Anno* to speak to the particular circumstances in which they lived, American Catholics authorized multiple perspectives on economic justice that were often in direct contradiction with one another. The texts provided a lexicon that made dialogue possible, though the terms of that lexicon were differently imagined. As we shall see, in naturalizing the culturally contingent and universalizing the particular, the players in this book were engaged in their own form of mythmaking,[30] as each employed the authority of the encyclicals to stake a claim for their distinctive visions of a Christian social order.

The first chapter examines the two social encyclicals themselves, *Rerum Novarum* and *Quadragesimo Anno*. I will illustrate how these important works can be understood as myths operating within the larger umbrella myth of natural-law theology. The remainder of the book will deal with the way these texts were used in different contexts of the American Catholic terrain.

Chapter 2 looks at an often-ignored element of American Catholic culture, that of rural life. Historian Richard Hofstadter coined the term

---

29. J. Dolan, *The American Catholic Experience*, 417.
30. On "mythmaking," see McCutcheon, "Myth," 201–4. McCutcheon cites Burton Mack as coining the term "mythmaking" in Mack's *Who Wrote the New Testament? The Making of the Christian Myth* (San Francisco: Harper and Row, 1995). Quoting p. 301 of Mack's work, McCutcheon writes: "the art of mythmaking 'turn[s] the collective agreements of a people into truths held to be self-evident'" (201).

"agrarian myth" to describe the collective image of Americans' relationship to the land. Catholics were also affected by this myth, while at the same time they reshaped it with their own mythic resources. This chapter will focus on the way in which the National Catholic Rural Life Conference and the Catholic Worker movement each made use of the social encyclical tradition in their own, sometimes incompatible, understandings of rural life's role in a just social order.

Chapter 3 examines industrial labor and Catholic attempts to sanctify it through the Social Action Department of the National Catholic Welfare Conference, the Association of Catholic Trade Unionists, and the Young Christian Workers movement. While these organizations worked to transform the American labor movement to reflect the Catholic ideology, the fortunes of the labor movement as a whole determined the fate of these Catholic organizations.

The fourth chapter explores the ways in which the social encyclicals were tapped to validate the conservative, free-market-based perspectives of Catholic thinkers like John Dinneen, Ferdinand Falque, and Edward Keller. The post-Depression years saw a conscious effort among the burgeoning corporate sector of America to improve the image of capitalism in the public eye. Led by organizations like the National Association of Manufacturers, attempts were made to shed the word "capitalism" of its social-Darwinist connotations and enshrine the term within the panoply of quintessentially "American" themes such as "democracy" and "freedom." Market-friendly Catholics saw in the social encyclicals the keys to a natural order in which competition, decentralization, and deregulation were central to justice and the common good.

Chapter 5 investigates the manner in which Catholic natural-law theology provided the mythic framework for making sense of right-to-work laws. Right-to-work laws addressed crucial questions relating to what constituted "freedom" of contract, the relation between the One and the Many, and differing notions of class. We will see how Catholic arguments reformulated and deviated from "secular" arguments both in support of and in opposition to right-to-work legislation.

Finally, Chapter 6 discusses the most popular Catholic proposal for reconstructing the American social order: the Industry Council Plan. Derived from the teachings of *Quadragesimo Anno,* the debates surrounding the Industry Council Plan illustrate vividly the multiplicity of strands that made up the Catholic economic imagination, as each figure measured the plan's worth against his or her own rendition of an *authentically* Catholic social order.

Historian of religion Jonathan Z. Smith once wrote that "the task of application [of religious canon] as well as the judgment of the relative adequacy of particular applications to a community's life situation remains the indigenous theologian's task, *but the study of the process, particularly the study of comparative systematics and exegesis, ought to become the major preoccupation of the historian of religion.*"[31] This book is a study of comparative exegesis in that it explores variations on the readings and applications of the social encyclicals before Vatican II. Each chapter reveals the adaptability of the myths articulated in *Rerum Novarum* and *Quadragesimo Anno* as the texts were refashioned to meet the needs of a diverse array of American Catholics. Like all myths, the meanings of these texts were both open-ended and contested. At the same time, they served to bind a community within a common discursive framework complete with its own terminology, its own system of authority, and its own axioms that pointed to a natural and divinely sanctioned economic order.

31. J. Smith, "Sacred Persistence," 43, emphasis added.

(1)

The Encyclicals

More than any other writings or commentaries emanating from Rome, two papal encyclicals informed American Catholics on issues of economic and social justice in the decades before Vatican II: *Rerum Novarum* and *Quadragesimo Anno*. Both outlined the principles of a Christian economy and painted a picture of a divinely ordained, organic social order to which all Catholics should strive to conform. In time, each encyclical took on the status of myth for Catholics in America and around the world, serving as the proof texts for a wide latitude of conceptions of justice, the common good, and *authentically* Catholic approaches to accessing, distributing, and controlling material resources.

In my Introduction, I used Genesis to illustrate a way myth may be understood. When seen in relation to the umbrella myth of its sacred tradition, the combination of Genesis's perceived credibility and its perceived authority among many Jews and Christians brought it to the status of myth. Catholics before the Second Vatican Council were bound by the umbrella myth of natural-law theology. Within the Roman Catholic context, natural law presupposed that God created an ordered universe—a universe in the process of moving toward a final end of reconciling with the God that created it. Morality consisted of conforming to the order that God had set forth, an order in which nature, with humankind as its centerpiece, was engaged in a process of achieving its ultimate potential: union with God. Hand in hand with this teleology, natural law involved "the belief that there exists in nature and/or human nature a rational order which can provide intelligible value statements independently of human will, that are universal in application, unchangeable in their ultimate content, and morally obligatory on mankind."[1] As such, key to the Catholic understanding of natural law was our ability to employ *reason* to discern this moral order. God's gift of reason enabled humankind to know right from wrong, and free will allowed us to conform to the will of God in our private lives and in our public intercourse.

It was Leo XIII, author of *Rerum Novarum,* who canonized natural-law theology in his 1879 encyclical *Aeterni Patris.* Leo XIII called for a revival of scholasticism in the tradition of Thomas Aquinas. He did not advocate reverting to a thirteenth-century way of thinking, but rather recapturing the presuppositions that guided philosophy and theology prior to the Enlightenment, especially human access to objective truth through reason. Of course, the quality of reasoning would, in turn, be validated in its conclusions by its correspondence to the magisterial teachings of the Church.[2]

To my knowledge, only one scholar, Winston Davis, has attempted a substantive examination of the mythic dimensions of natural-law philosophy and theology, though not in an exclusively Roman Catholic context.[3] "By the *myth* of natural law," Davis meant "the story of God's creation of certain values 'in nature' and—what is nearly the same story—His sanctification of certain relationships, acts, and attitudes as 'naturally choiceworthy.'"[4] The discursive field in which the ideology of Roman Catholicism was articulated between *Aeterni Patris* and Vatican II was bound by the umbrella myth of natural law. This study is interested in two particular applications of that natural law mythology, *Rerum Novarum* and *Quadragesimo Anno,* which themselves achieved the status of mythic texts, and in the manner those myths were imagined among Catholics in the United States.

---

1. Patrick Allitt, *Catholic Intellectuals and Conservative Politics in America, 1950–1985* (Ithaca, N.Y.: Cornell University Press, 1993), 7–8; cites Paul Sigmund, *Natural Law and Political Thought* (Cambridge, Mass.: Winthrop Press, 1971), viii.
2. The full text of *Aeterni Patris* may be accessed via the Vatican Web site at http://www.vatican.va/holy_father/leo_xiii/encyclicals/index.htm; for more on the context of Leo XIII's release of *Aeterni Patris,* see Robert D. Cross, *The Emergence of Liberal Catholicism in America* (Cambridge, Mass.: Harvard University Press, 1958), esp. 47.
3. Winston Davis, "Natural Law: A Study of Myth in a World Without Foundations," in *Myth and Philosophy,* ed. Frank Reynolds and David Tracy (Albany: State University of New York Press, 1990), 317–48; and Davis, "Natural Law and Natural Right: The Role of Myth in the Discourses of Exchange and Community," in *Myth and Philosophy,* ed. Reynolds and Tracy, 349–79.
4. Davis, "Natural Law: A Study of Myth," 319, emphasis in original.

Rerum Novarum

The Roman Catholic Church was in crisis when *Rerum Novarum* was written. For decades the Church had been losing a battle with the forces of liberalism, both territorially and intellectually. On the territorial front, liberal democratic nationalism had swept across Italy, resulting by 1870 in the complete loss of the Papal States. Peter D'Agostino has shown the profound extent to which what came to be known as "The Roman Question" preoccupied the Vatican between 1870 and 1929.[5] At the time, Church leaders assumed that spiritual authority could not exist without territorial authority, an assumption reinforced by the importance of revenues generated by its property to the fiscal health of the Church.[6] Peter Kent and John F. Pollard have pointed out that "like secular states, [the Vatican] seeks power, but power in the spiritual and cultural domain." Therefore, those institutions that "challenge its spiritual objectives and promote countervailing ideologies" will be cast as its enemies, while its allies will consist of those who can "assist it to achieve its goals of cultural hegemony."[7] The Vatican feared that losing temporal power would curtail its influence in other countries, eliminating the leverage needed to give it an authoritative voice on issues pertaining to education, marriage, the appointment of bishops and clergy, disposal of Church properties, and other items. And their fears were realized, not only in Italy, but in the anti-Catholic policies of the *Kulturkampf* in Germany as well as in passage of the "laic laws" in France between 1882 and 1886, prohibiting clergy from teaching at state schools, secularizing higher education, and legalizing Sunday labor.[8]

---

5. Peter D'Agostino, *Rome in America: Transnational Catholic Ideology from the Risorgimento to Fascism* (Chapel Hill: University of North Carolina Press, 2004).

6. Thomas Bokenkotter, *A Concise History of the Catholic Church* (New York: Doubleday, 1977), 267–70.

7. Peter C. Kent and John F. Pollard, "A Diplomacy Unlike Any Other: Papal Diplomacy in the Nineteenth and Twentieth Centuries," in *Papal Diplomacy in the Modern Age*, ed. Peter C. Kent and John F. Pollard (Westport, Conn.: Praeger Press, 1994), 15.

8. Miriam Lynch, "The Organized Social Apostolate of Albert de Mun" (Ph.D. diss., Catholic University of America, 1952), 7–8; the traditional Vatican allegiance to the aristocracy did not endear the Church to liberal republicans and the rising bourgeois class. It was precisely this antagonism between the Church and the liberal bourgeoisie that left many shocked by Leo XIII's release of *Au Milieu des Sollicitudes* in 1892. The encyclical was an attempt to unify a French Catholic community bitterly divided along lines of class and ideology. Remarkable was Leo's recognition of the reality of a republican government in France, leading him to direct Catholics to "accept the Republic and try to change its anti-religious laws by constitutional means." This tactic appeared to be an anomaly for several decades to come. See ibid., 8.

On the intellectual front, liberalism had also done much damage to the Church's authority. The defenders of revelation as a viable form of knowledge had suffered greatly with the impact of thinkers like Benedict Spinoza, John Locke, Immanuel Kant, Ludwig Feuerbach, and Karl Marx.[9] In many intellectual circles, confidence in an independent human reason had supplanted the idea that knowledge of Truth depended on God's grace through revelation. The Church answered these threats with *Aeterni Patris* and the scholastic revival. Predictably, non-Catholics received the encyclical with suspicion, characterizing it as a reversion to medievalism, despite Catholic claims to the contrary.[10]

Both territorial and intellectual threats to the Church violated the Catholic sense of order. The structure and identity of Roman Catholicism in the modern age have their roots in the medieval era, often portrayed as a "golden age" during which the Church sat atop the hierarchy of feudal society. As the violent and chaotic conditions from which the feudal order sprang began to transform—leading in turn to stable communities and a rise in urbanism—so, too, did popular assumptions about order and authority. Medieval historian Jacques Le Goff noted that "the great heresies" of the medieval period have often been understood as "anti-feudal" heresies, for they called into question the "very structure of society."[11]

In the year of Leo XIII's coronation, he found himself defending feudal conceptions of hierarchy and authority in his encyclical attack on socialism, communism, and nihilism, *Quod Apostolici Muneris* (1878). While recognizing equality among individuals before God, there remained "an inequality of right and authority which emanates from the Author of nature Himself, *of whom all paternity in heaven and earth is named*" (sec. 5). Leo XIII continued:

> Just then as the Almighty willed that, even in the heavenly kingdom itself, the choirs of angels should be of differing ranks, subordinated the one to the other; again just as in the Church God has established different grades of orders with diversity of

---

9. Richard P. McBrien, *Catholicism*, rev. ed. (San Francisco: Harper and Row, 1994), 242–43.

10. Lillian Parker Wallace, *Leo XIII and the Rise of Socialism* (Durham, N.C.: Duke University Press, 1966), 209–13.

11. Jacques Le Goff, *Medieval Civilization: 400–1500*, trans. Julia Barrow (Cambridge, Mass.: Basil Blackwell, 1991), 90–95.

functions, so that all should not be *apostles, all not doctors, all not prophets* [1 Cor. 12:29]; so also has He established in civil society many orders of varying dignity, right, and power. And this, to the end that the State, like the Church, should form one body comprising many members, some excelling others in rank and importance, but all alike necessary to one another and solicitous for the common welfare.[12]

As we shall see, this presupposition of a natural hierarchic order continued to guide Leo XIII's thinking in *Rerum Novarum*.

Rerum Novarum went through several drafts before being released on May 15, 1891.[13] The encyclical can be divided into four parts: a description of the problem being addressed, a naturalization of private property, a naturalization of social classes and their harmonious interaction, and a description of principles aimed at establishing a Christian socioeconomic framework.

Leo XIII began by describing a conflict precipitated by the "spirit of revolutionary change" that had infected the world during the modern age. This conflict was most acute in the burgeoning industrial economy, where "the changed relations of masters and workmen; the enormous fortunes of individuals and the poverty of the masses; the increased self-reliance and the closer mutual combination of the working population; and finally, a general moral deterioration" (sec. 1) all lent themselves to a society that threatened to explode in violence. A quick solution was necessary to alleviate the suffering of the poor. By the eighteenth century, "workingmen's guilds" of the medieval age had been destroyed and had not been replaced, leaving the worker vulnerable to exploitation.

---

12. *Quod Apostolici Muneris*, sec. 6. Quotation taken from "Socialism, Communism, Nihilism," in *The Great Encyclical Letters of Leo XIII* (New York: Benziger Brothers, 1903), 26, emphasis in original; also in "Quod Apostolici Muneris," December 28, 1878, at http://www.vatican.va/holy_father/leo_xiii/encyclicals/index.htm, and reads, "The inequality of rights and of power proceeds from the very Author of nature, 'from whom all paternity in heaven and earth is named,'" quoting from Ephesians 3:15.

13. For more on the composition of *Rerum Novarum*, see John T. McGreevy, *Catholicism and American Freedom: A History* (New York: W. W. Norton, 2003), 127; McGreevy cites John Moloney, "The Making of *Rerum Novarum*, April 1890–May 1891," in *The Church Faces the Modern World: "Rerum Novarum" and Its Impact*, ed. Paul Furlong and David Curtis (Hull: Earlsgate Press, 1994), 27–39; also, Paul Misner, "The Predecessors of *Rerum Novarum* Within Catholicism," *Review of Social Economy* 49 (Winter 1991): 444–64; and Jean-Marie Mayeur, *Catholicisme social et démocratie chrétienne: Principes romains, experiences francaises* (Paris: Éditions du Cerf, 1986), 47–65.

Though the immediate cause of labor victimization stemmed from the personal moral failings of the wealthy, with their "callousness" and "greed," the root cause of this immorality could be traced to a greater evil: the repudiation of "the ancient religion" (sec. 2). On top of this, the flames of crisis were being stoked by socialists who played on the envy of the poor to pervert the natural social order by relegating private property to the hands of the state. Such an attempt was deemed "futile" and "emphatically unjust," for in their attempt to "rob the lawful possessor of property," the socialists would "bring the state into a sphere that is not its own, and cause complete confusion in the community" (sec. 3).[14]

With Leo XIII's analysis, we can see that certain categories of a broad taxonomy have been established from the start: wealthy/poor, master/worker, private domain/state domain. Maintenance of a "just" society as opposed to an "unjust," confused, chaotic one depended on keeping these categories in a *proper* relationship to one another. From the start, *Rerum Novarum* imagines a world that was once ordered and whole, but is now broken and confused. It fell on the Church to lead the way toward a restoration of society as it was meant to be.

Naturalizing private property was central to restoring right order, and Leo XIII devoted the next fifth of his encyclical to this concern. The right to private property took on new importance for the Church decades earlier in the late 1840s when the first real threat to the Papal States, and consequently the Church's property, emerged from the Italian nationalist movement. When Pope Pius IX was consecrated in 1846, all signs pointed to his support of a unified Italy, and liberals viewed him as a catalyst for change. But they felt scorned when Pius IX refused to support the revolt of Milan and Venice against their Austrian rulers—Roman Catholic rulers, after all, who had never threatened the Papal States. By the end of 1848, Pius IX fled to a retreat in Naples as the liberal nationalists declared a republic and "the end of the pope's temporal power," then "secularized church property, and instituted freedom of worship." With the help of French and Austrian forces, the experimental republic was put down and the Papal States restored—only to be taken away again just over twenty years later. In Pius IX's *Nostis et Nobiscum*, written while in exile, he branded the republican experiment the work

---

14. The translation used is found in Leo XIII, "Rerum Novarum," in *Catholic Social Thought: The Documentary Heritage*, ed. David J. O'Brien and Thomas A. Shannon (Maryknoll, N.Y.: Orbis Books, 1992), 14–15.

of those whose goal was "to drive people to overthrow the entire order of human affairs and to draw them over to the wicked theories of this Socialism and Communism, by confusing them with perverted teachings" (sec. 6). He warned that they were conspiring to prepare workers, "especially those of the lower class . . . for plundering, stealing, and usurping first the Church's and then everyone's property" (sec. 18).[15]

Having experienced firsthand the loss of its property, Leo XIII set out to defend it by the natural law.[16] As John E. Kelly described it, for Leo XIII, "the right of private property is a relative right, relative to man's historical condition. Except for the fall, private ownership would not be necessary." But through human reason, its current necessity could be shown.[17] Private property was natural, Leo XIII maintained, because of the "undeniable" fact that the motive of remunerative labor "is to obtain private property" and to hold that property privately (sec. 4).[18] Furthermore, property was "one of the chief points of distinction between man and the animal creation," for Leo XIII believed animals lived on instinct from moment to moment, while human beings, graced with reason, planned for the future and regulated the use of their resources. Because humans possess reason, "it must be within [their] right to have things not merely for temporary and momentary use . . . but in stable and permanent possession" (sec. 5).[19]

One of the more interesting rationalizations for the naturalizing of private property grew from Leo XIII's understanding of the individual's relationship to the land. Presumably unaware of those traditional cultures that adapted to the environment to assure their survival, Leo XIII's thinking reflected the Genesis model that dominated the Western world in which we were called to "subdue" the earth and "have dominion"

---

15. D'Agostino, *Rome in America*, 26–32; Pope Pius IX, *Nostis et Nobiscum (On the Church in the Pontifical States)*, December 8, 1849, http://www.ewtn.com/library/encyc/p9nostis.htm, accessed February 2, 2007.
16. Aquinas had asserted "that something may be derived from the natural law in two ways: first, as conclusions from their premises, secondly, by way of determination of certain generalities." Leo used this second approach to derive the natural right to private property. See John E. Kelly, "The Influence of Aquinas' Natural Law Theory on the Principle of 'Corporatism' in the Thought of Leo XIII and Pius XI," in *Things Old and New: Catholic Social Teaching Revisited*, ed. Francis P. McHugh and Samuel M. Natale (Lanham, Md.: University Press of America, 1993), 112; Kelly cites Thomas Aquinas, *Summa Theologica* (New York: Benziger Brothers, 1947), I–II, q. 95, a. 2.
17. J. Kelly, "The Influence of Aquinas' Natural Law Theory," 112.
18. Leo XIII, "Rerum Novarum," 15.
19. Ibid., 16.

over it (Gen. 1:28). For Leo XIII, "the preservation of life and for life's well-being is produced in great abundance by the earth, but not until man has brought it into cultivation and lavished upon it his care and skill." Through taming the earth, one "makes his own that portion of nature's field which he cultivates—that portion on which he leaves, as it were, the impress of his own personality, and it cannot but be just that he should possess that portion as his own, and should have a right to keep it without molestation" (sec. 7).[20] Surely soil that had been "tilled and cultivated" must also be seen as "improved," he reasoned. Embedded in this distinctively Occidental ideology, Leo XIII reckoned that his arguments were "*so strong and convincing* that it seems surprising that certain obsolete opinions" would dare to contradict him (sec. 8).[21]

The family served as the final vehicle for the naturalization of private property. The category of "the family" precedes "the state" in Leo XIII's rendering of the primordial past, thus granting it primacy over the possession and use of property. In the gendered framework of the day, the natural right to private property "must also belong to a man in his capacity of head of a family." It was "a most sacred law of nature" that a "father" provide for *his* children, and this was deemed impossible without property ownership.

Characteristic of myth, *Rerum Novarum* succeeded in making contestable propositions appear obvious to all by weaving together a series of hegemonic ideological positions into a distinctively Catholic ideological tour de force. Cultural assumptions deeply embedded in the Western mind regarding the motivation for labor, the distinction between humanity and other animals, our relationship to the environment, and the shape and purpose of "the family" were all brought to the service of placing private property in the sphere of nature itself, sanctioned by God. Once this principle was firmly established, there could be no doubt that socialism represented a perversion of the divine order.

The third section of the encyclical was devoted both to the naturalization of social divisions that we commonly label as classes and to naturalizing their relationship of mutual harmony. Never using Marxist terminology, Leo XIII categorized a social division between the classes of "the rich" on the one hand and the apparently synonymous "poor" or "worker" on the other. The hierarchical relationship between these

---

20. Ibid., 17.
21. Ibid, emphasis added.

groups was vital for the preservation of right order. Contrary to the socialists, Leo XIII maintained "that humanity must remain as it is. It is impossible to reduce human society to a level . . . all striving against nature is in vain." Inequality was painted as a necessity.

> There naturally exist among mankind innumerable differences of the most important kind; people differ in capability, in diligence, in health, and in strength; and unequal fortune is a necessary result of inequality in condition. Such inequality is far from being disadvantageous either to individuals or to the community; social and public life can only go on by the help of various kinds of capacity and the playing of many parts, and each man, as a rule, chooses the part which peculiarly suits his case (sec. 14).[22]

With these words, Leo XIII subverted the notion that inequality was a problem by rendering the maintenance of "social and public life" the end to which the individual serves. *Rerum Novarum* maintained the organic understanding of society typical of pre-Enlightenment Europe, complete with bodily metaphors to authorize social inequality.[23]

Leo XIII rendered "irrational" and "false" suggestions that inequality must inevitably produce class hostility (sec. 15). Ultimately, class conflict was diagnosed as springing from moral failure, particularly greed and envy. As such, conflict could also be remedied through individuals of each class upholding their mutual "duties" to one another, particularly "the duties of justice" (sec. 16). Worth noting are the rhetorical differences in Leo XIII's phrasing of these duties. The lessons bestowed on each of the two classes reflected different tones. Worker's duties were almost all proscriptive, while the duties of the rich were almost all prescriptive. In addition to being implored to carry out freely made agreements honestly, the worker was cautioned to "*never*" damage capital, "*nor* to outrage the person of an employer; *never* to employ violence . . . *nor* engage in riot and disorder." Nor were workers to have anything "to do with men of evil principles," who might foolishly raise the workers' hopes (sec. 16).[24]

---

22. Ibid., 20.
23. Ibid. "Just as the symmetry of the human body is the result of the disposition of members of the body, so in a State it is ordained by nature that these two classes should exist in harmony and agreement, and should, as it were, fit into one another, so as to maintain the equilibrium of the body politic" (sec. 15).
24. Ibid., 21, emphasis added.

The prescription for the wealthy involved understanding "that their work people are not their slaves; that they must respect in every man his dignity as a man and as a Christian; that labor is nothing to be ashamed of . . . but is an honorable employment." Leo XIII added that it was "shameful and inhuman to treat men like chattel," and that "the employer is bound to see that [the worker] has time for duties of piety." The rich were obliged to protect workers from "corrupting influences," while also making sure that they were never worked "beyond their strength" nor in work "unsuited to their sex or age" (sec. 16).[25] These duties made it clear that not only was the class structure to be maintained, but the burden of responsibility for action fell on the wealthy. Leo XIII's paternalistic presuppositions reflected an ideology that held a hierarchical class arrangement to be natural and a proper moral disposition to be the key to maintaining the divine order. For good measure, Leo XIII invoked a life after death as both carrot to the poor and stick to the rich as leverage to ensure that each class would carry out its duties (secs. 18 and 19).[26]

With the inviolability of private property secured in nature, along with the harmonious relations of the classes, *Rerum Novarum* was ready to confront more practical measures designed to stave off the impending crisis facing the industrial West. Before addressing these measures, it was necessary to draw two distinctions. First, there was a distinction between the natural right to possess property, and the limitations of that property's use. While the former was sacred, the latter varied (a distinction supported by the teachings of Aquinas) (sec. 19).[27] Drawing this distinction was vital to authorizing claims as to the "proper" use of capital.

The second distinction involved the state. While Leo XIII had made clear that the rights of the individual and the family superseded those of the state, the preservation of the "common good" justified state action affecting individuals and families (sec. 28). For Catholics, the common good was not understood as being the sum total of individual goods in society, nor as a utilitarian principle in which "goodness" was judged

25. Ibid.
26. Ibid., 22.
27. Ibid. The encyclical quotes Aquinas as saying "it is lawful for a man to hold private property; it is also necessary for the carrying on of human life. . . . Man should not consider his outward possessions as his own, but common to all, so as to share them without difficulty when others are in need." Leo cites *Summa Theologica*, IIa IIae, q. 61, a. 2, q. 60, a 2.

by the sheer numbers of individuals who benefited. Instead, Catholicism held that because the ultimate end of the individual was union with God, then the common good must be understood as that social order that best allowed persons to pursue their ultimate ends in God.[28] Therefore, the state had an obligation to maintain an order that was "consistent with the common good," particularly in the area of public safety (sec. 28).[29] With these two distinctions made, Leo XIII was free to proceed with suggestions for creating and maintaining a just social order.

Rerum Novarum touched on four specific areas affecting the condition of labor: working hours, child labor, wages, and workers' associations. The proportion of working hours to resting hours, said Leo XIII, should relate a job's level of difficulty. Hard labor necessitated fewer hours and increased periods of rest (sec. 33). Leo XIII also warned against abuses in child labor, a controversial stance in the 1890s. Still, he took care to avoid specifying a suitable age to begin working. As for women, Leo XIII deemed them "not suited to certain trades, for a woman is by nature fitted for home work" (sec. 33).[30]

"Just wage" teachings were among the more contentious elements of *Rerum Novarum*. Leo XIII rejected the ideology that wages were "fixed by free consent." Because labor was a necessity for self-preservation, the idea that one is "free to work or not, so he is free to accept a small remuneration or even none at all," was rendered "a mere abstract supposition." This being the case, Leo XIII proposed a standard that he portrayed as "a dictate of nature": that wages "must be enough to support the wage earner in reasonable and frugal comfort" and sufficient to support a family (sec. 34).[31] Ideally, savings could go toward the purchase of property on which crops could be grown. Leo XIII's language highlighting the "great abundance of the fruits of the earth" to be reaped from a plot of land, reflected a vision of a society capable of retaining the vestiges of an idyllic feudal village (sec. 35).[32] Such bucolic imagery

---

28. For a discussion on the history of the Catholic conception of the "common good," see A. Nemetz, "Common Good," in *The New Catholic Encyclopedia* (Washington, D.C.: Catholic University of America, 1967), 15–19; see also Normand J. Paulhus, "Uses and Misuses of the Term 'Social Justice' in the Roman Catholic Tradition," *The Journal of Religious Ethics* 15 (Fall 1987): esp. 262–64.
29. Leo XIII, "Rerum Novarum," 27.
30. Ibid., 30.
31. Ibid., 31.
32. Ibid., 32.

must have seemed quite alien to the displaced workers of the industrial age facing desolate urban conditions.

The ambiguity of the terms "reasonable," "frugal," and "comfort" in *Rerum Novarum*'s standard for a just wage set the stage for a broad range of readings. So, too, did the corollary to workers' wages that appeared earlier in the text, which addressed the question of how much wealth was too much. On this issue, Leo XIII taught that "no one is commanded to distribute to others that which is required for his own necessities and those of his household; nor even to give away what is reasonably required to keep up becomingly his condition in life" (sec. 19).[33] In both the wages of the wage earner and the wealth of the wage dispenser, status inherent in a natural arrangement of social class figured into the dictates of "justice."

Among the most significant sections of the encyclical were those dealing with private associations. These were associations organized to promote the interests of specific social groups. Of particular interest to workers was Leo XIII's handling of labor unions. He naturalized them, sanctioned them, and encouraged them, though with stipulations. Unions were acceptable because they resulted from "the natural impulse" for individuals to work in cooperation. Societies resulting from this impulse "exist within the State, and are each a part of the state," but "nevertheless cannot be prohibited by the State absolutely and as such. For to enter into a 'society' of this kind is the natural right of man." Associations created for "evidently bad, unjust, or dangerous" purposes that posed a threat to the state or public safety, however, could be forbidden. Furthermore, he cautioned against unions mixing Christians with those hostile to Christianity (a caution presumably directed at those with Marxist inclinations). When faced with these circumstances, Christian laborers were enjoined to form their own associations among themselves as a means of preventing the exposure of "man's chief good to extreme danger" (sec. 40).[34] Bishops were urged to support and guide Christian unions, while wealthy Catholics were encouraged to bankroll them. Concerns and warnings notwithstanding, the Church's fashioning of labor unions as a natural right was received in many circles as a major victory for the working classes.

33. Ibid., 22.
34. Ibid., 34.

Encyclicals and Papal Authority

Papal encyclicals are written to address topics of concern to the Church and its members. At another level of analysis, however, encyclicals must also be seen as a means of constituting papal authority. Encyclicals are a distinctive apparatus employed in the production of a Roman Catholic ideology. They may be understood as not simply *giving* knowledge of that which is held to be "sacred truth," but also as shaping the boundaries of what constitutes knowledge.[35] Key to this act of shaping is portraying the authority of the Church as the necessary precondition for putting knowledge to proper use. *Rerum Novarum* is no different in this manner.

In the identification of the categories that combine to form the social order (individual, family, guild, state, Church), *Rerum Novarum* was engaged in classification according to a taxonomic scheme. The variables of that taxonomy shift with regard to power and authority based on circumstance. For instance, while the individual generally superseded the state, violating the moral order (as defined by the Church) validated the state in limiting the freedom of the individual. But regardless of taxonomic fluctuation, the Church (i.e., the earthly surrogate of the Divine) retained the position of greatest privilege in all classificatory equations. Lincoln has elaborated on the role of taxonomy in myth by noting that

> for all that the epistemological functions of taxonomy are undeniable, placing primary emphasis on them obscures the fact that all knowers themselves are *objects* of knowledge as well as subjects insofar as they cannot stand apart from the world that they seek to know. One consequence of this (and far from the least important) is that categorizers come to be categorized according to their own categories. Taxonomy is thus not only a means for organizing information, but also—as it comes to organize the organizers—an instrument for the classification and manipulation of society.[36]

---

35. See James H. Kavanagh, "Ideology," in *Critical Terms for Literary Study*, 2nd ed., ed. Frank Lentricchia and Thomas McLaughlin (Chicago: University of Chicago Press, 1995), esp. 310, 314.

36. Bruce Lincoln, *Discourse and the Construction of Society: Comparative Studies of Myth, Ritual, and Classification* (New York: Oxford University Press, 1989), 137, emphasis in original. Lincoln provides an instructive endnote: "One must, of course, grant that

Not only implicitly, as the final arbiter of what constitutes natural law, but explicitly as well, the authority of Church is woven into *Rerum Novarum* as the sine qua non of a just social order. The origin of the social crisis itself is grounded in the repudiation of "the ancient religion" (sec. 2). All efforts to restore order are rendered "in vain if they leave out the Church," whose teaching role cannot be surpassed. We are reminded that "there is nothing more powerful than religion (of which the Church is the interpreter and guardian) in drawing rich and poor together, by reminding each class of its duties to the other" (sec. 16). More important, the Church as mediator of God's grace holds the keys to eternal life, understood as the sole source of meaning to all human endeavor (sec. 18). *Rerum Novarum* quite pointedly reserved for the Church not only the responsibility for "pointing out the remedy," but also for applying it. Only through the agency of Church officials and organizations could the "commandments of God" be taught and enacted. "It is precisely in this fundamental and principal manner, *on which everything depends,* that the Church has a power peculiar to itself. The agencies which it employs are given it for the very purpose of reaching the hearts of men by Jesus Christ himself, and derive their efficiency from God" (sec. 22).[37] Even in the final section, we are reminded that "all men must be persuaded that the primary thing needful is to return to real [i.e., Roman Catholic] Christianity, in the absence of which all the plans and devices of the wisest will be of little avail" (sec. 45).[38]

When seen in this light, the subject of *Rerum Novarum* may be understood as not only the plight of the worker, but also the authority of the Church. Written in an age when papal power appeared critically wounded, the encyclical's composition sought to ensure that every facet of the social order could be measured in relation to the Church. When abandoned, chaos and turmoil would reign; when obeyed, peace and harmony.

---

diverse data of the phenomenal world being too numerous, varied, and complex for any individual mind or cultural aggregate to process, it is a move born of necessity to organize disparate bits of information into categories and to organize those categories into taxonomic systems. Such systems always remain, however, impoverished, oversimplified, and tendentious models of a fuller reality. Nor should their necessity or utility be taken uncritically: although taxonomies may render thought and action possible, it must be stressed that any given system renders only *certain kinds* of thought and action possible, simultaneously precluding infinite others" (197).

37. Leo XIII, "Rerum Novarum," 24, emphasis added.
38. Ibid., 38.

Rerum Novarum's success in achieving the status of myth results in large measure from the skill with which the ideology of the Roman Catholic Church was portrayed as simply the law of Nature itself. Even allowing for the intentional ambiguity of Leo XIII's text, in his hesitancy to move beyond statements of "principle" into the realm of specific policy recommendations, we find property rights, class inequality, gender roles, child labor, wages, and trade unions all accountable to Nature's rules. Because Nature has no voice but the voice given to it by particular individuals, with particular interests, living in particular times and places, then the voice of "Nature" always reflects those who invoke it. In the case of papal encyclicals, the "natural" is synonymous with "the Church sanctioned."

Quadragesimo Anno

Forty years after *Rerum Novarum,* Pope Pius XI revisited the question of economic order in his 1931 encyclical *Quadragesimo Anno.* As the first encyclical to use the phrase "social justice," a phrase that had become vogue in Catholic circles,[39] Pius XI continued turning to the natural law for solutions to economic problems. On most issues, *Quadragesimo Anno* can be seen as a reiteration of key principles established in *Rerum Novarum.* But forty years later the world had changed, and these changes are reflected in both the analytical nuances of Pius XI's words, his rendering of the "natural," as well as in substantive developments discernible in the text.

Pius XI's Europe was still suffering the effects of World War I— among them, a new suspicion of liberalism and damaged faith in human reason. This spawned the rise of dictatorial regimes commonly known as fascist. There were significant variations among these fascist regimes, and the context in which Pius XI worked was Italian fascism. Invited by the Italian king to form a new government in 1922, Mussolini envisioned an organic society entirely under the control of the Fascist Party and working for the party's expansion. In contrast to liberalism, fascism meant "the radical negation of particularity, the subordination of every kind of particularity to the 'total,' 'natural-organic' whole, 'the nation.'"[40]

---

39. Richard L. Camp, *The Papal Ideology of Social Reform: A Study in Historical Development, 1878–1967* (Leiden: E. J. Brill, 1969), 99.

40. Mihaly Vajda, *Fascism: A Mass Movement* (New York: St. Martin's Press, 1976),

When the Fascist Party took control, it was not long before accommodations had to be made to those features of Italian culture that seemed inextricable from the population's sense of national identity. Among those features was the pervasive Catholicism of the Italian people. It is important to note that attachment to Catholicism did not always translate to attachment to the institution or the teachings of the magisterium. Catholicism sometimes manifested itself within popular practice in ways that seemed utterly disconnected from the formal structure and teachings of the Church's hierarchy. Recognizing the centrality of the faith to Italian culture, however, Mussolini began to cultivate a relationship with the Vatican itself, and with Catholicism as a symbol of Italian national identity. In addition to having his children baptized and confirmed in 1923, crucifixes were hung in school buildings and government sanctuaries, a cross that had been taken away from the Coliseum with the revolution in 1874 was restored, and clerical salaries were raised. On the surface, at least, a rapprochement between the Fascist Party and the Church had been achieved.[41]

A superficial understanding of Italian fascism and Catholicism might lead one to see strong lines of continuity between the two, particularly in their rejection of liberalism and their conceptions of an organic, hierarchically arranged social order characterized by class cooperation. Indeed these elements of commonality, coupled with sheer opportunism, facilitated cooperation between the Holy See and Mussolini's government in the subversion of the left-leaning (though predominately Catholic) Partito Popolare, as well as in the Lateran Treaties of 1929, which secured the territorial rights to Vatican City that the papacy had sought for so long.[42]

Yet Italian fascism was a distinctive ideology in competition with the Catholic ideology for the hearts and minds of the people. It could not be reconciled fully with Catholicism because, like liberalism, the fascist ideology turned away from God as the ground and purpose of human

---

16–17; see also Adrian Lyttleton, *The Seizure of Power: Fascism in Italy, 1919–1929*, 2nd ed. (Princeton, N.J.: Princeton University Press, 1987); Claudio G. Segrè, *Italo Balbo: A Fascist Life* (Berkeley and Los Angeles: University of California Press, 1987).

41. See especially D'Agostino, *Rome in America*, chaps. 6 and 7, esp. 169.

42. Ibid., chaps. 6 and 7; see also Konrad Repgen, "Foreign Policy of the Popes in the Epoch of the World Wars," in *History of the Church*, vol. 10, ed. Hubert Jedin, Konrad Repgen, and John Dolan, trans. Anselm Biggs (New York: Crossroad, 1981), 47–59; see also Camp, *The Papal Ideology of Social Reform*, 64; Camp cites Pietro Scoppola, *Dal neoguelfismo all democrazia cristiana* (Rome: Editrice Studium, 1957), 142–50.

existence. As Pius XI himself commented regarding the Fascist Party's public posturing vis-à-vis the Church: "Fascism declares itself to be Catholic. Well, there is one way and one way only to be Catholic, Catholics in fact and not merely in name, true Catholics and not sham Catholics . . . and that is to obey the Church and its head."[43] The reality was that for all of the outward trappings of Catholicism adopted by Mussolini's regime, fascist totalitarianism undermined the authority of the Church by replacing loyalty to the Vatican—God's instrument for the mediation of Grace on earth, in the Catholic worldview—with loyalty to the party. Mussolini's fascism possessed an "instinctive" anticlericalism because the Church, after all, also demanded the full allegiance of its people. While fascists and Catholics both used words like "organic" and "natural" to describe society, fascists placed the individual in the service of the "organic" nation. Catholic teleology, meanwhile, viewed society as "organic" insofar as persons worked in harmony toward ensuring conditions enabling individuals to gain salvation.[44]

Along with Italian fascism, *Quadragesimo Anno* was written against the backdrop of global economic depression and the expansion of communism in Eastern Europe. The Vatican still felt bitterness engendered by failed negotiations with the Bolsheviks regarding Catholic privileges in the Soviet Union between 1917 and 1926. This only encouraged a tendency to view right-wing movements, which may themselves have been equally hostile to the Church, as a preferable option to communism.[45] The scope and scale of the global depression magnified the disparity between rich and poor, providing fertile ground for a persistent, though fractured, socialist movement throughout Europe and the United States.

In light of these circumstances, *Quadragesimo Anno* revisited the same themes as *Rerum Novarum*, appealed to the same "nature" as the source of its prescriptions, but added a few distinctive elements to the mythology

---

43. D'Agostino, *Rome in America*, 224; he cites Daniel A. Binchy, *Church and State in Fascist Italy* (London: Oxford University Press, 1941), 331, 517, and Tracy H. Koon, *Believe, Obey, Fight: Political Socialization of Youth in Fascist Italy, 1922–1943* (Chapel Hill: University of North Carolina Press, 1992), 132–34.

44. A description of fascist anticlericalism as "instinctive" can be found in Lyttelton, *The Seizure of Power*, 130, citing A. C. Jemolo, *Chiesa e stato in Italia negli ultimi centi anni* (Turin: Einandi, 1948), 591.

45. Stewart A. Stehlin, "The Emergence of a New Vatican Diplomacy During the Great War and Its Aftermath, 1914–1929," in *Papal Diplomacy in the Modern Age*, ed. Kent and Pollard, 81–82.

of a Christian social order. Pius XI attempted to distance Catholicism from what he saw as the two extremes of socialism and laissez-faire capitalism.[46] But the socialism of Pius XI's day was divided. Disputes regarding the acceptability of violent revolution as a vehicle for change had pitted moderate socialists against communists.[47] The emergence of a moderate socialism forced Pius XI to clarify the Church's stance regarding the compatibility of socialism and Christianity, because socialist programs "often strikingly approach the just demands of Christian social reformers" (sec. 113). Failure to acknowledge God as both the ground and the end of human life, Pius XI emphasized, meant that "no one can be at the same time a sincere Catholic and a true socialist," rendering the term "Christian-Socialist" an oxymoron.[48]

Pius XI also responded to those who interpreted *Rerum Novarum* as favoring "the wealthier classes against the proletariat" (sec. 44). He saw the Church's defense of private property, rather than its endorsement of class hierarchy, as the cause of these interpretations. Acknowledging that defending private property brought with it the "double danger" that the diminution of property's social character might lead to individualism while the diminution of its private character might lead to collectivism, Pius XI reiterated the distinction between the rights to possession and to use. Proper use must be judged in relation to both the individual and the common good. When the natural law failed to define the duties of ownership, the matter was to be left to the cautious discretion of the state. Yet Pius XI went further than Leo XIII in holding that the right to property is not abrogated by either its nonuse or even its misuse (secs. 47–49).[49]

The Catholic ideology of a divinely ordained hierarchical class order continued to shape papal teaching on wages and class harmony, though *Quadragesimo Anno* aimed to provide more specific suggestions for alleviating the strain of class divisions. Pius XI made a special plea for "a contract of partnership" between labor and ownership, in which workers

---

46. Pius XI differed from Leo XIII in his use of the term "laissez-faire." Where Leo pitted "the rich" or "the wealthy" against the socialists, Pius XI was explicit in his use of the term laissez-faire, and even points to the "so-called Manchester School" (sec. 54) as the opposite extreme of socialism and an unacceptable alternative.

47. Camp, *The Papal Ideology of Social Reform*, 67–68.

48. Pius XI, "Quadragesimo Anno," in *Catholic Social Thought*, ed. O'Brien and Shannon, 67–69.

49. Ibid., 52–53; see also Camp, *The Papal Ideology of Social Reform*, 66, on Pius XI's corrective of Leo XIII in regard to the rightful acquisition and possession of property.

would have a share in both profits and setting wages. While such a scheme could only come voluntarily, it proved to be a key aspect of the encyclical among its interpreters. A "just" wage, Pius XI contended, must not only be "sufficient" to support a worker and *his* family (Pius XI continued to see the role of women as exclusively domestic and judged their forced placement into the working world to be "most unfortunate"), but must also enable a profit for business ownership and keep with the common good by allowing for the employment of as many people as possible (secs. 70–75). This last stipulation reflected the staggering unemployment rate of the Depression era, though he insisted that the massive labor pool was no excuse for sub-subsistence wages (sec. 74).[50]

The most influential and durable feature of *Quadragesimo Anno* was the articulation of the *principle of subsidiarity*. This principle, again derived from natural law, was defined by Pius XI as that "right order" of society in which smaller bodies did not transfer "to the larger and higher collectivity functions which can be performed and provided for by lesser and subordinate bodies" (sec. 79). In other words, if something can be "performed and provided for" by a family, why leave it up to the city government? If it can be done at the factory, why leave it up to the state? Subsidiarity was indicative of a theology of *personalism* found in the writings of Pius XI and developed by later popes. The personalist maintained that "everything social is related to the person and must promote its perfection," culminating in union with God.[51] Sociopolitical systems were measured with respect to their impact on the individual, while the individual could never be denigrated for the sake of the system. The principle of subsidiarity was thought to be a vehicle for maintaining human dignity and, therefore, the common good. As we shall see in later chapters, however, the phrase "performed and provided for" resisted precise application and rendered the principle amenable to a broad range of policy perspectives.

Subsidiarity was at the heart of Pius XI's model for a Christian economic order. Leo XIII had referred to the guild system as a model for class harmony. Pius XI developed this idea further, arguing for a corporatist system. Essentially, this involved two tiers of professional and interprofessional groups. In the first tier, employers would work together

---

50. Pius XI, "Quadragesimo Anno," 59.
51. Wilhelm Weber, "Society and State as a Problem for the Church," in *History of the Church*, vol. 10, ed. Jedin, Repgen, and Dolan, 237–38.

with unions to control wages, prices, and production in an industry. In the second tier, representatives from the various industries would come together to regulate trade and production in the larger society, always aiming toward the preservation of the common good. The state would recognize these syndicates, could provide assistance in their organization, and could interact with them in a manner that Pius XI left ambiguous (secs. 88–98).[52]

To a great degree, the corporative order that Pius XI described mirrored the economic and organizational goals of Mussolini's fascist government (as we will discuss in greater detail in Chapter 6). The major difference, however, was the ideology underlying the corporative orders. As noted earlier, the fascists were motivated toward consolidation of power and the promotion of the Party, while the Catholics were motivated by the promotion of the common good directed toward union with God, mediated, of course, by the authority of the Church. Pius XI understood this distinction to be profound.[53]

---

52. Pius XI, "Quadragesimo Anno," secs. 88–98, 62–64.
53. On Italian fascist corporatism, see D'Agostino, *Rome in America*, chaps. 6–7; John F. Pollard, *The Vatican and Italian Fascism, 1929–32* (New York: Cambridge University Press, 1985), 11–12; Lyttleton, *The Seizure of Power*, 202–5. Lyttleton cites Alfredo Rocco, *Scritti e discorsi politici: Vol. II* (Milan: Giuffre, 1938), 631–45, noting that the corporatist "programme outlined by Rocco was, in all essentials, that finally adopted by Fascism" (205). Despite the differences between the Italian fascist and Catholic visions of the corporate order, there has been considerable confusion regarding their similarities over the years. As a result, Catholic historians have been concerned with distancing Pius XI and Catholic corporatism from fascism. David O'Brien wrote that Pius XI "took pains to distinguish his proposals from the existing system of Italian fascism" (O'Brien, *American Catholics and Social Reform: The New Deal Years* [New York: Oxford University Press, 1968], 21), while Wilhelm Weber asserted that "in *Quadragesimo Anno* Pius XI attacked fascist corporatism" (Weber, "Society and State as a Problem for the Church," 255). I suggest, however, that descriptive terms such as "took pains" and "attacked" distort the position of Pius XI as reflected in *Quadragesimo Anno*. Consider the following quotation from section 65 of *Quadragesimo Anno*: "There are some who fear that the State is substituting itself in the place of private initiative, instead of limiting itself to necessary and sufficient help and assistance. It is feared that the new syndical and corporative order [of Italy] possesses an excessively bureaucratic and political character, and that, notwithstanding the general advantages referred to above, it risks serving political aims rather than contributing to the restoration of social order and the improvement of the same." A close reading of this quotation, in relation to the encyclical as a whole, does not reveal a sterling indictment of fascist corporatism but a cautious distinction. Note that Pius XI writes in the passive voice, employing expressions like "it is feared" and "there are some who fear," instead of "we fear." Pius XI does not use this detached and objective voice in his denunciations of socialism or laissez-faire capitalism, the two errors resulting from liberalism (fascism's common enemy). Furthermore, Pius XI did not devote considerable space in his encyclical to Italian fascist corporatism in comparison to the attacks on laissez-faire capitalism and socialism. I do not make this argument to underplay the distinction between Roman Catholic and Italian fascist

The subtext of *Quadragesimo Anno*, like *Rerum Novarum*, was the authority of the Church. No less than Leo XIII, Pius XI attributed economic disorder and social tension to alienation from the Church. Original sin was to blame for "defection from the Christian law in social and economic matters" and was the ultimate cause "of the apostasy of many workingmen from the Catholic faith." It was due to original sin that "the marvelous harmony of man's faculties [had] been so deranged that now he is easily led astray by low desires, and strongly tempted to prefer the transient goods of this world to the lasting goods of heaven" (sec. 132).[54] A positive transformation of the economic order could only occur when a world that had "fallen back into paganism," and in which "whole classes of men" had denied Christ, would be made into "auxiliary soldiers of the Church," ready to do battle against those ideologies that challenged Catholic supremacy (sec. 141).[55]

While a theological analysis may be content to view the choice demanded by Pius XI as one between human-generated ideologies on the one hand and God on the other, the methods at our disposal in this study require that we redescribe the conflict as one between human systems of authority. Loyalty to class, party, or church are not, in this case, measured along a "secular/sacred" divide, but are instead all three ideological constructions claiming authority by appeal to the transcendent category of nature.

Like *Rerum Novarum* forty years earlier, *Quadragesimo Anno* presented the culturally specific as natural and put forward a distinctively Catholic ideology, complete with divinely ordained social hierarchies, gendered understandings of wage justice, standards for governmental action, and an activist role for bishops and clergy of the Church. In the hands of the Catholic faithful, both encyclicals took on the status of myth, seen as presenting a credible description of nature and the social order, and rendered authoritative in the advancement of individual and social causes relating to the economic order. In an American context, these myths would be refashioned countless times as Catholics struggled to establish their distinctive readings of a just socioeconomic order as authoritative and authentic.

---

corporatist visions, but instead to demonstrate the complicated context in which the encyclical was written, and the apologetic contexts in which the histories about the encyclical have been written.

54. Pius XI, "Quadragesimo Anno," 71.
55. Ibid., 75.

(2)

Sanctifying Life on the Land

For the faithful, sanctification is an ontological state. The holiness of people, places, times, and actions are understood as intrinsic and capable of revealing themselves. For the scholar of religion, however, lack of access to "natures" and "essences" renders holiness immeasurable and untestable. Instead, sanctity is conceived as a disposition toward those people, places, times, and actions that is cultivated through discourse. In other words, we produce holiness by our words and actions. The sacred becomes such by rhetorical and ritualistic postures that arise to meet specific social and personal needs. Sanctification, from this academic point of view, results from a change of perspective rather than a change in ontology, and transforming this perspective often requires substantial and intentional effort. The sanctity of life on the land in the Roman Catholic context, fueled by the language of the social encyclicals, is our first illustration of the production of the sacred in the service of a Catholic worldview.

The generation before Vatican II experienced profound transformation in the American economy, particularly with respect to its agricultural sector. Steadily since the Civil War, urban industrialization had been luring rural dwellers into the cities, rapid population growth necessitated higher crop yields, technology had been increasing the farmer's need for large capital expenditures, global trade had demanded the creation of mediating bodies that stood between farmers and those who consumed their crops, and the need for more land, better machines, and greater production to remain competitive in the marketplace assured that banks, mortgages, and debt would become permanent fixtures in the rural economy. By World War II, the role of the government in regulating agriculture appeared irreversible. The transforming social conditions of farm life brought with them many changes in ideological posture among rural Americans, all designed to navigate the new developments with the least amount of damage to personal integrity, social standing, and economic security.

Among the ideological responses were those colored by Roman Catholicism. Bound by the mythic narratives of *Rerum Novarum* and *Quadragesimo Anno* and armed with the lexicon these texts provided, Catholics on the land went about attempting to address their rapidly changing material circumstances. Viewed comparatively, the National Catholic Rural Life Conference (NCRLC) and the Catholic Worker (CW) movement, in their efforts to shape both rural living and Catholic culture in the American agrarian setting, illustrate a range of uses for which this mythology served. Though sharing many assumptions in common, both movements fashioned distinctive ways of living an "authentically" Catholic life through their own readings of the encyclicals.

Rural Life in America

We tend to describe ideological systems in linear terms, as coherently connected streams of ideas. But when manifested in the lives of real people, the image of a stream gives way to that of an estuary where ideological fragments collide, overlap, and morph. The ideology that produced the mythic encyclicals that spoke to the lives of agrarian Catholics at midcentury was no different, for Catholic mythology shared space with a number of other ideological strands that were brought to bear on the changing social conditions of the countryside. The most dominant of these strands, affecting nearly every rural reform movement, was the Jeffersonian agrarian ideal that saw yeoman farmers, with their own property and their self-subsistence, as the only economically free people in the nation and therefore the bedrock of democracy. In 1955 the historian Richard Hofstadter coined the term "agrarian myth" to describe this ideal — an ideal coupled with the belief that yeoman farmers developed a heightened morality from their supposed simplicity and close interaction with nature.[1] Whether the "agrarian myth" as it evolved really

---

1. Richard Hofstadter, *The Age of Reform: From Bryan to F.D.R.* (New York: Knopf, 1955), 23–30; Mary L. Schneider, "Visions of Land and Farmer: American Civil Religion and the National Catholic Rural Life Conference," in *An American Church: Essays on the Americanization of the Catholic Church*, ed. David J. Alvarez (Morgana: St. Mary's College

reflected Jefferson's own perspective,[2] there is no doubt as to the impact this myth had on American agrarian movements, beginning with Populism of the late 1800s and continuing today.

Though generally unsuccessful in rural communities, socialism also played a role in addressing agricultural transformation. While primarily an urban movement, socialism arguably had its most sustained American political success in rural Oklahoma during the first two decades of the twentieth century.[3] The coupling of Marxist principles with Protestant evangelical and charismatic Christianities proved a potent social force among those who celebrated the "proletarian Jesus."[4] Urban and secular socialists may have scoffed, but the ideological syncretism resonated with struggling farmers of Oklahoma and a handful of other rural communities.

Protestant responses to the rural life crisis coalesced around the American Country Life Association, founded in 1919 after more than a decade of Protestant activism on behalf of agrarian reform. The Country Life movement derived its theological outlook through the voice of the Social Gospel postmillennialists who sought to prepare the way for the kingdom by abolishing the poverty that went hand in hand with the industrial revolution.[5] Its strategy was also shaped by the burgeoning field of sociology, distilled especially through the mind of Presbyterian minister and Columbia University Ph.D. Warren H. Wilson. For Wilson and other Country Life advocates, the failure of American family farms could be traced to poor business management.[6] The movement spearheaded by figures like Wilson has been characterized as an attempt to bring the urban industrial values of efficiency, mechanization, and

---

of California, 1979), 102; Robert D. Cross, "The Changing Image of the City Among American Catholics," *Catholic Historical Review* 48 (April 1962): 33-35.

2. For more on this debate, see Joyce Appleby, "Commercial Farming and the 'Agrarian Myth' in the Early Republic," *The Journal of American History* 68 (March 1982): 833-49; Lance Banning, "Jeffersonian Ideology Revisited: Liberal and Classical Ideas in the New American Republic," *William and Mary Quarterly* 43 (January 1986): 3-19.

3. See Jim Bissett, *Agrarian Socialism in America: Marx, Jefferson, and Jesus in the Oklahoma Countryside, 1904-1920* (Norman: University of Oklahoma Press, 1999), 3.

4. Ibid., 83-104, esp. 89; Bissett cites *Beckham County Advocate*, November 27, 1913; *Appeal to Reason*, December 21, 1895; *New Century*, April 25, 1913; and *Ellis County Advocate*, May 15, 1919.

5. Jeffrey Marlett, *Saving the Heartland: Catholic Missionaries in Rural America* (DeKalb: Northern Illinois University Press, 2002), 12-13.

6. Jeffrey L. Gall, "Presbyterians, Warren Wilson, and the Country Life Movement," *The Journal of Presbyterian History* 76 (Fall 1998): 218-19, 226.

organization to the countryside.[7] Some have argued that the primary motivation for the movement rested in attempting to improve agricultural productivity as a means of lowering food costs for urban dwellers.[8] Still, the movement's guiding assumptions and solutions were to be influential to later reform movements, including the NCRLC.[9]

Another ideological strand developed in response to the centralization of property and the monopolization of wealth so characteristic of early twentieth-century economic life: the decentralist movement. For decentralists, large-scale industrial production was the enemy and was blamed for "the dispossession of the propertied middle class of shopkeepers and small manufacturers, the creation of a depersonalized and propertyless working class, and the centralization of economic and political wealth into fewer hands."[10] Decentralists saw the Great Depression as the inevitable result of a trend toward consolidation and "economic giantism." At the same time, the Great Depression was a prime opportunity to promote the restoration of widespread property ownership and a return to small-scale living.[11]

Decentralism appealed to a broad assortment of the disaffected, from the monarchist Seward Collins—founder of the pro-fascist magazine *American Review*—to the decidedly un-fascist Herbert Agar, Pulitzer Prize–winning journalist and London correspondent for the *Louisville Courier-Journal*. Agar was a founder of the decentralist magazine *Free America*, and he established close ties with perhaps the most prominent American decentralist advocates, a collection of writers, scholars, and intellectuals known as the Southern Agrarians.[12] Literary luminaries such as Robert Penn Warren and Allen Tate (before his conversion to Catholicism) joined in 1930 with ten others, all connected to Vanderbilt University, to publish a manifesto titled *I'll Take My Stand: The South and*

---

7. Ibid., 215. See also Marlett, *Saving the Heartland*, 12; both Gall and Marlett cite David Danbom, *The Resisted Revolution: Urban America and the Industrialization of Agriculture, 1900–1930* (Ames: Iowa State University Press, 1979), esp. 23–50.

8. Gall, "Presbyterians, Warren Wi4lson, and the Country Life Movement," 215; cites Danbom, *The Resisted Revolution*.

9. Marlett, *Saving the Heartland*, 13–14.

10. Edward Shapiro, "Decentralist Intellectuals and the New Deal," *The Journal of American History* 58 (March 1972): 938–57, quotation taken from 939.

11. Ibid., 939.

12. Albert E. Stone Jr., "Seward Collins and the *American Review*: Experiment in Pro-Fascism, 1933–37," *American Quarterly* 12 (Spring 1960): 3–19; Shapiro, "Decentralist Intellectuals and the New Deal," 938–39; Herbert Agar, *A Time for Greatness* (Boston: Little, Brown, 1942), esp. 3–39.

the Agrarian Tradition. The essays as a whole constituted a call for Southerners to return to the land and establish an economy built on small markets and subsistence farming. Replete with wistful allusions to a collectively imagined bygone era—an era marked by a sense of order and social connectedness grounded in shared religion, political, and economic independence, and a stable racial hierarchy (sentiments that some contributors later disavowed)—*I'll Take My Stand* advocated a way of life akin to a medieval feudal economy infused with a democratic spirit.[13]

In short, changes befalling rural America in the middle of the twentieth century were addressed by appealing to several ideological variants, though the support for widespread property ownership, self-sufficiency, and anti-industrialism of the decentralist movement, closely connected as it was to the Jeffersonian agrarian myth, held the broadest appeal to those facing the challenges of agrarian life.

Distributism

In addition to encountering the same economic dislocation, Catholics involved in the NCRLC and the CW movement shared one important thing in common with non-Catholic decentralists like Agar and the Southern Agrarians: they were all deeply influenced by an English (and predominantly Roman Catholic) movement known as distributism. Hilaire Belloc, G. K. Chesterton, Eric Gill, and the Dominican Vincent McNabb were the most influential distributist thinkers, and by the 1930s their impact on American audiences grew tremendously. This impact was fueled by the opening of a New York branch of the Sheed and Ward publishing house, a press notable for its publication of Catholic philosophers and theologians.

G. K. Chesterton had been a socialist before his conversion to Catholicism. When *Rerum Novarum* was released, he related, "nobody in our really well-informed world took much notice of it." The encyclical rejected socialism, after all, and was easy for the young Chesterton to

---

13. See Louis D. Rubin, introduction to *I'll Take My Stand: The South and the Agrarian Tradition* (New York: Harper Torchbook, 1962), iv–xxx; Paul V. Murphy, *The Rebuke of History: The Southern Agrarians and American Conservative Thought* (Chapel Hill: University of North Carolina Press, 2001), esp. "Introduction: The Rebuke of History," and chap. 1, "The Radical Conservatism of *I'll Take My Stand*"; Stone, "Seward Collins and the *American Review*," 13–14; Shapiro, "Decentralist Intellectuals and the New Deal," esp. 938–41.

dismiss. But eventually he concluded that the "obvious cure for private property being given to the few" was not consolidating property into the hands of the state, as socialists proposed, but instead, "to see that it is given to the many. . . . Then, having discovered that fact as a fact, we look back at Leo XIII and discover in his old and dated document, of which we took no notice at the time, that he was saying then exactly what we are saying now. 'As many as possible of the working classes should become owners.'"[14] And so it was that the founders of a movement they called distributism, formalized in an organization known as the Distributist League, discovered in Leo XIII what they believed to be an intellectual kinsman.[15]

English distributists, like their American cousins, took from *Rerum Novarum* the sacred right to private property. Both capitalism and communism were seen as two sides of the same coin, each leading to the monopolization of productive property and rendering people submissive to the larger system, thereby stripped of dignity.[16] If the term "capitalism" only referred to private property and the use of capital to ensure that "the economic operations of to-day must leave something over for the economic operations of tomorrow," neither the distributists nor Leo XIII would have objected. But Chesterton argued such a definition of the term would be so benign as to render it useless. Instead, the distributists defined capitalism as an "economic condition" that led to the creation of a proletariat class resulting from the concentration of wealth and the productive means in the hands of a few. Reminiscent of Marx, this proletariat class was defined by their servitude to capitalists in exchange for a wage.[17] Unlike Marx, however, the Distributist League promoted wider distribution of private property, to "be achieved by protecting and facilitating the ownership of individual enterprises in land, shops, and factories." The goal was not greater purchasing power—the

---

14. G. K. Chesterton, *The Catholic Church and Conversion* (New York: Macmillan, 1950), 99–100.
15. Michael Coren, *Gilbert: The Man Who Was G. K. Chesterton* (New York: Paragon House, 1990), 241; Hilaire Belloc, "The Faith and Capitalism," in *Essays of a Catholic* (New York: Macmillan, 1931), 295.
16. G. K. Chesterton, *The Outline of Sanity* (London: Methuen, 1926), 4; Hilaire Belloc, *The Servile State* (New York: Henry Holt, 1946), xix–xxvii.
17. Chesterton, *The Outline of Sanity*, 5–6; Hilaire Belloc, *The Restoration of Property* (New York: Sheed and Ward, 1936), 19. Belloc's definition of capitalism read, "a state of society in which a minority control the means of production leaving the mass of citizens dispossessed. Such a dispossessed body of citizens is called a 'Proletariat.'"

goal was economic freedom.[18] Government revisions of the tax structure, favoring small farmers and small businesses while penalizing capital consolidation, along with changes in the legal rights of small corporate shareholders allowing them greater influence in decision making, were key to the Distributist League platform.[19]

While not a formally Roman Catholic organization, the Distributist League was dominated by Catholic apologists, a fact leading to tensions between them and the league's non-Catholic members.[20] In keeping with the call of the papal encyclicals, league representatives like Belloc viewed the success of a distributist economy as inseparable from the restoration of Roman Catholicism. Though Belloc cautioned against linking Catholicism too closely with any temporal economic and political order, the pervasive presence of Catholic philosophy was a precondition for distributism's success. It was "in the reconversion of our world to the Catholic standpoint," wrote Belloc, that there "lies the only hope for the future."[21] Moreover, the cause of human misery, industrial capitalism, "arose out of the denial of Catholic morals at the Reformation," Belloc asserted.[22] Max Weber's *Protestant Ethic and the Spirit of Capitalism* and R. H. Tawney's *Religion and the Rise of Capitalism*, while not cited in Belloc's work, lent credence to his assertion, in the minds of some Catholic readers, that the development of modern capitalism and Protestantism went hand in hand. Such views did little to win over non-Catholics to the distributist cause.

With its naturalization of property, its frequent references to the golden age of the medieval guild system,[23] and its naturalization of social hierarchy,[24] it is not difficult to see the influence of the Roman Catholic

---

18. The Distributist League, *Do We Agree? A Debate Between G. K. Chesterton and Bernard Shaw with Hilaire Belloc in the Chair* (Oxford: Kemp Hall Press, 1928), 48, back-page advertisement; Belloc, *The Restoration of Property*, 9–10.
19. Belloc, *The Restoration of Property*, 28, 68–72, 96.
20. Coren, *Gilbert*, 241.
21. Belloc, *The Crisis of Civilization* (New York: Fordham University Press, 1937), 241–43, 4–5.
22. Belloc, "The Faith and Capitalism," 288; Belloc reiterated this sentiment in *The Restoration of Property*, 41.
23. See, for instance, Belloc, *The Crisis of Civilization*, 218, or Chesterton, *The Catholic Church and Conversion*, 63–64.
24. See, for instance, Belloc, *The Crisis of Civilization*, 223: "The fourth principle is perhaps the most important of all. If we are to prevent the arising of a proletariat, which evil it is the whole object of the guild to prevent, we must have hierarchy. Hierarchy is essential to all human affairs anyhow. It is essential to the management of a guild as to the management of any other social organism."

social ideology on the agenda of the distributists. *Quadragesimo Anno*'s principle of subsidiarity provided fodder for the distributists' preference for decentralization and smallness. Furthermore, the appeal that these English distributists held for a group so contextually dissimilar as the Southern Agrarians is also sensible. American Southern culture came to be built around the ideology of natural social hierarchies, especially those related to race. Since well before the Civil War, Southern divines made theological appeals to the medieval feudal system as a heavenly sanctioned means of authorizing their own social order in the context of slavery. Even without reference to categories of race, the distributist rhetoric was bound to strike a familiar chord.[25]

The National Catholic Rural Life Conference

By the late 1930s, encyclically inspired distributism had fused with the Jeffersonian agrarian myth in the strategies and rhetoric of the NCRLC. Mary Schneider has called the decade between 1935 and the end of World War II the "period for Americanization" of the NCRLC, when Catholic apologetics gave way to the imagery of Jeffersonian democracy. Catholic rural lifers also paralleled their situation to that of the Pilgrims who saw themselves as "saints" cultivating the garden of a new Eden.[26] But even in light of the "Americanized" language, we must understand that the NCRLC was not arguing that Catholicism had finally aligned itself with a distinctively American ethos that was better suited to address the rural problem, but instead from the perspective that resources from the American cultural menu could be used to support a vision of nature to which the Roman Catholic Church had had access all along. Therefore, the preservation of America's imagined soul—its farms and rural communities—rested on the cultivation and flourishing of rural Catholicism.

On the eve of World War II, Roman Catholics represented only 20 percent of rural Americans, and less than 20 percent of all Catholics lived in rural areas.[27] The low numbers were not for lack of effort. As

---

25. See Eugene Genovese, *The Slaveholder's Dilemma: Freedom and Progress in Southern Conservative Thought, 1820–1860* (Columbia: University of South Carolina Press, 1994).
26. Schneider, "Visions of Land and Farmer," 99–102.
27. David Bovée, "The Church and the Land: The National Catholic Rural Life Conference and American Society, 1923–1985" (Ph.D. diss., University of Chicago, 1986), 1:148; Marlett, *Saving the Heartland*, 4.

early as 1879, efforts by the Irish Colonization Association (ICA) to transplant urban Irish immigrants to rural communities had been initiated. Spearheaded by Bishop John Lancaster Spalding of Peoria over a decade before *Rerum Novarum,* the ICA coupled the promotion of Catholic piety with an appeal to the Jeffersonian democratic ideal.[28] So too did the German Central-Verein, an organization of German-American Catholics made up of a significant proportion of immigrant farmers. The Central-Verein appealed to the language of "organicism" that pervaded *Rerum Novarum*. Paradoxically, as Philip Gleason has pointed out, these appeals ran counter to the individualistic fervor so vital to the Jeffersonian agrarian ideal. They managed to live with paradox, however, and continued to promote the middle-class virtue embodied by the yeoman farmer while at the same time repudiating "the American dream of middle-class success."[29]

Though apparently not directly influenced by the English distributists, Frederick P. Kenkel, the key figure in the leadership of the Central-Verein's social reform program from 1908 to 1952, also turned his gaze to the Middle Ages to inspire his vision of the future. The son of German immigrants, Kenkel was an unlikely figure in the Catholic rural life movement, having been thoroughly irreligious into his mid-twenties and having been born to a fairly well-to-do family in the city of Chicago where he would spend most of his youth, with the occasional extended stay in Germany. A return to the Catholic fold after the tragic death of his first wife supplied Kenkel with an ideological framework in which to articulate his discontent with the modern age. The combination of German Romanticism and the Church's social teachings fueled his desire for a radical restructuring of the social order in which human interaction would be conceived organically and mediated through a vocational system ordered similarly to the arrangement of medieval guilds. The work of the nineteenth-century German bishop Wilhelm von Ketteler was especially inspiring to Kenkel, particularly Ketteler's focus on protecting the working class through a combination of private self-help organizations and trade unions, as well as carefully targeted legislation for the protection of the poor. The vision of the German Jesuit economist Heinrich Pesch also shaped Kenkel's outlook. Pesch's corporatist

---

28. Schneider, "Visions of Land and Farmer," 101–2; Cross, "The Changing Image of the City Among American Catholics," 33–35.
29. Philip Gleason, *The Conservative Reformers: German-American Catholics and the Social Order* (Notre Dame, Ind.: University of Notre Dame Press, 1968), 186–89, esp. 189.

vocational organizing principles guided Pius XI's own model in *Quadragesimo Anno*. In Kenkel's hands, Pesch's work laid the foundation for a revitalized agrarian system made up of "independent owners of small units of productive property," including "tradesmen, and shopkeepers," but most important, farmers. It was this emphasis that led Kenkel and the Central-Verein to be early and influential advocates of the NCRLC.[30]

Like its predecessors, the NCRLC promoted its version of economic justice through its rhetorical appeal to an array of mythic resources, but none as central as the social encyclicals of Leo XIII and Pius XI. The ideologies reflected in the encyclicals were reconstituted in rural America through hundreds of books, pamphlets, lectures, conferences, and societies generated by the NCRLC in the pre–Vatican II years. Changes in the American economic landscape by the late 1950s also brought with them changes in the rhetorical strategies of the organization. Moreover, the NCRLC's vision of an authentically Catholic social order differed not only from those of urban Catholic laborers and industrialists but also from those of fellow rural-life advocates, like the Catholic Worker.

Founded in 1923 by Edwin V. O'Hara, the NCRLC was formed by priests to promote ideas beneficial to rural life among laypeople and to help rural priests nationwide. From the beginning, improving the lives of Catholic farmers was closely tied to the promotion of the Catholic faith in America. Fear that low urban birthrates, coupled with the overwhelmingly Protestant character of the rural United States, would prevent the Church from thriving in the long term rested at the heart of what NCRLC leaders called "The Catholic Rural Problem."[31] Immigration restrictions in the 1920s aimed primarily at curbing the rise of the Catholic population in a nativist climate stoked the flames of Catholic concerns. The Great Depression forced the NCRLC to broaden its focus, however, and while never abandoning its missionary character, the immediate economic problems related to rural life consumed the organization's attention.[32]

---

30. Ibid., 90–143, and 188; see also Marlett, *Saving the Heartland*, 15–21, 61; on Ketteler, see William Edward Hogan, "The Development of Bishop Wilhelm Emmanuel von Ketteler's Interpretation of the Social Problem" (Ph.D. diss., Catholic University of America, 1946), esp. chap. 2.

31. Bovée, "The Church and the Land," 1:148; Luigi G. Ligutti, 4 *Working Aims of the Catholic Rural Life Conference*, Marquette University Archives (hereafter MUA), Milwaukee, Wisconsin, NCRLC Series 5/1, Box 1, "General Publications, 1940–1944." Ligutti's pamphlet outlined the argument of "The Catholic Rural Problem," which had been posed since the founding of the NCRLC, in a concise and clear manner.

32. George E. Mowry and Blaine A. Brownell, *The Urban Nation, 1920–1980* (New York: Hill and Wang, 1981), 30; Bovée, "The Church and the Land," 1:194.

The rapid growth of the NCRLC came with the appointment of an Italian immigrant priest, Luigi Ligutti, to be its executive secretary in 1940. Ligutti arrived in Des Moines, Iowa, with his family in 1912, joined the priesthood at the age of twenty-two in 1917, and became a U.S. citizen the following year.[33] His interest in rural life began in earnest with his appointment to parishes in the small rural towns of southwestern Iowa. One town Ligutti served, Magnolia, was an Irish settlement that he described as containing "the poorest of God's poor. The people were still primitive."[34] It was in these years that Ligutti familiarized himself with the work of Edwin O'Hara, became a student of the distributist works of Chesterton and Belloc, and discovered Leo XIII's *Rerum Novarum*. The words of pope Leo XIII informed his homilies and dealings with parishioners, and by 1931 Ligutti was an active participant in the NCRLC.[35]

One passage from *Rerum Novarum* in particular found its way onto the pages of NCRLC publications and Ligutti's own speeches and writings more than any other:

> If working people can be encouraged to look forward to owning a few acres of land, the result will be that the gulf between vast wealth and deep poverty will be bridged over, and the two orders will be brought nearer together. Another consequence will be the great abundance of fruits of the earth. Men always work harder and more readily when they work on that which is their own, nay they learn to love the very soil which yields in response to the labor of their hands, not only food to eat, but an abundance of the good things for themselves (sec. 35).[36]

This passage validated the necessity and sanctity of land ownership, while holding out the promise of "good things" coming with it. For Ligutti and the NCRLC, that promise was threatened by a rise in monopolies on

---

33. David S. Bovée, "Catholic Rural Life Leader: Luigi G. Ligutti," *U.S. Catholic Historian* 8 (Fall 1989): 143; Vincent A. Yzermans, *The People I Love: A Biography of Luigi G. Ligutti* (Collegeville, Minn.: The Liturgical Press, 1976), 51.
34. Yzermans, *The People I Love*, 17.
35. Ibid., 19–20, 31–32.
36. This is Ligutti's translation, which deviates from O'Brien and Shannon's with the words "owning a few acres of land," which is translated in the latter as "obtaining a share of the land"; see Luigi Ligutti and John C. Rawe, *Rural Roads to Security: America's Third Struggle for Freedom* (Milwaukee: Bruce Publishing, 1940), 99; Yzermans, *The People I Love*, 42.

capital, corporate farming, tenancy, the limited credit resources of a troubled economy, and a culture of urbanization that lured rural youth off the land and into factories and office buildings.

By the 1940s, if that threat were to be summarized in one word, it would be "bigness." Cries bemoaning "bigness" were common throughout the nation, but particularly within Catholic circles. Big collectives, at the root of communism, were seen as simply the flip side of the "big corporation" symptomatic of capitalism. Both trends toward consolidation of power and growth in size were viewed as threats to human dignity.[37] Such concerns were buttressed by Pope Pius XII's appeal to the teachings of his predecessor in *Quadragesimo Anno*. "Modern cities," said Pius XII in a speech to farm owners in 1946,

> with their constant growth and great concentration of inhabitants, are the typical product of the control wielded over economic life and the very life of man by the interests of large capital. As Our glorious Predecessor, Pius XI, has so effectively shown in his Encyclical, *Quadragesimo Anno*, it happens too often that human needs do not, *in accordance with their natural and objective importance,* rule economic life and the use of capital. On the contrary, capital and the desire for gain determine what the needs of man should be and to what extent they are to be satisfied.[38]

The NCRLC developed strategies to combat bigness rooted in its reading of the papal encyclicals. Beginning with accepting the sanctity of private property, like the English distributists before them, land ownership was interwoven with the centrality of the family in the NCRLC's ideology. Following Leo XIII's axiom regarding the family's anterior position to all other forms of social organization in the development of society, Ligutti and other NCRLC representatives painted a portrait of farm living with "traditional" families at its center. The NCRLC's *Manifesto on Rural Life* began its systematic outline of the Catholic rural ideology with a chapter on "The Rural Catholic Family" and accorded to the

---

37. For examples, see "Nationalization," *The Commonweal* 44 (August 2, 1946): 372–73; Rudolph Edward Morris, "Christianity and Collectivist Trends," *Thought* 23 (September 1948): 463–65, 468, 474.

38. *The Pope Speaks on Rural Life,* MUA, NCRLC Series 5/1, Box 1, "General Publications, 1944–1946," 8–9, emphasis added.

family a "place of primacy" among all other social organizations. Families were "both the source of population and the chief agency in the training and education of the child. The Christian family is the keystone of the arch which supports our Christian civilization," they wrote.[39] Echoing *Rerum Novarum,* private property was highlighted as vital to preserving the stability of the family, which consequently assured the stable preservation of the Roman Catholic tradition. The new urban society spawned by the industrial revolution, on the other hand, was seen as working "against the family in favor of divorce, desertion, temporary unions, [and] companionate marriage."

It is telling that the NCRLC's 1956 manual, *A Program for the Family Farm,* defined the family farm as "a socio-economic institution in which the capital, labor, and management of the family is organized toward the production of food and fibre for the benefit of family and society."[40] Note that the object of this definition was not the farm itself, but the family. This was in keeping with the NCRLC's mantra that family farming was "a way of life and not just another industry."[41] In the Jeffersonian tradition, Ligutti and others saw family farms not only as the core element in the preservation of Christianity, but also as bulwarks against political and economic tyranny. Whenever possible, papal statements were highlighted to illustrate the compatibility between the Catholic and Jeffersonian ideals.[42]

Not surprisingly, the NCRLC ideal family did not deviate significantly from that ideal generated by dominant Catholic teachings. The image of the Holy Family—Jesus, Mary, and Joseph—was iconic. "An enduring moral union of husband, wife, and children for a common good to be attained by their cooperative activity" was how one NCRLC publication described a family. The woman's role in this union was clearly

---

39. National Catholic Rural Life Conference, *Manifesto on Rural Life* (Milwaukee: Bruce Publishing, 1939), 3.

40. *A Program for the Family Farm,* MUA, NCRLC Series 5/1, Box 2, "Manuals & Programs, 1954–1957," 2.

41. Luigi Ligutti, "Agrarianism, Cooperatives, and the Bishops' Statement," *The Catholic Rural Life Bulletin* 3 (May 1940): 5; this phrase dates back to W. Howard Bishop, president of the NCRLC from 1928 to 1934. Through Bishop's relationship with Herbert Agar, the expression made its way into Agar's writings as well. See Christopher J. Kauffman, "W. Howard Bishop, President of the National Catholic Rural Life Conference, 1928–1934," *U.S. Catholic Historian* 8 (Fall 1989): 29–35; he cites Edgar Schmiedeler, O.S.B., "Herbert Agar, Land of the Free," *Landward* 4 (Spring 1936): 6.

42. Luigi Ligutti, "The Monsignor Says," *The Christian Farmer* 1 (February 1948): 1; "From Rome . . . ," *Land and Home* 9 (December 1946): 95.

delineated by the paternalistic assumptions of both the Church and the prevailing American culture of the day. The woman was to be the "queen" of the farm home. After all, "every woman's hope and ambition," Ligutti had written, "is to become queen of a home, and there is no better place in which to reign as queen than in a home on the land."[43] While husbands provided the resources and raw material for the family, wives took those resources and materials and created a home environment that was beautiful, comfortable, and pleasant. Because the home was the center of religious, cultural, and educational life for the children, the educational burden fell on the mother as well. And as the primary purchaser of domestic goods, the rural wife shared in the responsibilities of managing the family business affairs.[44]

Though tightly circumscribed, NCRLC documents emphasized the "dignity" and importance of the woman's role, which was thought to accord her the status of "interpreter" to the Holy Family ideal.[45] No greater threat was posed to that status than the lure of the labor force outside the home in urban population centers.[46] The NCRLC's founder, Edwin O'Hara, himself had said, "no small part of the rural exodus to the city has been occasioned by the hope of farm women that they might thereby escape some of the drudgery and inconvenience and discomforts which they experience in the farm home."[47] With this in mind, the NCRLC heavily promoted "modern sanitation, appliances, electricity, lighting," and other technological advancements among its top priorities, and its periodicals were filled with advice columns suggesting ways of beautifying the home, tasty recipes, and ideas for family recreation, all designed with women in mind.[48]

While gender hierarchy was ever present in the NCRLC, emphasis on class hierarchy, as naturalized in the social encyclicals, was virtually

43. Mrs. R. B. Sayre, "Nobility of the Queen in a Farm Home," address given on October 6, 1942, at the NCRLC convention in Peoria, Illinois, MUA, NCRLC, Series 8/1, Box 4; L. G. Ligutti, "Keep Youth on the Land," *Land and Home* 6 (September 1943): 71.
44. NCRLC, *Rural Life in a Peaceful World* (Des Moines, Iowa: NCRLC, 1944), 3; Ligutti and Rawe, *Rural Roads to Security*, 299.
45. Raymond Philip Witte, *Twenty-five Years of Crusading: A History of the National Catholic Rural Life Conference* (Des Moines, Iowa: NCRLC, 1948), 82–83.
46. See, for instance, Joint Subcommittee on Low-Income Families of the Joint Committee on the Economic Report, *Low-Income Families*, 81st Cong., 1st sess., December 21, 1949, 514.
47. Timothy Dolan, *"Some Seed Fell on Good Ground": The Life of Edwin V. O'Hara* (Washington, D.C.: Catholic University of America Press, 1992), 78.
48. Ibid; see any issues of *Land and Home, The Christian Farmer,* and *Feet in the Furrows* for examples of these articles and advice columns.

absent. In a sense, Catholic rural lifers believed they were advocating an escape from the class system altogether by promoting self-sufficiency as a hedge against the wage economy. *Rural Roads to Security: America's Third Struggle for Freedom,* coauthored in 1940 by Ligutti and John C. Rawe, diagnosed industrialism, urbanism, and monopolization of capital as the root causes of a class system. Invoking the names of Washington, Lincoln, and Jefferson, the authors saw the ideals of "liberty, equality, precious freedom, our inalienable, God-given rights" as antidotes to class stratification.[49] Apparently without any sense of irony, the American presidential trinity was co-opted in an attack on a liberalism spawned by the Reformation, which "saw only good in the ambitions of men, demanded fullest liberty for the satisfaction of personal aggrandizement without hindrance of law, or organization, or any effort to safeguard one man against the greed of another."[50] Liberalism thus set in motion the perilous course toward industrialism and the creation of a landless, proletarian class. Ligutti and Rawe's solution, of course, was "*family-unit operation and fee-simple, family-basis ownership of land* based on religious principles and spiritually motivated."[51] To those who advocated socialism, communism, or fascism, the authors were prompted to ask: "Do these leaders forget they are speaking to Americans?"[52] And so, two decades before John Courtney Murray's famous effort to do so in *We Hold These Truths,* Ligutti and Rawe penned a manifesto that wove together the dominant strands of American political ideology with the philosophy of Thomas Aquinas and key themes of post–*Rerum Novarum* Catholic thought.

Promoting the Family Farm

Restructuring the economic and social order would require practical measures, and the NCRLC actively promoted many. During the early phase of Ligutti's tenure with the organization, homesteading held the premier place in the NCRLC's list of strategic priorities. The opportunity to put the distributist ideology into action came with the passage of Section 208 of the National Industrial Recovery Act of 1933 that created a

---

49. Ligutti and Rawe, *Rural Roads to Security,* 3–49, esp. 8, 29.
50. Ibid., 3.
51. Ibid., 10, emphasis theirs; see chap. 3 on "Proletarianism."
52. Ibid., 8.

Subsistence Homesteads Division within the Department of the Interior. Thanks largely to Ligutti's petitioning, Granger, Iowa, was chosen as the first site for the new homesteads. Fifty homes were built (about two-thirds of these homes were inhabited by Roman Catholic families) on a 225-acre plot of land.[53] The ideal homestead involved subsistence farming coupled with "some carefully selected cash-crop enterprise only when a considerable supply of year-round home-grown food for the family and for the livestock ha[d] been provided for."[54] Granger was a mining town where workers averaged less than half-a-year's worth of labor. The remainder of the year, families were left wageless and often struggled to survive. The project was designed to address this problem specifically, and it met with some success. By the time official support for the experiment ended in 1951, thirty-two of the original fifty families chosen for the project were still living on the same plots of land.[55]

Homesteading, however, was not a solution for urbanites with no experience in farming, the NCRLC contended. Never did Ligutti or the conference give the impression that farming was anything less than a challenge. As early as Edwin O'Hara, the NCRLC rejected any characterization of being a "back to the land movement" to the extent that it involved those with no rural roots choosing a life of farming. "To send out of the cities families who have no acquaintance with farming cannot result in enriching the agricultural community either economically or socially," wrote O'Hara. Reflecting the animosity rural dwellers felt toward the city, O'Hara described the "back to the land movement" as being "essentially a city movement which seeks with wonted generosity to unload on the country groups of individuals who have failed to make a living in the city."[56] Ligutti shared O'Hara's attitude, leading the NCRLC to emphasize the importance of education and preparation for farm living. They hoped to retain families on the land, and to a lesser extent, recruit those city dwellers with substantial previous farm experience to return to their agrarian roots. Farming was not for disenchanted urbanites caught up in agrarian romanticism.[57]

53. Yzermans, *The People I Love*, 33–35, Bovée, "The Church and the Land," 1:243.
54. Ligutti and Rawe, *Rural Roads to Security*, 121.
55. Yzermans, *The People I Love*, 33–39; Bovée, "The Church and the Land," 1:243.
56. T. Dolan, "Some Seed Fell on Good Ground," 71; cites O'Hara, *The Rural Problem and Its Bearing on Catholic Education* (Columbus: National Catholic Educational Association, 1921), 3; reprinted in Witte, *Twenty-five Years of Crusading*, 45–47.
57. NCRLC, *Manifesto on Rural Life*, 14.

The success of homesteading depended on its coordination with a variety of other pragmatic ventures the NCRLC helped promote. First among these were cooperatives. Rural cooperatives involved independent small farmers pooling their resources to buy things like tools, machinery, seed, and fertilizer, then combining to market their goods. This cooperation eased the burden of the large capital outlays that were necessary to compete with corporate farms. In its earliest years, the NCRLC approached cooperatives with caution for fear of being branded "socialists" in their promotion of a collective endeavor. Only marketing cooperatives were mentioned in the first conference resolutions. But by the late 1930s and early 1940s, this fear had eased (in part because the circumstances of farm life had become more desperate), and production as well as purchasing cooperatives came to be at the core of the NCRLC's agenda. Conservative rural dwellers suspicious of collective action needed only to turn to the words of *Rerum Novarum* and *Quadragesimo Anno* to justify cooperatives, as NCRLC documents like *Rural Roads to Security* and *The Popes and the Social Principles of Rural Life* made clear. "To the citizens of every nation," read one conference source, "the Church says 'Unite and combine for self-help'; 'form associations of mutual help and service'; 'where you are in the same trade or the same profession or the same industry combine into *vocational* groups'; 'unite and combine into *occupational* groups for mutual help and service.'"[58] These citations of the social encyclicals pitted the authority of the papacy against any fears Catholic farmers might have of moving too deeply into socialism by pooling their resources.

For Catholic rural lifers, cooperatives were the agrarian equivalent to the guild system proposed for industrial labor in Pius XI's encyclical. Somewhat paradoxically, the NCRLC was left arguing that not only were these cooperatives a necessity, but at the same time they must remain voluntary, according to their reading of the principle of subsidiarity.[59] Pains were taken to emphasize the compatibility between cooperatives and the American way of life. One NCRLC publication appealed to democracy as the elemental quality of cooperatives, and for good measure used variations on the term "democracy" three times in rapid succession to drive the point home: cooperatives were "organized on a democratic basis

---

58. Ligutti and Rawe, *Rural Roads to Security*, 254; see also *The Popes and the Social Principles of Rural Life*, MUA, NCRLC Series 5/1, Box 1, "1932–1946," emphasis in original.
59. NCRLC, *Manifesto on Rural Life*, 56; NCRLC, *Rural Life in a Peaceful World*, 7.

and controlled by democratic methods" and were "among democracy's best defenses."[60] Clearly the association of cooperatives with socialism affected their rhetoric.[61]

The naturalization of labor unions in the social encyclicals was defended by the NCRLC. Though only a few attempts were made to organize farm unions prior to the late 1960s, when César Chávez organized the United Farm Workers, the NCRLC had begun supporting unionization early. The demise of the family farm could be traced to the rise of corporate farms that employed and exploited tenant and migrant farm workers. By encouraging these workers to unionize, it would benefit the family farms by preventing corporate farms from saving so much on labor costs. By the mid-1950s, the conference began emphasizing that agricultural workers not only had a right to form unions but a "duty" to do so. Only through unions could they have "the means of fulfilling their responsibility to live according to the dignity of their own nature, to care for the bodily and spiritual needs of their family [sic], and to carry out their obligations to the occupation in which they work and to the community [sic] in which they live."[62]

The NCRLC also vigorously promoted credit unions as essential to the success of homesteading. Though the federal government had established farm land banks by 1916 for agrarian assistance, the program became so complicated by the 1920s that many farmers were left bewildered by the system. With the Depression, the availability of credit diminished while the need for it increased, prompting the creation in 1934 of the Farm Credit Administration (FCA). The FCA divided the nation into twelve districts. Each district included a federal bank that issued bonds and first-time mortgages to farmers, a bank specifically for cooperatives in need of extra capital, and a productive credit corporation. The productive credit corporations had as their sole purpose lending to cooperative credit unions, more than five hundred of which existed nationwide by 1940. The NCRLC consistently pushed for more credit unions and lobbied the federal government for more credit at lower

---

60. NCRLC, *Rural Life in a Peaceful World*, 7.
61. For an example of accusations of socialism, see the debate regarding a collective farming movement in Terrebonne, Louisiana, in 1943, in Select Committee of the House Committee on Agriculture, *Farm Security Administration*, 78th Cong., 1st sess., March 18, 1943, 672-75.
62. NCRLC, *A Program for the Family Farm* (1956), MUA, NCRLC Series 5/1, Box 2, "Manuals and Programs, 1954-1957," 11.

rates.[63] For the most part, the FCA was underfunded and the NCRLC's hopes for massive federal commitment to agricultural credit were never realized, spawning criticism of the New Deal and a growing disenchantment among NCRLC leadership with the government's approach to rural life.[64]

Creating a Catholic Rural Culture

Though government support for credit unions did not meet NCRLC expectations, the parish credit union, free from state assistance, ultimately became the organization's model for thrifty financial planning and management. The NCRLC called on parish priests to start these credit unions and encourage all their parishioners to purchase low-cost shares in the venture. By 1959 there were a total of 936 Roman Catholic parish credit unions, representing 75 percent of the total denominationally based credit unions in the United States and Canada. On the whole, parish credit unions accounted for 6 percent of all credit unions nationwide.[65]

For Ligutti and other conference members, the economic success of family farms was inextricably bound to the cultivation of a distinctively Roman Catholic agrarian culture. This involved creating a rhetorical climate that successfully tied farming to doing God's will. The NCRLC accomplished this through retreats, farm schools, recreational activities, and the publication of magazines and pamphlets that promoted a way of thinking and speaking about rural life that placed it in a sanctified realm. If you were not "proud and happy" to be a farmer, Ligutti once wrote, "then you're not a Christian farmer," for the Christian farmer understood life as a means of service to God.[66]

Private property had been firmly established as a natural right in the Catholic ideology, and it was essential that the NCRLC treat this feature with delicacy. After all, while promoting private property undergirded the mission of the conference, the right to private property was also key to promoting an ideology that valued corporate farming and farm

---

63. Edgar Schmiedeler, O.S.B., "Credit for the Farmer," *The Catholic Rural Life Bulletin* 3 (August 1940): 12–13; NCRLC, *Manifesto on Rural Life*, 62; NCRLC, *A Program for the Family Farm*, 9–10.
64. T. Dolan, "*Some Seed Fell on Good Ground,*" 109.
65. Joyce Finnigan, O.F.M., "Starting a Credit Union," *The Priest* 15 (December 1959): 1008–10.
66. Ligutti, "The Monsignor Says," 1, MUA, NCRLC Series 6, Box 6.

monopolies, the bane of the NCRLC. The approach that the NCRLC advocated to temper the "abuse" of this sacred right was tied to the concept of stewardship. Validated by Piux XI's warning in *Quadragesimo Anno* that the right to possession of private property did not extend so far as to authorize its misuse (sec. 47), Ligutti and his cohorts hammered away at stewardship as the framework for understanding the role of property in God's plan. The earth was conceived as a gift from God for which we—especially those who farmed—bore responsibility to preserve and utilize in a socially beneficial manner.

As one of the first Catholic priests to promote tithing to maintain the financial health of the parish, Ligutti composed "A Tither's Creed," in which all of the elements of stewardship advanced by the NCRLC could be found.

> I believe God retains ownership of the earth and of all that grows and dwells therein. . . . I believe that we men are merely the stewards of anything we may legally possess. . . . I believe that God is not only the owner of the earth by right of creation but also by right of His continual care which He bestows upon it. . . . I believe that the sources of material wealth—Land—Labor—Capital—are God's and that which is produced by them is God's directly or indirectly. . . . I believe that in order to acknowledge in a practical way these my beliefs, I must return to God a share of what He has given to me for the establishment and development of His works in this world.[67]

This prayer expressed the belief that private property retained its sacred nature precisely because it was the gift of God's grace. Private property forfeited its sacred status when it was used in a manner that thwarted that grace. Ligutti and other members of the NCRLC were fond of quoting Pius XI's encyclical on communism, *Divini Redemptoris,* written six years after *Quadragesimo Anno*. "Is it not deplorable," Pius XI asked rhetorically, "that the right of private property, defended by the Church, should so often have been used as a weapon to defraud the working man of his just salary and his social rights?"[68] For the NCRLC, then, it was the relationship of God to property—and in turn, the importance of that

---

67. Yzermans, *The People I Love*, 20–21.
68. *The Popes and the Social Principles of Rural Life*, MUA, NCRLC Series 5/1, Box 1, "1932–1946"; Pius XI, *Divini Redemptoris*, sec. 50.

property to the maintenance of human dignity—that circumscribed the limits of property rights.[69]

Perhaps the clearest statement of the role of stewardship in the NCRLC ideology could be found in Ligutti's 1954 pamphlet, *A Christian Policy for Agriculture*. Ligutti began by establishing that the earth was God's greatest material gift, because it provided all the elements necessary to sustain life. The farmer, unlike the miner, works with a renewable resource: crops. Because God and not the farmer was the true owner of the soil, however, the farmer was obligated "to use properly and fully the good earth for himself, his family, and society, and at the same time, leave that good earth richer and in better condition than when he took up stewardship of it." As the primary food producer, farmers bore a grave responsibility to serve others and could not say, "I'll produce as I see fit and let the non-farmers go hang." As citizens of the world, farmers were obligated to distribute the fruits of the soil. Thus, farming was "more than money making"; it was a way of life deeply bound by social and sacred contract.[70] Conceptualizing the relationship of the farmer to the land in these terms was actively promoted in NCRLC literature, educational programs, retreats, and religious devotions specifically tailored to rural life.

Formal education was the most important way that farmers could improve their lot, and it was also essential to the success of cooperatives and credit unions. NCRLC leaders regularly complained that education, even in the country, was geared toward preparing children for urban life, not rural life. Even Catholic colleges in rural areas were designed to take youth away from the land, with courses reflecting the attitude that rural life equaled backward life. Ligutti wrote that "silently but surely, this has been the refrain, 'come to our college and leave the rural community and the baptismal parish.'" Ligutti himself did not know of any Catholic colleges that offered courses on agriculture. The NCRLC's 1944 pamphlet *Rural Life in a Peaceful World* attacked "the fact that parents have allowed their rural homes and schools to become the recruiting stations for cities and city jobs," thus fueling the ills of industrialization by driving people off the land and into urban sprawl, where "bigness" set the stage for immorality. "Too many urban-minded teachers

---

69. Aloisius J. Muench, "Statement by the President," *The Catholic Rural Life Bulletin* 4 (November 1941): 94.

70. Luigi Ligutti, *A Christian Policy for Agriculture*, MUA, NCRLC Series 5/1, Box 2, "General Publications, 1951–1954."

in rural schools, who lack the understanding and appreciation of rural living which is necessary to render a proper service to the rural home and the rural community," had fueled the exodus. "No teacher should attempt to teach rural children," the conference demanded, "unless that teacher has a social point of view and a social philosophy that includes a sympathetic understanding of rural living."[71]

In response, the NCRLC helped establish farm schools for boys and what they called "practical schools" for girls. The schools were intended to provide "the education and practical training necessary for success in farming."[72] Adult education programs were also founded by the conference that focused on new scientific developments and improved technologies affecting agriculture. Increasing the rural population demanded the use of "modern technology to the nth degree," along with a vision of "scientific progressiveness, and not the narrow reactionary conservatism of many agricultural economists," Ligutti argued.[73] Improved technology, techniques to prevent soil erosion such as crop rotation, terracing, strip cropping, contouring crop rows with grass waterways designed to push rainwater along to the edges of fields, and elements like these were all presented within the framework of stewardship.[74] Without exposure to these techniques, many rural farmers would be unable to be competitive with corporate farm factories.

Catholic agrarians made a direct connection between poor utilization of the land and birth control. Ligutti suggested that artificial birth control was directly linked to the poverty young couples experienced in an urban environment. Many rural advocates were actively involved with the Christian Family Movement (CFM), an organization designed to promote Catholic values in family planning. As historian Jeffrey Marlett noted, "Catholic agrarianism and the CFM shared a vision of natural fertility that was divinely constructed."[75] Birth control cut against a divine order in nature, much in the same way that urban industrialism was seen as an unnatural state of existence.[76] Some, like Msgr. John J. Heinz, a vice president of the NCRLC, believed that proper land use leading to higher

71. NCRLC, *Rural Life in a Peaceful World*, 10.
72. Ibid., 11.
73. L. G. Ligutti, *Post-War Homes on the Land*, MUA, NCRLC Series 5/1, Box 1, "General Publications," 1944–46.
74. Edward W. O'Rourke, "Soil Saving—A Plan," *Land and Home* 10 (March 1947): 22–23.
75. Marlett, *Saving the Heartland*, 39.
76. Ibid.; see also Bovée, "The Church and the Land," 373.

crop yields "may well prove to be the beginning of the end of the land wastage which has given the birth-controllers an excuse for their attempts to revive old discredited Malthusianism as one more stick with which to beat tomorrow's children."[77]

Another vehicle for educating came in the form of retreats that coupled learning and religious devotion. By 1949, the NCRLC was promoting a thirty-six-hour retreat aimed at the "refertilization not only of the farmer's soul, but of his farm as well." The retreats were typically composed of Catholic families from a single parish or district, because intimacy cultivated empathy. Retreats began early in the morning with a High Mass, followed by speakers—ranging from bishops to well-known agricultural professors—who would address topics like the dignity of farming. As Msgr. Heinz described it, retreatants were reminded that "Christ loved the fields and the mountains; in utterance after utterance He took His examples from growing things." These were allusions that farmers were thought to understand "more keenly than the city dweller." After lunch, participants reflected on the farmer's duties to the family and to the community. In keeping with the male-oriented bias of the NCRLC, which was not unusual in most sectors of society in the 1940s and 1950s, Heinz suggested that meetings dealing with duties might inspire the male farmer to see "himself suddenly in a patriarchal light, as the head of the family in the Christian sense of being the protector and servant of all." Presentations continued until dinner and would include at least one session devoted to practical concerns regarding farming techniques and the implementation of modern scientific agricultural methods or equipment. The first day's session closed with a benediction, only to resume again early the following morning with Mass and a Communion breakfast. After roundtable discussions on the topics addressed the day before, the retreat ended with a Rural Holy Hour and was over by lunchtime.[78]

These retreats have been characterized as among the "most successful methods of reaching rural laity."[79] Time constraints on the farmers made three- and four-day closed retreats impractical, so the thirty-six-hour retreats were well suited to their needs. On average, over 60 percent of the adult parishioners attended the retreats in those parishes

---

77. John J. Heinz, "Harvest Among the Harvesters," *The Priest* 5 (January 1949): 42.
78. Ibid., 42–43.
79. Bovée, "The Church and the Land," 327.

where they had been held, a remarkably high percentage compared to typical church functions.[80] All of this was helped by the Rural Retreat Bureau of the NCRLC, which recommended retreat "masters" and assisted with the scheduling and programming of these events.[81] The retreats blended all of the NCRLC's goals: fostering a spirit of community and cooperation, educating the farmer as to the latest advancements in science and technology, and imbuing the farm family with an invigorated commitment to their faith and to the Roman Catholic Church, which served as a partner in the task of improving rural life.

Rural Devotional Practices

The cultivation of a distinctively Roman Catholic approach to rural life also involved the development of devotional practices emphasizing the dignity of farming and its centrality to God's plan. As early as the 1930s, the NCRLC began an association with the movement for liturgical renewal spearheaded in the United States by Dom Virgil Michel, O.S.B. David Bovée's history of NCRLC characterized the conference's view of the liturgical movement in the 1930s "as providing the necessary spiritual glue for the hoped-for revived agrarian order."[82] The connection between the NCRLC and liturgical reform continued through the 1950s as conference members published collections of rural blessings, rural rituals, and rural songs. Pope Pius XII even granted the NCRLC special permission in 1945 to use English for "the special prayers on Rogation Days for the blessings of the fields, livestock, and other objects of rural life." The pinnacle came in 1958 with the publication of a 410-page *Rural Life Prayerbook*, edited by Alban J. Dachauer, S.J.[83]

Typical to these forms of devotion were parallels between the agricultural calendar and the liturgical year. The bread of the land supplied the body, while the bread of the Eucharist supplied the soul.[84] These parallels were easy to make given the roots of the liturgical calendar being

---

80. Heinz, "Harvest Among the Harvesters," 45.
81. *For This We Stand*, MUA, NCRLC Series 5/1, Box 1, "General Publications," 1944–46.
82. Bovée, "The Church and the Land," 2:327.
83. Ibid.
84. For example, see Rev. Benedict Ehmann, *Agriculture and the Liturgical Year*, MUA, NCRLC Series 5/1, Box 2, "General Publications, 1947." This pamphlet was reprinted from the September 1946 issue of *Land and Home*.

located in the growing seasons. Another element of religious devotion encouraged by the NCRLC was the veneration of St. Isidore. St. Isidore was the patron saint of farmers and was almost single-handedly elevated to devotional status by the efforts of the conference. This devotion began in the 1930s when Bishop J. H. Schlarman, the president of the NCRLC, wrote a prayer to St. Isidore. Within a few years, the NCRLC commissioned a painting of the saint and the creation of more prayers and devotional literature. These devotions became an important part of NCRLC-sponsored retreats, and soon the conference began selling statues of St. Isidore and his wife, St. Maria della Cabeza, "as well as a 'do-it-yourself' red cedar wood 'outdoor shrine kit' to put them in."[85] By 1956, over one hundred thousand people participated in a novena (a nine-day devotion) on the saint's feast day. Luigi Ligutti even believed himself to be in the constant companionship of one of St. Isidore's angels and recorded conversations with the angel in his journal.[86] In short, agricultural prayers and devotional literature, as well as devotion to St. Isidore, became a regular feature of the NCRLC's annual list of resolutions and were vital elements of the production of the NCRLC's rural Catholic ideology.

Reflecting the social encyclicals, the restoration of an agrarian social order was not thought possible without the guidance of the institutional Church, with the rural parish priest playing the pivotal role. One NCRLC publication written in 1946 illustrates this well. *To Save the Farm: A Story* was printed and distributed by the conference, complete with illustrations, to serve as a model for what the organization hoped to inspire. It told the story of a fictional family, the Wexlers, who were being driven out of business by "big-company farmers." When the seven Wexler children realized that being displaced to the city would mean abandoning their favorite horse, "Trip," they vowed to work together to save their farm. They agreed to create a family cooperative, involving sacrifices that would enable them to do what was necessary to make the farm work efficiently. Yet even with all of their effort, their dairy cows and crops were not earning them enough to compete with the neighboring "Storm Hill Farm," a factory farm that exploited its workers and did damage to the land. Their only option was to turn to their parish priest, "Father Vanhoeven," who spearheaded efforts among parishioners to

---

85. Bovée, "The Church and the Land," 2:328–29.
86. Yzermans, *The People I Love*, 87.

create cooperative ventures that would benefit the whole community. They formed a production cooperative, a marketing cooperative, and even a cooperative store. Parishioners were sent to complete course work on cooperatives and the latest agricultural techniques. In the end, the cooperatives were successful and the community was enriched. The story ended by reminding readers that all because little Sam Wexler refused to give up his favorite horse, a chain of events was touched off that restored hope. Sam "had Trip. The Wexlers had the farm. Life was happy. God was good."[87]

Among the many things this story illustrated about the NCRLC's approach to rural life, perhaps the most important was the role of the parish priest. The fortunes of the Wexler family, and others like it, began to change when they turned to the Church for guidance. The priest was called on to play the role of organizer and educator in rural America. In fact, during the early years of the NCRLC, the overwhelming proportion of priests making up the membership of the organization was a matter of some concern. As late as 1930, circular letters generated by the conference were still addressed "Dear Reverend Father." Ligutti, himself the prototype of the priest described in *To Save the Farm*, was successful in increasing lay participation during his tenure as director of the NCRLC.[88]

The NCRLC and the Government

The final element of the NCRLC's program for the restoration of rural life in America was its active attempt to involve the federal government in addressing issues of concern to the conference. These lobbying efforts reflect the NCRLC's stance on the principle of subsidiarity as defined by Pius XI. The principle's insistence that those activities that could be "performed and provided for" by smaller social units should not be transferred to larger ones had the potential to undercut reform efforts on a grand scale. Indeed, the conference consistently leaned toward promoting private initiatives before governmental activities. But the NCRLC did

---

87. *To Save the Farm: A Story* (1946), MUA, NCRLC Series 5/1, Box 1. "Reprinted from *These Our Horizons*, the Eighth Reader of the Faith and Freedom Series. By permission of the Commission on American Citizenship of the Catholic University of America and of the Ginn and Company, publishers."

88. Bovée, "The Church and the Land," 1:140; 2:321.

not read the principle of subsidiarity restrictively and saw the government as the "custodian and promoter of the common good." Before all else, this meant that the government had "the grave duty to promote the widest possible distribution of land ownership."[89] The conference stance on all legislation in the 1940s and 1950s was measured against this goal, leading to intense lobbying efforts for increased credit for farmers, tax reform, price controls, technical assistance, immigration reform, rural resettlement, and a living wage for farm workers.

Taking their cue from the social encyclicals, the NCRLC fought hard against taxes that they believed to be burdensome and discouraging to private initiative by unfairly punishing ownership.[90] If taxes had to be levied, the conference argued that "the burden should properly fall upon absentee owners of large estates or upon agricultural corporations, or upon the various agencies that obtain the smaller farmer's money." The small family farm, however, played too important a role in the culture of the nation to be saddled with high taxes.[91]

Farm prices were another major issue with the NCRLC. Since the New Deal, the federal government tried to guarantee stable agricultural prices by regulating the production of agricultural goods. In doing so, the government subsidized farmers to grow certain crops, while subsidizing other farmers to let portions of their fields remain fallow. Prices were directly affected through the regulation of scarcity. For the conference, this scarcity production system was anathema, particularly in light of global hunger. Instead, the NCRLC proposed that "efforts must be exerted towards agricultural production to full capacity with justice and charity in distribution."[92] Profit, in other words, could not override the basic material needs of the many when it came to food production.

On the surface, NCRLC opposition to scarcity production appears counterintuitive because the economic benefits reaped by the program were believed to be gained by the farmers themselves. Instead, the conference asked that the government rectify the disparity between the prices of agricultural goods and industrial goods. Surplus values of industrial goods were considerably higher, placing farmers at a disadvantage when

89. Ligutti and Rawe, *Rural Roads to Security*, 3.
90. *Rerum Novarum*, sec. 35; *Quadragesimo Anno*, sec. 49.
91. NCRLC, *Manifesto on Rural Life*, 65; John LaFarge, S.J., "Catholic Agrarians Swing into Action," *America*, November 14, 1936, 129–30.
92. "Summary of Resolutions Adopted at the 23rd Annual NCRLC Convention, Des Moines, Iowa, October 23–25, 1945," *Land and Home* 8 (December 1945): 92.

purchasing these products. Though intentionally diminishing the disparity "bristle[d] with difficulties," the reduced costs of farm equipment would assure greater profits for those farmers with limited capital. Cooperatives, credit unions, technical training, and other methods would also increase the small farmer's profit margins.[93] Furthermore, the programs that benefited most from the government price control policies were the large commercial farms, which, while making up only half of the total farms in the 1950s, produced approximately 90 percent of total agricultural output in that decade. Even the government's 1959 *Economic Report of the President* admitted that "the majority of farm people derive little or no benefit from our agricultural price support legislation," while the 2.5 million small farmers—making up less than 10 percent of the total market—"receive only very small supplements, or none at all, to their incomes from Government expenditures for price support."[94]

Specifically, the NCRLC supported farmers' demands for "a 10 per cent margin above parity" in price supports. The extra 10 percent was designed to compensate for seasonal variations in prices that placed farmers at a disadvantage when compared to industrial workers and to compensate for past injustices in farm pricing.[95] The conference wanted to take improved technology as well as "changing tastes and nutritional needs" into account, so it urged flexibility in implementing parity pricing. Still, they believed that the government had to establish minimum prices for farm goods to compensate for frequently dramatic drops in prices that had occurred in the 1930s and 1940s.[96]

For all the NCRLC promotion of price supports, the organization's leaders were not sold on the idea that more income would mean a better life if that income resulted in an inflationary spiral. Private initiative and cooperative ventures were still the bedrock for rural reform. "A better living cannot be bought," wrote Ligutti, "it must be created, even with a meager income."[97]

93. Aloisius J. Muench, "Justice for the Farmer," *Land and Home* 5 (June 1942): 1; *For This We Stand*, MUA, NCRLC Series 5/1, Box 1, "General Publications, 1944–1946," 4; NCRLC, *Rural Life in a Peaceful World*, 6; NCRLC, *Manifesto on Rural Life*, 64.
94. Harold G. Vatter, *The U.S. Economy in the 1950s: An Economic History* (1963; Chicago: University of Chicago Press, 1985), 250–52. The "small farmer" was one whose total annual sales did not exceed $2,500 at the time of this 1959 report.
95. Muench, "Justice for the Farmer," 1.
96. NCRLC, *Rural Life in a Peaceful World*, 6.
97. *For This We Stand*, MUA, NCRLC Series 5/1, Box 1, "General Publications, 1944–1946," 4.

Though a better living could not be bought, financial security could certainly bring greater peace of mind. This realization was behind the NCRLC's advocacy of Social Security benefits for farmers. It was not until January 1955 that farmers were included in the Social Security plan, and the conference had lobbied for this inclusion for years.[98] Ligutti testified in 1949 before the Congressional Joint Subcommittee on Low-Income Families that "farm workers, full-time, part-time, resident or migrant, must not be considered nonentities in the social, religious, or economic fields. As a rule their lot is low pay, no minimum wage, poor working conditions, part-time employment, slum housing, no social security or old-age benefits. In other words, they are the economically left-out people.... In a democracy they cannot be left out."[99] Indicative of the divisions between agriculture and industry, Ligutti went on to complain that "most of the labor unions" were "unaware of the existence of such laborers in the United States." When the situation of the farm worker is brought up to union leaders in the hopes that they will lobby for reform, the leaders decline, saying "we have to compromise" or "it is too hard." Ligutti insisted that it was "never too hard if it were just for their own interests."[100]

Lobbying at the federal level included the promotion of a national program to combat soil erosion. When the Agricultural Act of 1948 placed soil conservation in the hands of individual states, NCRLC leaders testified before the Senate that "in practice," the decentralized efforts "would mean a break-down in our coordinated attack upon the problems of erosion and conservation."[101] This stance won the NCRLC praise on many fronts, including the Protestant weekly *The Christian Century*. It was "encouraging," NCRLC editors wrote, "to find at least one church organization that is not wary of challenging government policy on behalf of community welfare."[102]

Finally, formal lobbying efforts with the federal government took aim at the handling of the migrant farming population. Small farmers, unable

98. Vatter, *The U.S. Economy in the 1950s*, 252. One of the many examples of the NCRLC's promoting Social Security and health benefits to farmers can be found in "Summary of Resolutions Adopted at the 23rd Annual NCRLC Convention," 93.
99. Joint Subcommittee on Low-Income Families of the Joint Committee on the Economic Report, *Low-Income Families*, 81st Cong., 2nd sess., December 21, 1949, 515.
100. Ibid., 515, 525.
101. Senate Committee on Agriculture and Forestry, *Agricultural Act of 1948*, 80th Cong., 2nd sess., April 21, 1948.
102. "The Christian Century and the NCRLC, February 9, 1955," *Feet in the Furrow*, March 17, 1955, MUA, NCRLC Series 6, Box 7.

to compete with corporate farms, were put out of business and often ended up as hired tenants on large farms at low wages, working in squalid conditions. The problem was compounded when the U.S. government began a program during World War II to import seasonal labor from Mexico and Central America to harvest crops in light of male labor shortages. The "bracero" program, named after the Spanish term for male manual workers, guaranteed cheap labor costs for influential agricultural businesses. More often than not, these workers were forced to work outrageous hours and consigned to live in dilapidated shacks, provided by the government itself, while receiving "only a small fraction" of the pay that they were due, thanks to often unspecified "deductions" made for food and housing. Braceros who complained were labeled "trouble makers" and sent back home.[103]

In addition to the attention the NCRLC felt these migrant workers warranted in their own right due to their working conditions, conference representatives testified before Congress regarding the detrimental impact migrant workers had on the family farmer, whose labor was "dragged down by the competition of the tragically depressed wages of the migratory worker."[104] Indeed, after seven hundred Mexicans were imported to California to pick peaches in 1957, wage rates dropped from an average of fifteen to eighteen cents per box to twelve cents. Between 1948 and 1958 there was a 40 percent drop in the wages of tomato pickers in the San Joaquin Valley, while during the same period the number of Mexican braceros in the region increased by 90 percent.[105] The NCRLC appealed to both the consciences of Congress members as well as their fears. In the Cold War climate of 1952, NCRLC representative James Vizzard warned, "God help us if a new Karl Marx should arise to urge them to riot and revolution, for they truly have nothing to lose but their chains."[106]

The NCRLC protested the standards of these federally funded camps throughout the late 1940s and 1950s. They condemned "all legislation or agreements with any other country by which aliens are temporarily

---

103. Ted Le Berthon, "The Church and the Bracero," *The Catholic Worker* 24 (September 1957): 1.

104. Senate Subcommittee on Labor and Labor-Management Relations of the Committee on Labor and Public Welfare, *Migratory Labor*, 82nd Cong., 2nd sess., part 1, February 11, 1952, 209.

105. Elizabeth Rogers, "Report on Migrant Labor," *The Catholic Worker* 25 (April–May 1959): 1, 8.

106. Senate Subcommittee on Labor and Labor-Management Relations, *Migratory Labor*, 210.

admitted as agricultural workers, except in cases of absolute and *objectively* proved necessity," knowing full well that such objective proof was nearly impossible. Refusing to blame the workers themselves, the conference emphasized that it was "out of their own necessity" that these workers competed unfairly with the family farm and "undercut the value of the farm family's labor." Immigrant laborers were "denied the freedom to change" occupation once here in the United States and were "consequently kept segregated in field labor camps under penalty of arrest and deportation." Finally, the conference reminded its constituency that these immigrants were "denied as a condition of their employment the God-given right to family life and the fulfillment of their conjugal and parental duties to their wives and children," thus undercutting the sacred social unit of the family.[107] The situation improved by 1955, when agricultural workers began to reap the benefits of social legislation they had previously been denied, such as Social Security, health care, and a minimum wage. The bracero program continued, however, until 1964.[108]

Though the NCRLC frequently invoked the principle of subsidiarity in its reasoning, it was clear that the conference judged that some services could only be "performed and provided for" adequately by the highest social order, the federal government. In fact, the groundwork laid by increasing appeals for government intervention in rural affairs forecast potential consequences for the NCRLC by the 1960s. David Bovée's study of the conference noted that by then, the NCRLC risked its reputation as a grassroots organization in rural America by being seen by some as "an advocacy group for rural liberal Christian causes."[109] At that time the word "liberal" had come to be understood as describing people who supported social programs and government intervention in social problems.

The goal of preserving the family farm clearly ran against the economic tide, a tide that did not ebb during the 1950s. By 1963, one hour of farm labor was producing five times the crops it had when the NCRLC was founded in the early 1920s.[110] Family farms were becoming a rarity,

---

107. Bovée, "The Church and the Land," 2:479–81; George Higgins and William Bole, *Organized Labor and the Church: Reflections of a "Labor Priest"* (New York: Paulist Press), 84–86; NCRLC, *A Program for the Family Farm*, MUA, NCRLC Series 5/1, Box 2, "Manuals and Programs, 1954–1957," 6, 10–11.
108. Higgins and Bole, *Organized Labor and the Church*, 86.
109. Bovée, "The Church and the Land," 2:515–16.
110. James L. Vizzard, S.J., "The Agricultural Revolution," in *The Church and Social Progress: Background Readings for Pope John's "Mater et Magistra,"* ed. Benjamin Masse (Milwaukee: Bruce Publishing, 1966), 141.

though some cooperative ventures remain successful even today. The conference's dire predictions of urbanization resulting in the depopulation of Roman Catholics in America were incorrect. At the same time, the total Catholic population in rural America had dropped only two percentage points in fifty years from its 1920s average of 20 percent. Given that the overall rural population declined by nearly 35 percent in the same period, the NCRLC's objective of preserving a Catholic component on the land must be judged remarkably successful, thanks in part to the efforts of the conference.[111]

In sum, the National Catholic Rural Life Conference enacted a multifaceted program aimed at creating a culture that viewed rural life as sanctified life. The program was based on the teachings of *Rerum Novarum* and *Quadragesimo Anno,* and it focused on the reproduction of distinctive elements of those encyclicals in the community of discourse in which the conference engaged. The Catholic ideology culled from the encyclicals dovetailed with the Jeffersonian agrarian myth that dominated rural America. Liberty, equality, and democracy were cast as Catholic values; the Church would ultimately lead the way in defending them. The co-opting of these values was a remarkable feat in a pre–Vatican II Catholic culture.

The Catholic Worker Movement

Promoting rural life played an important role in the outlook of another Roman Catholic group in the United States, the Catholic Worker (CW) movement. Like the NCRLC, members of the CW understood themselves to be living the mandate of a just social order called for by the Roman Catholic Church's teachings since Leo XIII's *Rerum Novarum*. As we shall see, however, this mandate was often understood differently by CW members than by representatives of the NCRLC, particularly with respect to the CW's antipathy to the state and its radical approach to personalism. Still, there were ties between the two organizations. Dorothy Day, the dominant figure of the CW movement, attended a conference sponsored by the NCRLC in Peoria, Illinois, in 1942, where she came into contact with Luigi Ligutti.[112] The lessons she learned from Ligutti were

---

111. Bovée, "The Church and the Land," 2:514.
112. Witte, *Twenty-five Years of Crusading,* 126.

important to the movement, and *The Catholic Worker* newspaper often published articles by members of the NCRLC emphasizing the value of rural living. But CW activists sought to sanctify life on the land through a different reading of the Roman Catholic ideology.

The CW movement grew out of the combined efforts of Dorothy Day and Peter Maurin. Day, born in 1897 to a middle-class family, began her career as a journalist working mainly for socialist newspapers. She became friendly with many renowned leftist radicals while living in Greenwich Village during the First World War. A torrid love affair with a fellow journalist resulted in pregnancy and an abortion in late 1919. Day later married a literary promoter with whom she had a daughter, Tamar. The marriage ended when her husband abandoned Day following her conversion to Catholicism and her decision to baptize their daughter. In 1929 Day moved to Mexico with Tamar and submitted articles to the Catholic weeklies, *The Commonweal* and *America,* regarding the volatile Mexican political situation. Eventually, she returned to New York where she met Peter Maurin.[113]

Peter Maurin was a French peasant who had been active in the Sillon movement in Paris at the turn of the century, a movement seeking to blend tenets of liberal republicanism with Roman Catholicism. By 1909 Maurin had become disillusioned with Sillon as well as the Church and immigrated to Canada, eventually arriving in the United States in 1911. He made his living teaching French and engaging in manual labor. More important, while in the United States Maurin renewed his commitment to Roman Catholicism and began "reading and copying from Catholic literature, composing his own succinct verses on social themes and engaging in a kind of nonstop propaganda for social Catholicism that he called 'clarification of thought.'"[114]

Maurin lived a mendicant lifestyle, wandering the streets, sleeping "wherever he found a spot," eating only one bowl of soup a day, and applying his meager earnings to either charity or the publication of

---

113. Mel Piehl, *Breaking Bread: The Catholic Worker and the Origin of Catholic Radicalism in America* (Philadelphia: Temple University Press, 1982), 3–24, esp. 14, 18, 23; Dorothy Day, "A Human Document," *Sign* 12 (November 1932): 223–24.

114. Ibid., 57–58; Dorothy Day, *The Long Loneliness* (New York: Harper and Row, 1952), 199; Dorothy Day, "I Remember Peter Maurin," *Jubilee* 1 (March 1954): 34–39; Arthur Sheehan, *Peter Maurin: Gay Believer* (Garden City, N.Y.: Hanover, 1959), 10–39; Anthony Novitsky, "The Ideological Development of Peter Maurin's Green Revolution" (Ph.D. diss., State University of New York, Buffalo, 1977), 171; Mark Ellis, *Peter Maurin: Prophet in the Twentieth Century* (New York: Paulist Press, 1981).

pamphlets that contained his verses. In his book on the CW movement, Mel Piehl described these pamphlets as "Maurin's best hope as an agitator, for his speeches, shouted at close range in an almost incomprehensible, thick French accent, were largely ineffective and, indeed, often somewhat comic."[115] Yet it appears that Maurin's fervent devotion to his cause was central to his charisma and impressive to many of those who knew him.

At the suggestion of *The Commonweal* editor George Schuster, Maurin met Day in 1932. Despite some disagreements, fueled in part by Maurin's unintelligibly thick accent, Maurin convinced Day to start a Roman Catholic newspaper aimed at the unemployed. The paper was called *The Catholic Worker* and it reflected the distinctive perspectives of its founders.[116] The program developed for the CW movement was quite similar to the one that Maurin proposed. He outlined three essential components of the movement in one of his earliest essays for the newspaper.

> We need round-table discussions
> To keep trained minds from becoming academic.
> We need round-table discussions
> To keep untrained minds from being superficial.
>
> We need Houses of Hospitality
> To give the rich the opportunity to serve the poor.
> We need Houses of Hospitality
> To bring social justice back to Catholic institutions.
>
> The unemployed need food.
> They can raise that
> In an agronomic university.
> The unemployed need to acquire skill.
> They can do that in an agronomic university.[117]

The roundtable discussions consisted of lectures and talks sponsored by the CW and often took place at their Houses of Hospitality, the most famous of which was on Mott Street in the East Village. At Mott Street

---

115. Piehl, *Breaking Bread*, 58.
116. Ibid., 59–60.
117. Peter Maurin, "Easy Essays," *The Catholic Worker* 2 (June 1933): 3; Piehl, *Breaking Bread*, 60.

and other houses, volunteers would clothe, shelter, and feed the hungry. Houses of Hospitality soon sprang up in cities across the country, peaking in the late 1930s when these houses often served well over 1,000 meals a day. One house in St. Louis fed 2,700 people daily while distributing 700 more meals throughout neighborhoods in need.[118]

While the Houses of Hospitality and the newspaper were the means through which the CW had the greatest impact, the third part of its program, "agronomic universities," succeeded in giving the organization a foothold in the Catholic rural life movement. Agronomic universities evolved into farming communes that sought to embody the "utopian" elements of the Catholic Worker ideology. Maurin described these communes in language that echoed Marx: places "where each one works according to his ability and gets according to his need."[119] The result was an approach to rural life that differed significantly from that of the NCRLC while borrowing extensively from the same mythic resources.

Personalism, Anarchism, and Distributism

To make sense of these communes and their reading of the ideology put forth in the social encyclicals, we must look at the three philosophies that prompted their development: personalism, anarchism, and distributism. The personalism espoused by the CW was deeply influenced by Maurin's connections with activists involved in the publication of the French journal *Esprit*.[120] In the same year that Day and Maurin met, a group of young French Catholic intellectuals, eager to break away from the traditionalist, royalist wing of the French Church—while unwilling to align with the socialist and communist left—founded the review. The group's leader, Emmanuel Mounier, described *Esprit* as belonging to "neither the Left nor the Right," though it clearly sided with the interests of the working class.[121] They coined the term "personalist" to describe their ideological framework, pointing to the individual person as the ultimate end of all systems, be they political or economic. As such,

118. Piehl, *Breaking Bread*, 110.
119. Ibid., 62–64.
120. Ibid., 69–70.
121. John Hellman, "The Opening to the Left in French Catholicism: The Role of the Personalists," *Journal of the History of Ideas* 34 (July–September, 1973): 385–86.

personalists rejected "all doctrines that deny man's temporality and historicity in the name of a transcendent order."[122]

Maurin infused this personalist perspective into the ideology of the CW. For members of the CW, personalism was meant to be a radical commitment to living the message of the Sermon on the Mount and working toward spiritual perfection through a life of prayer, charity, and voluntary poverty. Like *Esprit,* the CW differentiated itself from the philosophical neo-Thomism of men like Jacques Maritain and Etienne Gilson by applying ideas in the form of a radical social activism.[123] As one article in *The Catholic Worker* summarized it, "Personalism means that instead of waiting for society or agencies outside of the individual to act, each person will take upon himself the moral responsibility of combating evil and correcting that which is wrong in the world as far as he is able." This required "the reform of each person as a prerequisite to the reform of society as a whole."[124]

Day wrote that "those principles of subsidiarity laid down in the Popes' encyclicals" authorized not only the CW's personalism but Maurin's opposition to the modern state as well. Subsidiarity also validated the support of Maurin, Day, and others at the CW for cooperatives, credit unions, and even "folk schools" springing forth from private initiative.[125] The principle as worded in *Quadragesimo Anno* was often quoted in full within the pages of *The Catholic Worker* and trumpeted as committing Catholics to a personalist response to problems at all levels of society.[126]

Subsidiarity and its value in promoting the philosophy of personalism was also key to undergirding perhaps the most distinctive element of the CW ideology, its Christian anarchism.[127] Stripped of its atheistic roots in the writings of nineteenth-century thinkers like Bakunin—sometimes to the dismay of secular anarchists whom Day and others encountered in the 1940s and 1950s—the Catholic Worker employed anarchism

---

122. Piehl, *Breaking Bread,* 70.
123. Hellman, "The Opening to the Left in French Catholicism," 385.
124. J. Michael McCloskey, "The Catholic Worker Movement," *The Catholic Worker* 23 (May 1957): 4.
125. Dorothy Day, "May Day," *The Catholic Worker* 23 (May 1957): 2.
126. For example, see Dorothy Day, "On Pilgrimage—January 1959," *The Catholic Worker* 25 (January 1959): 1, 2, 7.
127. Peter Maurin never used the term "anarchism" in public, according to Day, but privately aligned himself with the position. See Dorothy Day, "The Pope and Peace," *The Catholic Worker* 21 (February 1954): 1, 7.

in the service of promoting an agrarian Christian order.[128] Ammon Hennacy, a radical pacifist and promoter of "the simple life" who had chosen prison over military service and refused to pay taxes earmarked for military use, was among the most celebrated advocates of anarchism in the CW movement. He cited two definitions of anarchism that he felt placed the term within reasonable reach of being compatible with Roman Catholic theology. The first definition understood the term as "the philosophy of a new social order based on liberty unrestricted by man-made laws; the theory that all forms of government rest on violence, and are therefore wrong and harmful, as well as unnecessary." His second definition spoke of a theory by which society could live in harmony without government "by free agreements concluded between various groups, territorial or professional." In essence, CW anarchism was to be a collection of "voluntary associations" — invoking the encyclical language — that would live peacefully with one another.[129]

Hennacy's trouble with government reflected the overall attitude of the CW's membership, who were convinced that the authority of the state rested on violence and coercion. At no time was this more evident than during war, prompting the movement to endorse a pacifist stance. Prior to World War II, there was still some ambiguity as to whether the pacifist position of the CW was absolute or conditional. After a heated dispute between Dorothy Day's New York branch of the CW and the Chicago branch of the group in the early 1940s, it became clear that the pacifist position was absolute. The stance prompted the exodus of many CW members who believed that even violence could be justified under certain conditions, including those that led to World War II.[130] With the introduction of atomic weapons, the CW's pacifism became even more recalcitrant.

Christian anarchism advocated the elimination of the state, as well as the commitment of the individual to do her or his best to separate from those systems deemed to be oppressive. Hennacy compared the position of the CW to a swarm of bees described by Tolstoy. The swarm had congregated in a tree and

---

128. For more on the response of secular anarchists, especially Italian anarchists who felt insulted by the association of anarchism with Roman Catholicism in light of the Church's historic role in the promotion of authoritarian systems in Italy, see Ammon Hennacy, *The Book of Ammon* (Salt Lake City, 1965).

129. Ammon Hennacy, "Christian Anarchism Defined," *The Catholic Worker* 22 (July–August, 1955): 3, 7.

130. Piehl, *Breaking Bread*, 151–58.

thousands of them buzzed in useless activity. Finally some of those on the outside of the swarm sensed that there was a hive nearby where they could enter and start again making honey. As a few hundred left they made room for those next to them to see the light and gradually the whole swarm was in the hive. So it is with those of us to the left who must secede from this capitalist swarm of misery. When we refuse to register for the draft, or refuse to pay income taxes, or when we refuse to hide away in air drills we are moving away from the swarm. If we intellectualize about life away from the swarm but remain there by conforming in daily action with the status quo we are still a part of the swarm.[131]

The word "anarchism" caused some confusion not only among outsiders but among those associated with the CW as well. A 1955 debate in the pages of *The Catholic Worker* pitted Hennacy against Robert Ludlow, Hennacy's own godfather, who had left the movement by the early 1950s. Ludlow wrote an article questioning the utility of the term "anarchism" in the CW lexicon. He judged its use to be "unwise," especially given the term's association with rejecting not only temporal but also divine authority. As such, in a strategy similar to that of Pius XI, who rendered the notion of a Christian socialist oxymoronic, Ludlow held that the term was necessarily incompatible with the centrality of hierarchy to Roman Catholicism's theological self-conception. Ludlow went so far as to use the words of Leo XIII in several encyclicals to buttress his case and maintained that after much reflection, he was forced to conclude that it was "simply not in the Catholic tradition to make the realm of God so large that there is no room left for Caesar."[132] Government authority should not be assumed to be "evil and unjust" and therefore automatically disobeyed. "The national State is a hindrance to man," Ludlow agreed, though "not because it is a State but because the concept of national sovereignty makes of each State a strutting egoistic maniac ready to pull the trigger at any offense to its vanity." Yet to insist "an anarchist society would be possible, is like insisting that all become celibates or that all become Trappists."[133]

---

131. Hennacy, "Christian Anarchism Defined," 3.
132. Robert Ludlow, "Anarchism and Leo XIII," *The Catholic Worker* 22 (September 1955): 3, 8.
133. Robert Ludlow, "A Re-evaluation," *The Catholic Worker* 21 (June 1955): 2, 8.

To Hennacy, Ludlow's argument opened the door to continued participation in systems of oppression. The terms "personalist" and "anarchist" were, to Hennacy, simply two ways "of saying the same thing." Recalling Ludlow's analogy, he wrote, "we are not all called to be celibates or Trappists . . . but we cannot achieve freedom as sons of God by talking about ideals and not living them."[134] This argument encapsulated the perfectionist impulse that infused the activities of the CW.

Anarchism also put the CW's approach at odds with that of the NCRLC. While the CW still invoked the Jeffersonian ideal of small family farms and property ownership, it deleted appeals to Jefferson himself. But the ideal was not invoked as a means of preserving American-style democracy, as the NCRLC advocated. Instead, it was seen as a means of dismantling the American system that had taken on totalitarian proportions resulting from a runaway capitalism that bore fruit in the form of industrialism and compulsory military service. The enlightenment agenda found in the "American" ideals of democracy, freedom, and social harmony remained at the core of the CW's beliefs, yet it could not find those ideals in *America,* the state.

Personalism and anarchism fed easily into the ultimate economic goal of the CW movement: "the establishment of a *Distributist economy* wherein those who have a vocation to the land will work on farms surrounding the village, and those who have other vocations will work in the village itself."[135] The work of Chesterton and Belloc inspired the distributist agenda of the CW, as did that of Chesterton's close friend, Eric Gill, an English craftsman.[136] *The Catholic Worker* regularly advertised books and pamphlets advocating distributism, and its pages were peppered with articles from prominent English distributists such as the Dominican Vincent McNabb, along with transcriptions of papal writings and speeches that were understood to advocate the distributist philosophy.[137]

Directly tied to its Christian anarchism, the movement hoped that a decentralized distributist economy would result in America's being able

---

134. Hennacy, "Christian Anarchism Defined," 3.
135. "Catholic Worker Positions," *The Catholic Worker* 21 (September 1954): 5, emphasis in original.
136. Kerran Dugan, "Eric Gill: A Special Kind of Artist," *The Catholic Worker* 17 (November 1950): 4, 7.
137. Examples of these include Vincent McNabb, O.P., "An Economic Creed: From 'The Church and the Land,'" *The Catholic Worker* 12 (December 1945): 6; "Distributism: A Draft for Action," *The Catholic Worker* 13 (October 1946): 5, taken from the English distributist periodical *The Plough;* "Popes on Distributism," *The Catholic Worker* 20 (May 1954): 3; "The Holy See and Distributism," *The Catholic Worker* 21 (April 1955): 1.

to "dispense with the state as we know it," rendering the country "federationist in character as was society during certain periods that preceded the rise of national states." This brand of worker ownership, the CW stressed, was not to be confused with socialism but was instead to be achieved through "decentralized co-operatives," similar to those encouraged by the NCRLC. "It is a revolution from below," announced *The Catholic Worker* in 1954, "and not (as political revolutions are) from above." This revolution had as its first phase the "widespread and universal ownership" of property "as a stepping stone to a communism that will be in accord with the Christian teaching of detachment from material goods and which, when realized, will express itself in common ownership." Where Soviet communism was driven by an all-powerful state, members of the CW envisioned a voluntary communism. To skeptics who dismissed their dreams as pie-in-the-sky rhetoric, they responded that "success, as the world determines it, is not the criterion by which a movement should be judged." In fact, they were ready to accept failure if it meant that they continued to "adhere to these values which transcend time and for which we will be asked a personal accounting, not as to whether they succeeded . . . but as to whether we remained true to them even though the whole world go otherwise."[138]

Their distributist ideology was constituted in the form of farming communes. The first commune associated with the CW was established in 1936, thanks to a donation of twenty-eight acres of farmland near Easton, Pennsylvania. They hoped that this land would provide the initial step toward "a community of families living in separate establishments, and given the exclusive use of a parcel of land."[139] Over the years, more farming communes developed, each with its own personality. As Mel Piehl noted, whereas "St. Benedicts Farm in Massachusetts became an important Catholic art and liturgical center," another farm, Our Lady of the Wayside in Ohio, was known for taking care of "the retarded."[140] But all were inspired by the distributist and personalist teachings propagated by leadership of the CW.

By the mid-1930s, virtually every issue of *The Catholic Worker* included letters from those whom the movement had encouraged to relocate to the land. One regular contributor, Larry Heaney, on a farming commune in Rhineland, Missouri, complained of "shortages of stock

---

138. "Catholic Worker Positions," 5.
139. Piehl, *Breaking Bread*, 129; cites *The Catholic Worker* 3 (April 1936): 8.
140. Pichl, *Breaking Bread*, 130.

and equipment" as well as the high costs of getting started. His family shared 160 acres with another family and found it too much to handle. Letters to *The Catholic Worker* provided him, and others, with the opportunity to invite more families to join them. "Our vision of a farmer-craftsman village economy," he wrote, "entails the gradual grouping of a nucleus of convinced communitarians. One family each year, or perhaps every other year, could be established here [in Rhineland] on the farm that is dedicated to the Holy Family."[141]

Heaney acknowledged that as farmers, his family and the family he shared acreage with were still "greenhorns" and considered themselves "apprentice agrarians."[142] Six months after this acknowledgment, another letter from Heaney detailed the disappointing impact of a drought, combined with a "chilly, wet Spring, the seed rotting in the ground, the flourishing weeds, the loss of animals due to disease, the errors of judgment of inexperienced minds, [and] the blundering of untrained hands."[143] His report seemed to confirm the sort of warnings doled out regularly by the leadership of the NCRLC about the perils of "city slickers" attempting to take up farming. But Heaney reminded his readers that they were "not here merely to farm. We are living and working on this farm in order to build a community—a community about a church." As if his comments were aimed precisely at the cynics of the NCRLC, with its more organized, hierarchically bound, and bureaucratic program, Heaney decried the "social attachments of most Catholic thinkers" when it came to rural life. The focus of these thinkers on "political maneuverings, changing of the money system" and "large scale cooperatives," instead of "personal revolution, voluntary poverty, the welding of community and family ties, [and] intense participation in the liturgy," revealed their self-evident shortcomings to the readers of *The Catholic Worker*. For all the challenges families like his own faced on the land, it was imperative that they "group themselves about a church as though their very life depends on it."[144]

The struggles, disappointments, commitment, and persistence of Heaney's family was typical of many of the CW farm communes.[145] The

141. Larry Heaney, "Toehold on the Land," *The Catholic Worker* 14 (June 1947): 4.
142. Ibid.
143. Ibid., p. 5.
144. Ibid.
145. For example, see letter from The Carotas, "Agnus Dei Farm," *The Catholic Worker* 17 (1951): 5; and Jack and Mary Thornton, "Five Years on the Land," *The Catholic Worker* 18 (February 1953): 1, 5.

inherent problems with surviving on the land were compounded by the fact that many of these houses became agrarian extensions of the urban Houses of Hospitality.[146] Communes felt compelled to take in the homeless and indigent, irrespective of whether they possessed a strong work ethic. While the living dynamics were trying in the city, they could prove disastrous in an environment where survival depended on intensive farm labor. As Jeffrey Marlett explained, "the farm communes invited failure because too few persons did the needed work." The result was that by the end of the 1950s, "all the Catholic Worker communes either shrank or ceased operation altogether."[147]

While the NCRLC rejected any characterizations that saw itself as promoting a "back to the land" movement, the CW program of agrarian anarchism fit that characterization perfectly. Where the NCRLC focused on stopping the hemorrhaging of rural residents who opted for jobs in factories and office buildings, the Catholic Worker hoped for a more radical form of deindustrialization by reversing the migratory flow entirely. Though both agendas were shaped by the ideology of distributism as it had been described by the English Catholic readings of *Rerum Novarum*, they differed in the manner through which distributism was put into practice. Still, both the NCRLC and the CW accepted as given G. K. Chesterton's observation that while their hopes and dreams may not come to fruition, there was adequate proof that capitalism had failed to produce a society that balanced the distribution of goods and power.[148]

The NCRLC and the CW interpreted *Quadragesimo Anno*'s principle of subsidiarity in substantially different ways. The NCRLC, while suspicious of the state, put forward an agenda that clearly viewed the state as a vital partner in promoting a just social order. Legislation aimed at initiating homesteads, tax supports for cooperatives, a tax structure that benefited family farms to the detriment of corporate, tenant-based farms, federally backed credit programs, and government price controls were all seen as functions that could be "performed and provided for" most efficiently via the state. NCRLC leadership made themselves readily available to testify before congressional panels and actively lobbied the government for their causes. The CW infused the principle of subsidiarity with a different meaning that eschewed cooperation with the modern

---

146. See Marlett, *Saving the Heartland*, 82; James Fisher, *The Catholic Counterculture in America, 1933–1962* (Chapel Hill: University of North Carolina Press, 1989), 43.
147. Marlett, *Saving the Heartland*, 72–73, 86.
148. Chesterton, *The Outline of Sanity*, 8.

state. City-states, reminiscent of medieval Europe, could perhaps be reconciled with subsidiarity and the need for individuals to be free, but the modern state could not.[149] As such, while the pages of its newspaper were filled with denunciations of government policies, the perfectionist impulse promoted by the CW assured that cooperation with the government was impossible. The truly Christian social order must begin and end with the individual, the family, and the small agrarian community. Clearly the clerical character of the NCRLC and the overwhelmingly lay membership of the CW movement influenced the perspective of both movements' participants, with the former having a greater tolerance for top-down authority systems and the latter being inclined to a grassroots approach.

Despite their differences, the NCRLC and the CW movement reproduced the distinctive ideology of the social encyclicals on their own terms. The principle of subsidiarity, the naturalization of private property, the inviolability of the traditional family as the foundational cell in the social organism, the naturalizing of a self-sustaining life on the land, and the intrinsic right of workers to form associations were all fundamental to the outlook of both groups. Notably, the class system was not naturalized by either group as they saw the self-sufficiency of farming as a means of avoiding the class system altogether. Where the NCRLC promoted that ideology by employing a discourse reflecting the cultural context of its constituency through comfortably blending the language of natural-law theology with that of Jeffersonian liberalism and American populism, the CW promoted it by borrowing from the lexicon of the socialism and anarchism on which many of its own activists had been nourished. It was the language of the encyclicals and the overriding concern that the Roman Catholic Church lead the way toward transforming the social order that distinguished these agrarian movements from the Jeffersonian populists, the Oklahoma Marxists, Protestant Country Lifers, and the Southern Agrarians.

As has been noted, the tide toward large-scale farming amenable to feeding a rapidly growing urban population base was unyielding through the 1950s. The political agendas of both movements, each accused by detractors of being utopian and backward looking, were largely unsuccessful. Yet, in their own ways, both the NCRLC and the CW movement fashioned discursive communities that viewed life on the land, self-sufficiency, and the role of the farmer as sacred. *Rerum Novarum* and

149. Day, "The Pope and Peace," 1, 7.

Quadragesimo Anno took on the status of myth for each movement as they sought to address the seismic shifts in the material circumstances of Americans in the decades before the Second Vatican Council in a manner they hoped reflected "authentic" Roman Catholicism. Like all durable myths, the multivalence of the encyclicals enabled them to be brought to life in a variety of forms.

(3)

Sanctifying Industrial Labor

Members of the National Catholic Rural Life Conference and the Catholic Worker movement were both steeped in a distributist philosophy that colored their readings of the social encyclicals. For both groups, industrial capitalism and the urbanism that sprung from it posed a great threat to both Catholic morality and their distinctive conceptions of what it meant to be a human person. Rural living went hand in hand with preserving the possibility of an authentically Christian social order. Yet these movements cultivated ideologies that appealed not only to a decreasing minority of Americans but to a dwindling number of Roman Catholics in the United States as well.

By World War II, industrial capitalism and urban life dominated the day-to-day realities of most Americans. The seismic cultural shifts that accompanied the industrial revolution had taken on the hue of normalcy. Roman Catholics—concentrated in Northern cities—along with most Americans were more apt to seek out ways to improve their situations in that environment than to commit to escaping it. Like Catholics on the farm, many of those in the cities made use of the papal encyclicals to authorize changes in their working conditions. Validating these changes through their readings of Catholic social teaching, the encyclicals were understood to be divinely sanctioned means of engaging their material circumstances. The Social Action Department (SAD) of the National Catholic Welfare Conference of U.S. bishops, the Association of Catholic Trade Unionists (ACTU), and the Young Christian Workers movement (YCW) each attempted to apply the teachings of *Rerum Novarum* and *Quadragesimo Anno* to an industrialized society to sanctify the very way of life that Catholic rural groups had considered irredeemable. Encyclical language relating to class, property, family, wages, workers' associations, and the principle of subsidiarity were all brought to bear on the particular realities these men and women faced in a manner that invested their arguments with the imprimatur of God, Nature, and Holy Mother Church.

Catholic positions on urban working life need to be put into the context of those ideological tendencies present in industrial society, especially in the labor movement, on the eve of World War II. Since the nineteenth century, there had been multiple fault lines dividing the American labor movement, including racial, ethnic, gender based, regional, skilled worker versus unskilled worker, and trade versus industry, to name a few. At the risk of oversimplification, underlying each of these fault lines was a key issue that functioned as a variable in the dynamics of all the social divisions: class consciousness.

Since Alexis de Tocqueville observed in the preface to his 1835 edition of *Democracy in America* a general "equality of conditions" among the American people, it has been common to describe the U.S. social order as "classless."[1] The point of comparison, of course, was Europe, with its relatively static social order arising from its feudal past. Tocqueville's remark provided grist for the mill that touted American "exceptionalism," the effort to distinguish the nature of this nation from that of all others.[2] While the argument over class in America has deep roots and continues to inspire salvos on all sides of the ideological spectrum, the comments of sociologist Rick Fantasia on the diversity of perspectives among scholars regarding the existence of class consciousness rings true: "such differences have tended to reveal more about the preconceptions of the researchers than they have about any collective consciousness of class in society."[3]

That social stratification can be found in any society of the slightest complexity is undeniably true.[4] Whether circumstances arise that allow for that stratification to be conceptualized in terms of classes or not varies

---

1. Alexis de Tocqueville, *Democracy in America*, ed. J. P. Mayer, trans. George Lawrence (New York: Harper and Row, 1966), 9; see also Harold M. Hodges Jr.'s introductory section on "The Myth and Creed of Classlessness" in *Social Stratification: Class in America* (Cambridge, Mass.: Schenkman, 1964), 1–16; Rick Fantasia, "From Class Consciousness to Culture, Action, and Social Organization," *Annual Review of Sociology* 21 (1995): 269–87.

2. For more on the use of Tocqueville toward laying the foundation of a doctrine of American exceptionalism, see Philip Abbott, *Exceptional America: Newness and National Identity* (New York: Peter Lang, 1999), 97–120.

3. Fantasia, "From Class Consciousness to Culture, Action, and Social Organization," 270.

4. Hodges, *Social Stratification*, 1.

according to time and place. So the question of whether there is "class" in America may not be as important as whether there is consciousness of "class" in America. By the mid-to-late nineteenth century, the term "class" itself was deeply linked to Marx's analysis of class conflict as it developed in the rising Occidental capitalist order. With this linkage, those who saw class did so along lines divided between the proletariat and the bourgeoisie, workers and owners. We have even seen this division reflected in the social encyclicals themselves.

Whether the conditions of social stratification in America during the generation before Vatican II really were changing or not (and arguments have been made for either position), it appears that a growing majority of Americans came to be uncomfortable with rhetoric that accentuated class divisions and that painted capitalism negatively. By the 1920s, open castigation of capitalism was common. The Great Depression then unleashed a torrent of movements aimed at a radical transformation of the economic order. The rise of communism and fascism in Europe only sharpened the expectation that capitalism would soon give way to a new economic paradigm in the United States, and with capitalism's immanent demise, the class system it spawned would surely die.[5]

Few sites lend themselves to an exploration of the dynamics of class consciousness as transparently as the labor movement. In the United States, until the mid-1930s, most labor unions were affiliated with the American Federation of Labor (AFL). The AFL was a collection of trade unions. In other words, workers were united according to their particular trade or craft, ranging from electrical workers to ship captains. AFL union membership was made up primarily of skilled laborers, while semiskilled and unskilled workers were often left unorganized. Among the consequences of this format was a situation in which AFL trade unionists often shared interests with not only the lower classes but the middle classes of society as well, resulting from their higher levels of training and skill. Some have pointed out that this arrangement also facilitated the maintenance of social boundaries marked by ethnicity and race, because caste systems emerged within industries in which particular racial and ethnic groups were consigned to distinctive roles that reflected their status in the United States.[6]

5. See Virgil Michel, "What Is Capitalism?" *The Commonweal* 28 (April 29, 1938): 6.
6. See, for instance, Gwendolyn Mink, *Old Labor and New Immigrants in American Political Development: Union, Party, and the State, 1875–1920* (Ithaca, N.Y.: Cornell University Press, 1986).

Some were not satisfied with the trade union format of the AFL. By 1935 there emerged from within the AFL a group of union leaders committed to industrial unionism. Unions divided by craft rather than by industry pitted skilled workers against the unskilled, thereby weakening the force of labor overall. Organizations like the United Mine Workers, the Amalgamated Clothing Workers, and the International Ladies' Garment Workers formed a caucus they called the Committee on Industrial Organization (CIO). Their push for a "big-tent" policy within the AFL failed, and by 1936, industrial unions were effectively suspended from the AFL, leaving the CIO to organize industry on its own.[7]

Not surprisingly, Marxists who saw the world through the prism of distinct class divisions were more inclined to favor the CIO approach. Communists and socialists had played a significant role in organizing American workers since the late nineteenth century — a role that lasted into the 1950s — as well as in shaping American culture among policy makers and the intelligentsia. By the 1930s, radicals, communists, and New Deal liberals found themselves in frequent alliance against the rising tide of fascism, an alliance that earned the nickname the Popular Front.[8] The comparative prominence of communists and socialists in the unions of the CIO marked this organization's greater inclination to radicalism in relationship to the AFL. Consciousness of workers as a "class" — one that transcended the boundaries of ethnicity, race, and skill level — was far more common among the leaders of those unions affiliated with the CIO, and for the communists and socialists within the organization, working-class interests were deemed incompatible with those of their employers. Many, no doubt, dreamed of a classless society in which the workers themselves took not only management but ownership into their own hands.

Both the AFL and, especially, the CIO benefited greatly from the passage of the National Labor Relations Act (better known as the Wagner Act) in 1935. The Wagner Act not only guaranteed the right of collective bargaining for unions, but it also put strict limitations on employers who tried to interfere with the formation of unions and established

---

7. Melvyn Dubofsky, ed., *American Labor Since the New Deal* (Chicago: Quadrangle Books, 1971), 9–11.

8. The name "Popular Front" was derived from a similar, though far more structured, alliance against fascism that arose in France. For more on the Popular Front in the United States, and its lasting impact on American culture, see Michael Denning, *The Cultural Front: The Laboring of American Culture in the Twentieth Century* (New York: Verso Books, 1996).

an independent federal agency, the National Labor Relations Board (NLRB), to investigate and address concerns relating to union organizing.[9] The result was that organized labor, which had once been distant from American party politics—unlike its European counterparts—found itself tied to the political fortunes of Franklin Roosevelt's Democratic Party. Though the marriage went through periods of separation and turmoil, it provided labor with its first substantial link to the political and social establishment and would have significant long-term consequences for the trajectory of the ideological currents that dominated unionism in America.

Melvyn Dubofsky began his 1971 anthology on the labor movement since the New Deal with a vivid juxtaposition of contrasting scenes. The first scene was the summer of 1934, when striking workers in Kohler, Wisconsin; Minneapolis; and San Francisco were brutally beaten by police and members of the National Guard, both of which protected the interests of the companies that suffered from the labor disruption. The other scene was that of New York City union workers beating and maiming antiwar protesters in the spring of 1970. "What had happened over the course of four decades," Dubofsky asked, "to transform American workers from victims of the 'system' to its defenders?"[10]

While the answer is complicated, few would deny the significance of World War II and its aftermath in shaping the path of organized labor in America. Mobilized on behalf of the war effort, unions took their seat at the table with the other elements of the "establishment," providing organized labor with a level of power and status few in the 1920s would have imagined possible. After the war's conclusion, tensions that had been simmering during the first half of the 1940s boiled over, unleashing a series of bitter strikes nationwide in the winter of 1946 during a postwar recession. Though most of the strikes were successful in terms of meeting union demands, businesses had begun to force unions to accept more clearly demarcated lines of management authority. Furthermore, the strikes were terribly unpopular with the public at large, and for perhaps the first time since the labor movement began, business

---

9. Walter Galenson, "The Historical Role of American Trade Unionism," in *Unions in Transition: Entering the Second Century*, ed. Seymour Martin Lipset (San Francisco: Institute for Contemporary Studies Press, 1986), 54; George E. Mowry and Blaine A. Brownell, *The Urban Nation, 1920–1980* (New York: Hill and Wang, 1981), 85–86; Kenneth J. Heineman, *A Catholic New Deal: Religion and Reform in Depression Pittsburgh* (University Park: Penn State University Press, 1999), 69.

10. Dubofsky, ed., *American Labor Since the New Deal*, 3.

interests were successful in portraying labor as the "bully" in negotiations. America's newly acquired status as a superpower—more specifically, a superpower in the midst of a Cold War with a Marxist rival—forced a more deeply enfranchised labor movement to contend with the nation's new role whenever advocating on behalf of its members.[11]

The acrimony caused by the strikes of 1946, coupled with a resurgence of the Republican Party in Congress, led to the passage of the 1947 Taft-Hartley Act. This act was designed to weaken the Wagner Act and did so by handing over to the federal government substantial power to intervene when unions opted to strike. Furthermore, participation in NLRB elections required that union leaders publicly declare themselves noncommunist.[12] Workers previously supportive of communists were now backed into a corner; they could maintain their principles or maintain their clout.

The repercussions of Taft-Hartley were significant. In 1949 and 1950, the CIO expelled eleven unions, representing between 17 percent and 20 percent of its total membership, for being "Communist-dominated" (though a few unions had already seen the writing on the wall and left voluntarily).[13] A communist-free CIO, having abandoned much of the class consciousness and rhetoric that precipitated its original formation, was poised for reunion with its progenitor, the AFL. The reunion took place in 1955 under the banner of a new organization: the AFL-CIO.

The AFL-CIO's first leader was George Meany of the AFL, an Irish Catholic from New York who began as a plumber and rose through the ranks to become one of the most powerful labor leaders of the twentieth century. He made a name for himself with his blunt demeanor, ardent anticommunism, and efforts to fight racketeering in the unions. When CIO President John L. Lewis publicly urged labor leaders to protest the Taft-Hartley noncommunist affidavit by refusing to sign, Meany was the first to challenge him. He called out Lewis—who, despite being a conservative Republican, had tolerated communists in the CIO for their organizational skills—as being among the "stinking America haters who love Moscow." Meany proclaimed: "I'm prepared to sign the affidavit

11. Joshua Freeman et al., *Who Built America? Working People and the Nation's Economy, Politics, Culture, and Society, Volume Two: From the Gilded Age to the Present* (New York: Pantheon Books, 1992), 475–77.
12. Ibid., 492.
13. Steve Rosswurm, "Introduction: An Overview and Preliminary Assessment of the CIO's Expelled Unions," in *The CIO's Left-Led Unions*, ed. Steve Rosswurm (New Brunswick, N.J.: Rutgers University Press, 1992), 1–2.

that I was never a comrade of the comrades."[14] His speech on the future of the labor movement, given on the eve of the AFL-CIO reunion, reflects the comparatively conciliatory tone of organized labor a decade after the war. "Certain facts and considerations" needed to be taken into account for success at the bargaining table, Meany declared.

I. "The interests of labor and management are interdependent, rather than inimical."
II. "Free labor and free enterprise can exist only under a free system of government."
III. "The totalitarian threat of our day is communism."
IV. "Certain business leaders may consider 'big government' or socialism more of an immediate threat to their interests than communism." Labor, said Meany, shares their concern.
V. "The vast majority of labor-management disputes can be settled amicably."[15]

The struggle of the working class, which defined Marxism and typified a significant strand of the early labor movement in the United States, was absent from Meany's rhetoric. By the mid-1950s, organized labor was more likely to define itself as a vital element of a "free market" system than as a force for the abolition of free-market capitalism. This did not mean that union workers were now satisfied with their lot and had joined hands with management. It did, however, mean that the causes of discord between labor and management were more likely to be traced to the personal failings of managers in particular industries or shops than to the intractable struggle of the working class to free itself from the chains of the capitalists.

Roman Catholics represented an enormous bloc within labor and, consequently, played a role in laying the foundation for the changes in the labor movement during the 1940s and 1950s. Moreover, the transforming status of labor that characterized these decades was reflected in the fate of those Catholic organizations devoted to sanctifying the environment of industrial labor. The SAD of the National Catholic Welfare

---

14. Lester Vilie, *Labor U.S.A.* (New York: Harper and Brothers, 1959), 3–17; Charles A. Madison, *American Labor Leaders: Personalities and Forces in the Labor Movement* (New York: Frederick Ungar, 1950), 185.

15. George Meany, "On Labor's Future," in *American Labor Since the New Deal*, ed. Dubofsky, 167–68.

Conference, the ACTU, and the YCW reproduced the ideologies of the social encyclicals to suit their encounters with the industrial market economy of mid-twentieth-century America.

The Social Action Department

The Social Action Department (SAD) was an arm of the National Catholic Welfare Conference (NCWC), an organization of American Catholic bishops. During World War I, American bishops organized to coordinate the Catholic war effort as well as to provide a centralized voice that could negotiate with and lobby the federal government. This effort proved so successful that after the armistice, the organization continued under the name National Catholic Welfare Conference. The NCWC was administered by a group of bishops who oversaw various departments committed to promoting the Church's interests in the areas of education, legislation, the press, lay groups, and social action.[16] The bishops appointed priests to serve as the heads of the various agencies, including the SAD.

It is worth noting that in the early days of the NCWC, a Rural Life Bureau (RLB), headed by the eventual founder of the NCRLC, Edwin O'Hara, was a central component of the SAD. From the start, however, the RLB was viewed as a "poor stepchild" of the department. Centered on the other side of the continent in Eugene, Oregon (where O'Hara had been assigned), far away from the SAD's Washington, D.C., headquarters, the RLB often acted outside the orbit of the SAD's leadership. O'Hara's biographer, Timothy Dolan, noted that the SAD "seemed riveted to urban-industrial concerns" to the perceived exclusion of rural life.[17] Soon afterward, the RLB evolved into the National Catholic Rural Life Conference, and while maintaining ties with SAD, it ultimately pursued its own agenda.

John A. Ryan was the first, and perhaps the most influential, director of the SAD. Ryan came to prominence when his 1906 dissertation,

---

16. Thomas J. Reese, S.J., *A Flock of Shepherds: The National Conference of Catholic Bishops* (Kansas City, Mo.: Sheed and Ward, 1992), 23–24; Dorothy M. Brown and Elizabeth McKeown, *The Poor Belong to Us: Catholic Charities and American Welfare* (Cambridge, Mass.: Harvard University Press, 1977), 69.

17. Timothy M. Dolan, *"Some Seed Fell on Good Ground": The Life of Edwin V. O'Hara* (Washington, D.C: Catholic University of America Press, 1992), 91.

A Living Wage, was published under the same title. Using *Rerum Novarum* (sec. 34) as his key proof text, he set out to make the argument that all workers were entitled to wages "sufficiently high to enable the laborer to live in a manner consistent with the dignity of a human being."[18] Ryan successfully corralled the bishops to put forward a remarkably progressive set of recommendations aimed at enhancing the quality of life for laboring Americans. The 1919 plan, known formally as "The Bishops' Program of Social Reconstruction," called for a wide range of social legislation, including minimum-wage laws, standardized health and safety regulations in the workplace, public insurance for the sick and the elderly, controls on monopolies, and an end to child labor.[19] In part because the Bishops' Program followed many of the same ideological currents as Franklin Roosevelt, and in part because of the close personal relationship John Ryan eventually cultivated with FDR, Ryan could claim that nearly all of what the bishops proposed in 1919 had become law in some form by the end of the 1930s. While Ryan was an ardent supporter of union organizing, George Higgins (a later director of the SAD) characterized his "main remedy" for social ills as legislation. The transformations necessary to lift workers out of poverty could not take place in a reasonable amount of time if left solely to organizing workers, Ryan believed. Government intervention was a necessity.[20]

The SAD functioned, in many ways, like a clearinghouse of information on Catholic social thought. The department reproduced the Church's ideology by sponsoring conferences, promoting labor schools, providing speakers for events, and printing pamphlets advocating its positions on social justice. SAD staff members were fairly prolific, publishing articles addressing the pressing economic and social issues of the day in a wide array of Catholic periodicals. Those who supported their positions

18. Jay Dolan, *The American Catholic Experience: A History from Colonial Times to the Present* (Notre Dame, Ind.: University of Notre Dame Press, 1992), 342; John A. Ryan, *A Living Wage: Its Ethical and Economic Aspects* (New York: Macmillan, 1906), viii.

19. See Joseph M. McShane, *Sufficiently Radical: Catholicism, Progressivism, and the Bishops' Program of 1919* (Washington, D.C.: Catholic University of America Press, 1986); see also James Hennessey, S.J., *American Catholics: A History of the Roman Catholic Community in the United States* (New York: Oxford University Press, 1981), 228–29; J. Dolan, *The American Catholic Experience*, 244–46; Charles R. Morris, *American Catholic: The Saints and Sinners Who Built America's Most Powerful Church* (New York: Vintage Books, 1997), 151; Chester Gillis, *Roman Catholicism in America* (New York: Columbia University Press, 1999), 70–72.

20. Msgr. George G. Higgins and William Bole, *Organized Labor and the Church: Reflections of a "Labor Priest"* (New York: Paulist Press, 1993), 27; cites J. Ryan, *A Living Wage*.

took pleasure in characterizing the SAD as a mouthpiece for the bishops. Those who opposed the department—typically for its general sympathy for New Deal–style economic planning and for its active support of labor unions—expressed concerns that their positions would become conflated with those of "the Church." Like all arguments emerging from the Roman Catholic Church or any such organization, successfully popularizing the notion that one's political and social outlook was synonymous with that of *the* organization, movement, or party itself, as such, was pivotal in establishing the necessary authority to shape that group. The SAD's direct link to the American hierarchy, in a Church dominated by a hierarchically bound self-understanding (certainly prior to Vatican II), lent force to the economic vision promoted by the department.

Adapting to a Changing Climate

By the 1940s, most of the work coming out of the SAD was being led by Raymond McGowan, Ryan's assistant. It was primarily through McGowan's leadership that a formal system of cooperation between labor, management, and the government—eventually labeled the Industry Council Plan—became the centerpiece of the SAD's vision, where it remained through the 1950s. McGowan had advocated something along these lines as early as the 1920s and was validated by *Quadragesimo Anno*'s description of an ideal social order as something resembling a modernized medieval guild system along corporatist lines. As such, McGowan spearheaded a SAD agenda that focused especially on organizing unions and establishing systems that enhanced labor-management cooperation.[21] (Because Chapter 6 will be devoted to the role of the Industry Council Plan in Catholic economic thought, we will postpone a fuller discussion of the plan until then). When Msgr. Ryan died in 1945, McGowan took over the role as director of the SAD until retiring in 1954.

A comparison of two articles McGowan penned for *The Commonweal* in 1936 with a statement he released on Labor Day in 1953, shortly before his retirement, is instructive in illustrating changes in the SAD's approach to the American economy in those years. In 1936, McGowan used recently released statistics from the Brookings Institution to show

21. Ibid., 32–34.

that America, still recovering from the Depression, was failing to live up to *Quadragesimo Anno*'s demand that "the wage paid to the working man must be sufficient for the support of himself and his family." The distribution of income, McGowan argued, only provided "the greatest number of jobs in broker offices and stock exchanges," leaving the overwhelming majority of Americans in the cold. By the Brookings Institution study's reckoning, prices, production, and property distribution were also skewed to benefit the wealthy. These findings reflected Pius XI's own description of "the immense number of propertyless wage earners on the one hand and the superabundant riches of the fortunate few on the other." From this, *Quadragesimo Anno* concluded that "earthly goods so abundantly produced in this age of industrialism are far from rightly distributed and equitably shared among the various classes of men." McGowan added his own opinion that "the encyclical might have been speaking of this very table [made available by the Brookings Institution about the American economy]."[22]

McGowan's diagnosis was that the wealthy saved too much and failed to put their profits to work for the majority of people. If liberty "to buy at the lowest price and sell at the highest" was God's greatest gift, then the evidence would suggest that God was a "monstrosity," he argued. If this was "the American way," he asked, "is there anything in the 20-percent underproduction, the $10,000,000,000 superfluous savings made by 2.3 percent of the families and the 12,000,000 families receiving less than $1,500 a year, to make an American willing to call it 'the American way'?" Appeals to a return to "the good old days," now that the Depression was ending, prompted McGowan to ask whether "the dog hungers for its vomit."[23]

Interpreting the principle of subsidiarity always raises the question of whether government intervention is needed to attain justice in individual cases. McGowan pushed aside the arguments of those who maintained that state governments, as opposed to the federal government, were the proper forum to address these issues. "Usually," he protested, "those who appeal to action by the states do not want anything done." The American economy reflected what Pius XI termed "the Individualistic school," McGowan held. The irony was that the battle cry of "free

22. Raymond A. McGowan, "Footnotes to a Document," *The Commonweal* 24 (May 8, 1936): 38–39.
23. Ibid.

competition and open markets" was not really what the individualists wanted. Instead, they wanted "liberty to dominate undiluted by labor unions, farm cooperatives, consumers' organizations and government."[24]

In a follow-up article published two months later, McGowan focused on the difficulties in remedying widespread economic injustice that was posed by the American Constitution itself. Whereas *Quadragesimo Anno* held that government could "go beyond the demands of the natural and divine law and specify in further detail what owners shall do for the common good," the U.S. Supreme Court had interpreted the Constitution as forbidding federal interference in industry and private commerce. "A constitutional amendment," McGowan proposed, "is the only practicable way to avoid the unconstitutionality of Catholic social teaching. It should be an amendment that permits the federal and state governments to act both directly and through organized industries and professions."[25] Clearly, McGowan's reading of subsidiarity held that without federal government action, those steps necessary to establishing a Christian social order could not be "performed and provided for." In McGowan's eyes, as it stood in 1936, "the American governmental system is individualistic. It commands Individualism to race us over the cliff to our destruction."[26]

The tone of McGowan's 1953 Labor Day statement cast a far different light on the American economic scene. Guarded but genuine optimism ruled the day, and a more positive assessment of America's compatibility with a Catholic social justice platform colored McGowan's rhetoric. "Genuine, if limited, progress has been registered in recent years," McGowan proclaimed. "More people are gainfully employed than at any other time in the history of the United States. More employees than ever are now organized into bona fide trade unions. The standard of living of most of the working people is relatively good in spite of the continuing problem of inflation." Times had changed. The "Individualism" that pervaded American society seemed to have been defeated, in McGowan's accounting. "There was a time in the history of this country," he began his reflections on the past, "when many property owners and workers regarded their personal rights as absolute. In economic life—as contrasted with domestic life, which at that time was more directly influenced by Christian morality—they acted as though

24. Ibid., 39–40.
25. Raymond A. McGowan, "Further Footnotes," *The Commonweal* 24 (July 31, 1936): 339–40.
26. Ibid., 341.

they were alone in God's universe or as though they and their neighbors were meant to be enemies to one another." The tide had turned by 1953. "Thanks be to God, we are slowly getting over that way of thinking and acting in the field of economics."[27]

While McGowan's outlook had grown significantly more positive in the intervening seventeen years, there was still much to be done. If the Cold War were to come to an end, unemployment could rise substantially. Labor-management cooperation still had a long way to go, despite a more "mature" collective bargaining system and a rise in profit sharing. The "natural community" of those who participate in the same industry had yet to develop into full-blown industry councils, and inflation continued to pose a risk. But wholesale characterizations of an "individualist" America had given way to a description of a nation beginning to "repent" of its individualistic past, having "made a good beginning in our efforts to reconcile the rights of the individual in economic life with the corresponding rights of the community." Labor Day was therefore an occasion "to express our gratitude for this salutary improvement in our national life."[28] The contrast in McGowan's words, separated by nearly two decades, speaks volumes of the changing economic attitudes of the period.

By the time George G. Higgins became the director of the SAD in 1954, the organization had gone through many transformations. But its agenda continued to be steered by the primary features set forth in the American bishops' 1919 plan, particularly greater worker participation in ownership and management decisions. Organizing labor unions was still a vital part of the SAD agenda in some industries and in some regions, yet improving the quality of union leadership and sparking greater activism and interest among the rank-and-file members was of primary concern. The right of unions to exist had been won by the 1950s, both in law and even in the eyes of much of the management class. Assuring that those unions served the best interest of their members and society as a whole was now the central task. In the decade following World War II, while corruption and incompetence were a constant struggle, the SAD believed that the primary threat to healthy unions was communism.

27. Raymond A. McGowan, "1953 Labor Day Statement," pamphlet (Social Action Department, NCWC), found in Rockhurst University Archives (hereafter RUA), "Institute of Social Order," Box 1.
28. Ibid.

Catholics and Communism

To make sense of the SAD's anticommunist agenda, along with the anticommunist agenda of other organizations tied to the Church, it is important that we look at the long history of the Catholic conflict with Marxism globally and in the United States. Roman Catholic antipathy to communism dates back to the early propagation of Marxist ideology. While socialists and communists often fiercely distinguished themselves from one another, the popes of the nineteenth and early twentieth centuries drew no fine lines between the two and saw both, along with any other forms of secularist or materialist worldview, as part and parcel of a broader scourge of liberalism—all traceable in origin to the Protestant Reformation.[29] One of the earliest public denunciations of communism from the Church came in Pius IX's 1849 *Nostis et Nobiscum* (discussed in Chapter 1) and later in his 1864 letter *Quanta Cura*. Both encyclicals attack the materialist and antireligious postures of Marxism, while the latter goes further in chastising communism and socialism for subjugating the rights of the family in relation to those of the state (*QC* sec. 4).

Hostility toward these derivations of Marxist thought was heightened by the perception that the very forces of Italian republicanism that sought to overthrow the Papal States and strip the Church of her temporal authority were ultimately inclined toward instituting a brand of Marxism in Italy. The reality was that while some were certainly inclined toward or inspired by socialism, the republicans had a broad range of ideological leanings while bound by a commitment to a united Italy under a representative government. Nonetheless, the perception that communism and socialism were root causes of the subjugation of the Papal States went far toward initiating the role of the Church as the premier anticommunist voice worldwide.[30]

---

29. On the lack of distinction drawn between communism and socialism, along with other isms, by the nineteenth-century papacy, see Donald F. Crosby, S.J., *God, Church, and Flag: Senator Joseph R. McCarthy and the Catholic Church, 1950–1957* (Chapel Hill: University of North Carolina Press, 1978), 4.

30. In his 1849 *Nostis et Nobiscum*, Pius IX writes of the Italian republican movement that "the goal of this most iniquitous plot is to drive people to overthrow the entire order of human affairs and to draw them over to the wicked theories of this *Socialism* and *Communism*, by confusing them with perverted teachings. But these enemies realize that they cannot hope for any agreement with the Catholic Church.... This is why they try to draw the Italian people over to Protestantism, which in their deceit they repeatedly declare to be only another form of the same true religion of Christ.... Meanwhile, they know full well

In the following decades, many factors contributed to cultivating a visceral hostility toward communism among Roman Catholics both in the United States and globally. First and foremost among these was the treatment of Russian Catholics during and after the Bolshevik Revolution. As Lenin himself once wrote: "the materialist theory of knowledge is a universal weapon against religious belief."[31] Consequently, with the communist ascendancy in Russia, Church property was confiscated and many bishops and priests were killed or sent to labor camps. The Russian Orthodox Church bore the brunt of the repression, but the historical division between it and the Roman Catholic Church only served to calcify Catholic suspicion of this strange and powerful revolutionary force emerging from Russia. In the same year that the Bolshevik Revolution began, three Portuguese children claimed to have witnessed an appearance of the Virgin Mary in the town of Fatima. The children recounted the Virgin's admonition: "I come to ask the consecration of Russia to my Immaculate Heart. . . . If [the world's Catholics] listen to my request, Russia will be converted and there will be peace. If not, she will scatter her error through the world, provoking wars and persecution of the Church." From that point on, Catholic opposition to communism was crystallized in the veneration of Our Lady of Fatima. Indeed, in a few years many millions of Catholics were praying "for the conversion of Russia" in the pews on Sunday mornings and in various devotional groups.[32]

Few events united Roman Catholics in their opposition to communism as the Spanish Civil War. From 1936 to 1939, battle lines were drawn between General Francisco Franco's nationalists and the republican forces of Spain. Communists fought alongside the republican forces, including a number of American communists (among other Americans) who volunteered for the Abraham Lincoln Brigade. While atrocities on both sides were significant, Roman Catholics around the globe were

---

that the chief principle of the Protestant tenets, i.e., that the holy scriptures are to be understood by the personal judgment of the individual, will greatly assist their impious cause." *Nostis et Nobiscum*, sec. 6, accessed February 12, 2007, http://www.ewtn.com/library/encycl/p9nostis.htm; on the Church's conflict with Italian republicans, see Peter D'Agostino, *Rome in America: Transnational Catholic Ideology from the Risorgimento to Fascism* (Chapel Hill: University of North Carolina Press, 2004), 26–59.

31. David McLellan, *Marxism and Religion* (New York: Harper and Row, 1987), 100; cites V. Lenin, *Materialism and Empiriocriticism* (Moscow: Progress Publishers, 1970), 330.

32. C. Morris, *American Catholic*, 228–29.

drawn to the conflict by reports of Churches being burned, along with thousands of priests and nearly three hundred nuns executed. The close association of the Church with the conservative wing of Spanish politics, coupled with leftist disdain for the Roman Catholic worldview, enabled Franco to successfully cast himself as the protector of the Church. In the United States, the Spanish Civil War served as a proxy in public debates for liberal Protestants to express hostility toward American Catholics, rendering Catholic support for Franco as evidence of their latent fascist tendencies. For Catholics, strong Soviet backing in the form of both troops and weapons for the Spanish republicans validated their view of the Church as the one great hope for the preservation of Western civilization and the front line of attack on the communist menace.[33]

President Roosevelt acceded to Stalin's territorial claims over eastern Poland at the Yalta Conference in early 1945, and many Roman Catholics in the United States who had previously aligned themselves with Roosevelt over the New Deal felt betrayed. As they predicted, Poland, an overwhelmingly Catholic country, fell completely within the Soviet orbit shortly after the conclusion of World War II.[34] Triggered by the "appeasement" at Yalta, figures like New York's Francis Cardinal Spellman, always vocally anticommunist, pushed his public efforts to marshal communist opposition into high gear. Soon Spellman was one of the most significant supporters of Joseph McCarthy's investigations into communism within the borders of the United States.[35] More influential still was Bishop Fulton J. Sheen, whose Sunday evening radio program *The Catholic Hour* had been broadcasting for two decades before the debut of his television program *Life Is Worth Living*. Watched in nearly six million homes nationwide—both Catholic and Protestant—until it went off the air in 1957, Sheen devoted special attention to instructing his audience on the perils of communism. The American Legion even awarded Sheen a medal for his "exemplary work on behalf of Americanism." Historian Donald Crosby, S.J., ventured to write that "if Spellman

---

33. Crosby, *God, Church, and Flag*, 6–7; Heineman, *A Catholic New Deal*, 179–81; Patrick Allitt, *Catholic Intellectuals and Conservative Politics in America, 1950–1985* (Ithaca, N.Y.: Cornell University Press, 1993), 24–25.
34. George Sirgiovanni, *An Undercurrent of Suspicion: Anti-Communism in America During World War II* (New Brunswick, N.J.: Transaction Publishers, 1990), 157–63; Crosby, *God, Church, and Flag*, 9–10.
35. Robert I. Gannon, S.J., *The Cardinal Spellman Story* (Garden City, N.Y.: Doubleday, 1962), 348–50; Crosby, *God, Church, and Flag*, 13–15, 200–201.

was the political leader of Catholic anticommunism, then its prophet and philosopher was Bishop Fulton J. Sheen."[36]

As many have noted, Catholic displays of anticommunism in the United States served the dual purpose of reflecting the orthodoxy of Church teachings while simultaneously securing Roman Catholics' credentials as "authentic" Americans in a time when the majority of Americans continued to view Catholic loyalty to the nation with suspicion. Within the labor movement, this dual purpose was intensified in light of the disproportionate representation of communists in unions. Catholic labor leaders like Philip Murray and John Brophy—both leaders of the CIO, where communist activism persisted until the early 1950s—became outspoken critics of the Communist Party.

Murray, the son of an Irish miner in Scotland who immigrated to the United States in 1902, frequently noted that his labor activism grew not only from the frustrations he encountered as a miner himself and later as a steelworker but also from the inspiration he drew from *Rerum Novarum*. Though tolerant of communists in the CIO early for their efforts in union organization—provided that they kept their politics to themselves—he consistently made his opposition to communist principles widely known. A member of the Knights of Columbus and the Ancient Order of Hibernians, two organizations that took pride in their anticommunist credentials, Murray was central to engineering the purging of communists from the CIO as it became clear to him that their presence was an impediment to the success of the labor movement in the United States. As he wrote of communism in 1951, "any organization of fanatics working secretly and on a program so clearly devoid of moral principles is, of course, a threat to our American democracy and to our democratic labor movement." Though opposed to noncommunist affidavits in the Taft-Hartley Act, his Catholic faith authorized his efforts to rid unions of communists.[37]

Like Murray, John Brophy also came to the labor movement through the United Mine Workers of America, but while Murray shifted to the

---

36. Mark S. Massa, *Catholics and American Culture: Fulton Sheen, Dorothy Day, and the Notre Dame Football Team* (New York: Crossroad, 1999), 82–91; Crosby, *God, Church, and Flag*, 15.

37. Madison, *American Labor Leaders*, 311–34; Neil Betten, *Catholic Activism and the Industrial Worker* (Gainesville: University Presses of Florida, 1976), 113–15; Heineman, *A Catholic New Deal*, 147–48, 175–78, 202–4; Philip Murray, "American Labor and the Threat of Communism," *Annals of the American Academy of Political and Social Sciences* 247 (March 1951): 128.

United Steelworkers of America, Brophy stayed with the miners. Early in Brophy's career, he joined with a priest in Pittsburgh to form a labor school and educate unionists in the social teachings of Leo XIII. Brophy's fairly strident hostility to communism did not serve to shield him entirely from accusations that he himself was a "fellow traveler," simply for his association with organized labor and the CIO. Yet Brophy believed that the Church called him to be "a radical" in the "fight against greed and privilege." He lectured frequently on the compatibility of the social encyclicals with the aims and methods of the CIO and later eagerly joined Murray in the purge of communist factions within the organization. Like so many Roman Catholics in the labor movement, Brophy's public anticommunism, though genuine, also served to mark his status as both Catholic and American.[38]

The Social Action Department and Communism

Within the broader context of Catholic anticommunism and the special attention given to the labor movement as a hotbed of "Red" activity, it is not surprising that the SAD saw communism as the greatest threat to a successful union movement. Scholars such as Steve Rosswurm have gone so far as to claim that the Roman Catholic Church in the United States, including the SAD, changed radically at the close of World War II and adopted an "entirely negative" campaign in an "effort to destroy communism," which replaced a positive program aimed as much at uplifting the working classes as eliminating communists from their ranks.[39] While the totalizing language of Rosswurm's characterization is unsupportable, the Cold War clearly shifted the SAD's focus toward anticommunism until the early 1950s, when the influence of the Communist Party on the union movement had been irreparably damaged. It is worth noting, however, that this may have been as much a tactical maneuver on the part of the SAD's staff as a reflection of an ideological turn. With the new political climate fostered by the Cold War, as evidenced by the Taft-Hartley Act that delegitimized communist-led unions (an act that, tellingly, was opposed overwhelmingly by the SAD, including John F.

---

38. Betten, *Catholic Activism and the Industrial Worker*, 114–15; Heineman, *A Catholic New Deal*, 41.
39. Steve Rosswurm, "The Catholic Church and the Left-Led Unions: Labor Priests, Labor Schools, and the ACTU," in *The CIO's Left-Led Unions*, 120.

Cronin, assistant director of the SAD from 1951 to 1960 and the most noteworthy anticommunist activist on the staff),[40] SAD activists feared that Red-baiting would be an effective tool for undercutting union gains. To the extent that communists could be removed from unions, the unions might be sheltered more effectively from outside attacks.

Ironically, the labor schools promoted by the SAD that proved so successful in informing unionists and potential unionists of Catholic social teachings were patterned on the Worker Schools sponsored by the Communist Party in the United States. One analysis of "Catholic Worker's Schools" penned by John M. Hayes of the SAD in the early 1940s asks:

> should we imitate the Communist technique in deliberately seeking to create leaders in the labor movement? While all may need instruction, isn't it possible to reach the others through sermons, lectures, study clubs and papers? In general it seems advisable to aim constantly at discovering and encouraging the most energetic and intelligent. It may be possible to gather a large number for the usual classes and to select from them a few who will be given special attention. The Communist [sic] have, or had, a standing offer to conduct a workers' school wherever twelve people sign up. Whether a rigid rule should limit attendance to Catholic unionists or a "preferential clause" should govern the situation depends on local circumstances.[41]

Perhaps Hayes would have been more cautious in invoking the Communist Party as a model had he written this report some years later. All the same, Catholic labor activists clearly saw communists as their primary competition for the hearts and minds of the working classes and after World War II intensified their focus on defeating their opponent.

The SAD reproduced the teachings of the social encyclicals for an American audience in countless ways. Its reading of the texts was colored by the New Deal activism of the department's pioneer, John Ryan. Though the SAD, under the leadership of McGowan, shifted its emphasis from legislation to organizing workers, it remained heavily involved

---

40. John F. Cronin, *Catholic Social Principles: The Social Teaching of the Catholic Church Applied to American Economic Life* (Milwaukee: Bruce Publishing), 22, 248.

41. John M. Hayes, "Analysis of Catholic Worker's Schools," 2, The American Catholic History Research Center and University Archives (hereafter ACUA), Catholic University of America, Washington, D.C., Collection 10, Folder 29.

in lobbying efforts aimed at shaping laws that strengthened the hands of labor unions, encouraging worker-management relations, and paving the way toward industry councils. In doing so, they worked to sanctify industrial labor in a manner distasteful to some rural-life activists. Though many in this organization of priests, including McGowan and Higgins, became regular fixtures in union halls and picket lines, none were actually union members. The reproduction of the Catholic ideology from the "bottom up" was left to organizations like the Association of Catholic Trade Unionists (ACTU).

The Association of Catholic Trade Unionists

The ACTU was a lay organization composed only of actual union members intent on spreading the message of *Rerum Novarum* and *Quadragesimo Anno* to fellow unionists. The movement sprang from the experiences of people like George R. Donahue and Edward W. Scully. Donahue, a young college graduate, was beaten several times by men working for organized crime bosses as he tried to organize checkers working on New York City's waterfront in the mid-1930s. He also had difficulty obtaining support for his efforts from rank-and-file members of the International Longshoremen's Association. Edward Scully was a freshly minted graduate of Harvard Law School. His interest in unions was sparked by stories told to him by members of the local New York Teamsters. They had complained that anywhere from 10 percent to 15 percent of their wages was being skimmed off the top by crooked union operatives, so that when their contract stipulated a wage of $40, they only received between $32 and $35 from their union agents.[42]

Experiences like these led Donahue and Scully to join an organization founded by eleven Catholic laymen while conversing around a kitchen table at the headquarters of the New York branch of the Catholic Worker on February 27, 1937. The ACTU was the brainchild of a group of "utility workers, seamen, several carpenters, a garment-worker, two journalists, a relief-worker and an office-worker," nearly all of whom were union members.[43] It was not the only organization of its kind to form during this time period. Groups like the Chicago Catholic Labor

---

42. John F. Burns, "ACTU Bores from Within," *Catholic Digest* 13 (April 1949): 50.
43. John C. Cort, "Nine Years of the ACTU," *America*, April 6, 1946, 4.

Alliance and the Labor Guild in Boston were also founded to inject Catholic teachings into the worker's movement. Prior to these Catholic organizations, only the Jewish Labor Committee, established in 1934, had been organized to formally bring religious interests to bear on unions. But the ACTU was the most broadly based of these Catholic groups, and certainly gained the most notoriety.

After months of debating between founding members, the organization outlined a statement of guidelines that was retained throughout its existence.

> Basing our stand on the papal encyclicals, the writings of other recognized Catholic authorities, and the basic principles of common sense and justice, we believe that:
>
> The worker has a right to: 1) Job security. 2) Income sufficient to support himself and family in reasonable comfort. 3) Collective bargaining through union representatives freely chosen. 4) A share in the profits after just wages and a return to capital have been paid. 5) Strike and picket peacefully for just cause. 6) A just price for the goods he buys. 7) Decent working hours. 8) Decent working conditions.
>
> And that the worker has a duty to: 1) Perform an honest day's work for an honest day's pay. 2) Join a bona fide union. 3) Strike only for a just cause after all other legitimate means have been exhausted. 4) Refrain from violence. 5) Respect property rights. 6) Abide by the just agreements freely made. 7) Enforce strict honesty and a square deal for everybody inside his union. 8) Cooperate with decent employers who respect his rights to bring about a peaceful solution to industrial war by the setting up of guilds for the self-regulation of industry and producer-cooperatives in which the worker *shares as a partner* in the ownership, management or profits of the business in which he works.[44]

These guidelines intentionally reflected key components of the papal encyclicals. In keeping with the wording of *Quadragesimo Anno* (and,

---

44. John C. Cort, "Catholics in Trade Unions," *The Commonweal* 30 (May 5, 1939): 34–35, emphasis in original.

in fairness, with the dominant ideas of the day), the issue of just wages was framed around the assumption of a male breadwinner supporting *his* family. The same rhetoric had pervaded the work of the SAD in its advocacy of a "living wage." (Notably, the SAD Assistant Director John Cronin's 1959 *Social Principles and Economic Life*—a revised and updated version of his 1950 tome *Catholic Social Principles*—included new gender-neutral language connected to the idea of a living wage. For instance, the 1950 sentence "The first need in social justice is a proper structure of economic society, so that all able and willing men can earn a living wage for the care of their families" was replaced by 1959 with the phrase "heads of households" in lieu of "men.")[45] Thus, the ACTU preserved what was thought to be a "traditional" family arrangement in the promotion of justice.

Leo XIII approached the notion of a right to strike with much caution (sec. 31), and Pius XI only added to the confusion when he took note of the fascist model outlawing strikes as well as lockouts (sec. 94) and announced that "little reflection is required to perceive advantages in the institution thus summarily described" (sec. 95). The ACTU, however, saw the right to strike as natural provided that it was only used as a last resort. Furthermore, also reflective of the pervading view of the SAD, the ACTU saw unionizing as not just a good option but a duty among the working classes. Having listed among the duties of the worker the need to "join a bona fide union," understood by association members as excluding company unions with no ties to the larger labor movement, *Quadragesimo Anno*'s reaffirmation of the rights of workers associations provided the ACTU (not to mention the SAD) with language that could be mustered to buttress the duty to unionize, despite the inconclusive wording of the encyclical (secs. 31–36).

The duty to unionize was not restricted to Catholics, and this belief was reflected in the ACTU's frequent attempts to make alliances with non-Catholic union members. It was precisely on the issue of involvement in non-Catholic, or "neutral," unions that the encyclicals were most hesitant. By 1931 Pius XI had conceded that in some contexts, the maintenance of a viable union movement that was strictly Catholic had become "impossible" (*QA* sec. 35). At the same time, he left it to the discretion of the local bishop to "permit Catholic workingmen to join

---

45. Cronin, *Catholic Social Principles*, 355; Cronin, *Social Principles and Economic Life* (Milwaukee: Bruce Publishing, 1959), 208.

these unions, where they judge that circumstances make it necessary and there appears no danger for religion" (*QA* sec. 35). Participation of Catholics in these religiously "neutral" unions had become standard practice in the United States, and the ACTU worked hard to cultivate connections to non-Catholics, in part to subvert suspicions that the association served as a divisive sectarian force. The invitation to participate in "Conferences"—meetings aimed at bridging differences between managers and workers—was extended to "non-Catholics, Negroes and Whites, Democrats and Republicans, any and all right-minded workers interested in correcting some abuse within their union."[46] These non-sectarian tendencies were exemplified by the New York ACTU's active support of Walter Reuther, a Protestant, over Albert E. Fitzgerald, an Irish Catholic, in a CIO election—support stemming from Fitzgerald's publicized ties to the communist wing of the trade union movement.[47] Opposition to communism contributed greatly to breaking down religious and social divisions within the ACTU sphere of action. "I don't think the ACTU has ever been so stupid as to confuse good guys with Catholic guys," a founder of the ACTU once wrote.[48] When a group of Jewish hat blockers appealed to the ACTU for assistance in fighting what they saw as antidemocratic forces in their union shortly after World War II, the ACTU obliged.[49] Inter-denominationalism became commonplace over the span of the ACTU's existence.

The authority of the encyclicals assured that no ideology could be properly labeled "Catholic" that did not accept the right to private property. It was on this issue that the ACTU was clearly most distinguishable from unionists of the Communist Party. After all, class difference—also accepted as natural in Catholic circles—was grounded in the differentiation of private property across the social spectrum. The ACTU, like the SAD, hoped to limit that differentiation in the promotion of worker "partnership" with the wealthier classes through joint management, ownership, and profit sharing that would emerge from the implementation of the Industry Council Plan, patterned after the corporatist vision of *Quadragesimo Anno* (see Chapter 6). Class division was a given from

46. George Kelly, "The ACTU and Its Critics," *The Commonweal* 49 (December 31, 1948): 300.
47. Norman McKenna, "The Story of the ACTU," *Catholic World* 168 (March 1949): 455; Burns, "ACTU Bores from Within," 53.
48. John C. Cort, "Lay Apostles in the Field," *The Commonweal* 54 (July 20, 1949): 356.
49. John C. Cort, "What Kind of Labor?" *Catholic Digest* 10 (April 1946): 26.

this perspective, but the ACTU believed that the gap between classes—the very size of which bred social discontent—could be effectively reduced if a modern guild system were to be instituted. As we shall see in the following chapters, it was on the issue of where the line was drawn between the laboring and managerial classes and the share of the latter's duties absorbed by the former that most disturbed conservative Catholics.

Chapters of the ACTU sprang up in cities across the nation. Detroit, San Francisco, and Pittsburgh were among the most noteworthy. By 1940 there were fifteen chapters in all, although at least four of them were not officially chartered.[50] It was not until 1947 that the chapters of the ACTU were formally federated. The Articles of Federation proclaimed that the movement took "as its charter" the "mandate" of *Quadragesimo Anno* that "side by side with these trade unions, there must always be associations which aim at giving their members a thorough religious and moral training" (sec. 35).[51] In the same way the NCRLC lifted a paragraph dealing with life on the land from *Rerum Novarum* to serve as its authorizing agent, the ACTU cited this passage in nearly all of its literature as a battle cry and a shield against those Catholics who questioned its legitimacy.

The federation created the post of a national chair who would preside over a national council representing each chapter. The purpose of both the chair and the council involved, among other things, serving as a conduit of information between all of the member organizations. Much as the SAD functioned as a pivot point for the dioceses across the nation who would turn to it for guidance in handling special matters or for assistance in educating the Catholic laity about social teachings, the national chair of the ACTU, in conjunction with the council, would serve as the "go-to" figure in the federation's structure, generating new chapters, organizing conferences, and promoting the ACTU's work among student groups on college campuses.[52]

Each chapter developed according to its own needs and interests, leading to a situation by 1956 in which it could be said that some chapters were "distinctly more active than others." By that year, official ACTU

---

50. J. Dolan, *The American Catholic Experience*, 405; Richard J. Ward, "The Role of the Association of Catholic Trade Unionists in the Labor Movement," *Review of Social Economy* 14 (September 1956): 92.

51. "Articles of Federation of the ACTU," Fordham University Archives (hereafter FUA), New York, "The Association of Catholic Trade Unionists, 1949–1967," Box 2, Folder 53.

52. Ibid.

membership had reached twelve thousand, with chapters in "New York, Detroit, Philadelphia, Gary, Indiana, Camden and Cleveland, Ohio and Pittsburgh" being "the largest and most active."[53]

John C. Cort, a Catholic convert and an original member of the ACTU, described the organization's aim as "nothing less than building a new, Christian world—nothing less than the realization of the kingdom of God 'on earth as it is in heaven.'"[54] Hoping to do this through the largely urban and industrial trade-union movement situated the organization far from the imagination of most Catholic rural lifers. Essentially, the ACTU understood itself to be both a religious and a teaching organization. As a religious group, the association wanted to save the souls of individuals and sanctify both the labor movement and industrial society. Its teaching component involved exposing workers not only to Catholic social teachings but also to tried-and-true methods of organizing and maintaining healthy unions—defined by the ACTU as not only striving for the worker's best interests and being free from corruption but also being free from communist influence. Differentiating between religious and secular motivations and methods in most—if not all—cases requires imposing necessarily artificial descriptive categories on human motivation and action. Organizing workers, learning strike tactics, assuring that local and national union elections were democratic, or discerning what might constitute a just wage might be seen as "secular" activities distinguishable from prayer meetings and novenas, but for the ACTU member, all these activities were considered part and parcel of doing the work of God and the Roman Catholic Church.

Tools for Spreading the ACTU Message

Promoting Catholic economic principles involved activities ranging from the establishment of labor schools to the publication of newspapers, participation in strikes, and providing legal aid to vulnerable workers. The proliferation of labor schools began in 1921 with the Worker's Educational Bureau of America, which eventually became a part of the AFL. A handful of colleges and universities established these schools, typically

---

53. Ward, "The Role of the Association of Catholic Trade Unionists in the Labor Movement," 92.

54. Cort, "What Kind of Labor?" 26; Norman C. McKenna, "ACTU," *The Catholic Mind* 45 (February 1947): 117–18.

with a curriculum lasting no more than a few weeks.[55] The Communist Party "Worker Schools" began in earnest during the 1920s and were greatly expanded during World War II in an effort to combat fascism. Worker Schools were quite successful at organizing laborers and empowering those sympathetic to the party's cause to assume leadership roles in their local unions.[56]

Among Catholics, labor schools were actively promoted through the SAD and often attached to Catholic colleges and universities, especially those of the Jesuit order. The New York ACTU opened its first school for union members in November 1937. It was free for all participants and sponsored in conjunction with Fordham University. While the ACTU was a lay organization, this did not exclude the active participation of Roman Catholic clergy (indeed, each chapter had its own chaplain). Participation of the clergy was almost a necessity given the lack of familiarity among Catholic laity with the encyclical tradition, if only to convince school participants that the ideas being taught were sanctioned by the Church. Some of these ideas seemed radical, after all, and suspicion as to their "Catholicity" would have been expected had the priests not participated. Father John Boland, who doubled as chairman of the New York State Labor Relations Board, taught a course on "Labor Relations," joined by Father John P. Monaghan, the chaplain to the New York chapter of the ACTU, who also taught classes in "Labor Ethics." Monaghan was especially instrumental in helping the ACTU gain the acceptance of the diocesan officials and the bishop.[57]

The curriculum of labor schools varied depending on location and sponsorship, but the description provided by Vincent J. McLaughlin in a 1940 article written about an ACTU labor school in New Rochelle, New York, reflected a fairly typical approach. Teachers were culled largely from the ranks of the priesthood. Classes were held weekly and were open to Catholics and non-Catholics alike, "regardless of race, color or creed." McLaughlin also emphasized the "heterogeneous character of the student body which insures a composite picture of labor conditions." Of the 102 students at this particular ACTU-sponsored school, 75 were

55. John F. Cronin, *Catholic Social Action* (Milwaukee: Bruce Publishing, 1948), 81–82.
56. Marvin Gettleman, "The Lost World of U.S. Labor Education: Curricula at East and West Coast Community Schools, 1944–1957," conference paper delivered at Gotham History Festival, New York, October 5–14, 2001. Available at http://www.gothamcenter.org/festival/2001/confpapers/gettleman.pdf; accessed June 16, 2004.
57. Cort, "Catholics in Trade Unions, 35; McKenna, "ACTU," 118.

union members representing 19 individual unions. The course lasted ten weeks. When the ten weeks had ended, students were asked to conduct their own final meeting that involved making presentations to the group. By encouraging this sort of active participation, it was believed that students would leave the program feeling confident and energized to take the lessons they had learned back with them to their locals. Topics included the social encyclicals, speeches by famous labor leaders like Samuel Gompers and Terrence V. Powderly, lectures on labor ethics, as well as tutoring in public speaking. The two hours allotted to coursework per night allowed time for presentations, discussions, and short breaks in between events.[58]

Several prominent ACTU members, including John Cort, were journalists and members of newspaper guilds. The *Labor Leader*, published by the New York ACTU, and *The Wage Earner*, the Detroit ACTU's paper (which began as *The Michigan Labor Leader*), were vital in winning an audience beyond Catholic unionists for the movement. Both papers could easily be distinguished from other papers advocating the cause of labor by their being peppered with quotations from the social encyclicals in every issue, employing these passages as proof texts in support of nearly every editorial position taken. The title, *Labor Leader*, was picked up by several chapters of the ACTU nationwide in the publication of their own papers.[59] Next to the New York ACTU's *Labor Leader*, the Detroit ACTU's paper, *The Wage Earner*, was the most successful. Paul Weber, the founder of *The Wage Earner* and a former assistant city editor for *The Detroit Times*, moved the paper from a biweekly, eight-page tabloid format to a weekly, twelve-page standard format in 1946. While emphasizing "straight" reports of union activities as well as investigative reporting, *The Wage Earner* took an editorial stance appealing to Catholic social teachings and focused its attack on communist activities within the unions. Even *Fortune* magazine credited *The Wage Earner* with contributing significantly to the defeat of communist unionists in the United Auto Workers elections of 1946. The paper's estimates of communist membership at one Michigan CIO convention were so accurate that when election returns for the communist candidate nearly mirrored *The Wage*

---

58. Vincent J. McLaughlin, "A Labor School Takes Inventory," *The Commonweal* 31 (January 12, 1940): 261–62.

59. Ted Le Berthon, "Detroit and the Nation," *Catholic Digest* 9 (September 1945): 41; McKenna, "The Story of the ACTU," 455–56.

Earner's estimations, the Detroit ACTU was accused of rigging the election—despite a lack of evidence that rigging had taken place.[60]

In April 1938, New York ACTU activists Ed Scully and John Sheen organized the Catholic Labor Defense League (CLDL), a subsidiary of the ACTU, with the goal of protecting unionists who believed their rights were being denied as a result of corruption or heavy-handed tactics of labor leaders, especially communists. Soon, the caseload expanded to include workers who faced management resistance to organizing, as well as unionists contesting penalties for violating union rules.[61] Originally composed of ten Catholic attorneys serving the New York ACTU, soon every chapter of the ACTU had its own CLDL unit or maintained a lawyer on its executive board to deal with legal issues affecting its constituencies.[62]

Reflecting the language of *Quadragesimo Anno,* the ACTU considered strikes to be a weapon of "last resort," though at times necessary. It was essential that the ACTU could convincingly argue that a particular strike met the standards of "justice" before endorsing participation in that strike. Detroit's Paul Weber held that a just strike demanded that four requirements be met: first, strikes were considered just only after all other peaceful attempts at negotiating a "fair" deal for unionists had been exhausted. Second, realpolitik figured into the equation in that a "reasonable prospect for success" was a necessary prerequisite for a strike to meet the standard of justice. Third, the gravity of worker grievances had to be serious enough in nature to justify striking. And finally, the harm done as a result of the strike to the community as a whole could not outweigh the positive results to be gained from work stoppage.[63] The similarities between Weber's "just strike" theory and the better known Catholic "just war" theory[64] should not be surprising when we consider that for the unionist, the strike was an act of war against management that involved the willing sacrifice of wages and security in the act of bringing production to a grinding halt. Though both theories are ultimately heuristic and depend for their utility on the disposition of the individual crafting and assessing the variables of each moral calculation, at the very least Weber's standards for justice demanded that ACTU

---

60. McKenna, "The Story of the ACTU," 456.
61. Burns, "ACTU Bores from Within," 51; Cort, "Catholics in Trade Unions," 36; Betten, *Catholic Activism and the Industrial Worker,* 133.
62. Betten, *Catholic Activism and the Industrial Worker,* 133.
63. Arthur Jentunen, "Leaven in the Unions," *Catholic Digest* 11 (November 1946): 59.
64. "Just War," in *The New Catholic Encyclopedia* (Washington, D.C.: Catholic University of America, 1967), 14:796.

endorsement of a strike followed a thoughtful and deliberate process of assessment.

ACTU participation in strikes also helped to spread its reading of Catholic social teaching. For instance, shortly after the ACTU's formation, members joined the picket lines in a strike against the Woolworth company, aimed at increasing the low wages of its employees. Barbara Hutton, the heiress to Woolworth's, became the focus of the strikers' ire after several of her friends publicly came to her defense by pointing out that she had given as much as $11 million to charity. The irony was not lost on the ACTU membership, who crafted a poster for display on the picket lines that read: "BABS GAVE $11,000,000 TO CHARITY, BUT 'THE WORKER IS NOT TO RECEIVE AS ALMS WHAT IS HIS DUE IN JUSTICE'—Pope Pius XI." Years later, John Cort remarked that "this was the first time that the pope ever appeared on a picket line in an American strike."[65]

Competing Catholic Interests

ACTU support for strikes sometimes put them in conflict with other Catholics. In 1939, the United Auto Workers local in Detroit went on strike. In response to worker requests for a say in setting the speed of production, their company had locked them out. The Detroit press was firmly aligned on the side of management, and the populist Catholic radio personality Father Charles Coughlin joined the chorus in condemning the workers' demands. The ACTU went on the offensive, pushing the workers' cause in their newspapers and enlisting a prominent "labor priest," Raymond S. Clancy, to rebut Coughlin's charges on the radio. Such public intra-Catholic conflict was rare, but the ACTU's actions significantly improved its status in the eyes of Catholic autoworkers, while enabling the association to engage workers in the substance of Catholic social teaching.[66]

Support for and participation in strikes did not always result in an improved reputation and increased membership for the association. In 1949, the ACTU of New York City supported a Gravediggers Union strike that resulted in substantial delays and, in some cases, the improper burial of corpses. Catholics were among the many outraged by the strike,

---

65. Cort, "Nine Years of ACTU," 4; John Cort, "Side by Side with the Unions," *The Commonweal* 59 (March 5, 1954): 552.
66. McKenna, "The Story of ACTU," 453.

and that outrage extended to New York's Archbishop Spellman, who had once been a supporter of the ACTU. Spellman publicly accused ACTU members of being communists, and the strike eventually failed, leading to a general decline in popular support for the association in New York City and among influential members of the hierarchy.[67]

In another example, the Printing Pressmen's Union announced a strike in 1962 against *Columbia Magazine,* the official organ of the Knights of Columbus (KOC), arguably the most prominent of all the Roman Catholic service organizations in the United States. The New York ACTU, led by its president, Daniel J. Schulder, took the side of the Pressmen's Union in the conflict that pitted Catholic interests against one another. In a personal letter to Luke E. Hart, the Supreme Knight of the KOC in New Haven, Connecticut, Schulder expressed his dismay on behalf of the ACTU, identifying the KOC's position as "contrary to a sound application of the social teachings of the Church." Schulder wrote,

> We frankly cannot understand your reluctance, in view of the robust financial position of the Knights cited at your convention last week, to extend medical benefits to the families of the 12 workers involved. We cannot understand your refusal to even consider the union's basic request to bring their wages to a par with similar wages for similar work in the New Haven area. We cannot understand how a fair minded employer can reject, out of hand, the offer of binding arbitration made by the Pressmen's Union. Finally, we are appalled by your decision to, in effect, break this union and its strike by contracting with a non-union printing firm in Atlanta, Georgia to complete the work and thus throw out the work of some thirty union magazine binders who are not a party to the dispute. . . . We are concerned . . . with the fate of the public image of the largest Catholic laymen's organization.[68]

In taking public positions against other prominent Catholic leaders, the ACTU often found itself getting under the skin of American Catholic leaders and laypeople alike.

67. Douglas P. Seaton, *Catholics and Radicals* (Lewisburg, Pa.: Bucknell University Press, 1981), 245.
68. Letter from Daniel J. Schulder, President of the New York ACTU, to Luke E. Hart, Supreme Knight, the Knights of Columbus, September 9, 1962, ACUA, Box 23 (ACTU Folder), George Gilmary Higgins Papers.

Concern about the ACTU was not limited to conservative forces in the Church. Some liberal Catholic clergy were unsure what to make of this influential lay movement. Philip A. Carey, a Jesuit and founder of Fordham University's Xavier Institute of Industrial Relations, despite a long relationship with members of the association, had misgivings about the role the organization was playing in the labor movement. In a letter to a fellow Jesuit in 1948, Carey revealed concerns, despite having "the profoundest respect for most of the men of the ACTU" in his home city of New York. "In fact," Carey wrote, "Often they [the ACTU] seem to arrogate to themselves an omnipotence and infallibility to decide the most perplexing and difficult questions that is hard to take. Often, too there is real difficulty in my mind as to whether there is a 'Catholic' solution to some of these problems and whether there is only ONE Christian solution. You know the immense perplexity one goes through in reducing the principles of Faith to the very mundane things."[69] Oversimplification of complex problems posed a greater risk in the mind of this Jesuit than admitting that the Church could not provide a simple solution. But the deepest concern for Carey appeared to be the status the ACTU had attained in the public eye.

> For some strange reason, ACTU doesn't appear as a private or voluntary organization but is taken and assumes the role of the Teaching Church on these matters. It is a real danger.... I know for a fact, that many good labor leaders here in town and many good Catholic leaders will have nothing to do with them and that they are unalterably opposed to it. To them it is introducing sectarianism into a field badly enough divided as it is. They feel that they can do their work much better, if they are not labelled [sic]. And I stress that word labelled. Perhaps, it is here that I find my most serious difficulties with the ACTU. Were they called the LaFayetter Society, or the Sturzo Guild, I'd not have so much difficulty, but there are overtones to the name.[70]

It is worth bearing in mind that although the Catholic Action movement's aim of energizing the laity was now in its third decade at the time of Carey's writing, the kind of authority this lay organization was claiming

---

69. Philip A. Carey, letter to R. McKeon, S.J., FUA, Box 1, Folder 53, "Association of Catholic Trade Unionists, 1949–1967."
70. Ibid.

for itself was out of the ordinary and potentially disconcerting. Interestingly, despite Carey's issues with the ACTU, he was still offering to speak at ACTU events into the mid-1950s.

Carey pointed to two prominent coconspirators among those "not in the ACTU camp": Fr. George Higgins and Fr. John Cronin of the Social Action Department.[71] Higgins addressed his feelings toward the ACTU in a letter to Rev. Francis J. McDonnell of the Catholic Labor Guild of Boston. McDonnell was seeking Higgins's advice as to whether the Labor Guild should forsake its independent status and become a "branch of the ACTU," as ACTU activists were encouraging them to do. In a letter dated March 19, 1954, Higgins advised against establishing formal ties with the ACTU. Instead, he appealed to the style of the Catholic Labor Alliance of Chicago, which promoted the union movement without becoming enmeshed in the tactical maneuvers of unions themselves, as a preferable model.[72] The Catholic Labor Alliance eventually changed its name to the Catholic Council on Working Life with the very intent of distancing itself from being seen as too closely tied to the unions themselves.[73] Of the ACTU's limited expansion, Higgins continued, "I have the feeling that the reason is that the majority of Catholic priests and laymen in the field of Catholic social action instinctively shy away from the ACTU approach" in favor of less politically charged tactics.[74]

Communism and the ACTU

The ACTU fought its battles along two fronts. The first, as described, pitted the organization against business owners and management who undermined the efforts of their employees to unionize and failed to provide wages and working conditions the association viewed as just. The second front, however, pitted the ACTU against elements within the labor movement itself. Communists and corrupt union leaders who led by dictatorial practices were the bane of the association, and it was in this intra-union context that the ACTU stirred up the most controversy.

71. Ibid.
72. Msgr. George Higgins, letter to Francis J. McDonnell, March 19, 1954, ACUA, Box 23 (ACTU Folder), George Gilmary Higgins Papers.
73. Harry J. O'Haire, Executive Secretary, Serra International, letter to All Members of the Board, September 20, 1956, ACUA, Collection 10, Folder 3.
74. Msgr. George Higgins, letter to Francis J. McDonnell, March 19, 1954, ACUA, Box 23 (ACTU Folder), George Gilmary Higgins Papers.

Association members took the position of the encyclicals that "no Catholic can remain in a union that is run along Marxist or unChristian lines."[75] At the same time, the ACTU thought the reality on the ground demanded that they acknowledge the inevitable damage a Catholic exodus from the labor movement would pose, which inspired a policy of constructive engagement. "No real Catholic can resign from that [Marxist or anti-Christian] union, and thereby surrender it to the Marxists or racketeers," the association held, "until he had made every possible effort to cure the corruption of that union."[76] With this as its charge, the ACTU continued to be active in many unions dominated by communists or controlled by criminal influences.

The language ACTU members used as they worked against corruption and communism in the unions focused on the need for "democracy" in the trade union movement, and this term was invoked almost instinctively in articles and pamphlets penned by association members across the United States.[77] The focus on democratic unionism reflected not only the genuine aspirations of these Catholic unionists, but also functioned to counteract pervasive suspicions that the Catholic Church sought to use the labor movement as a vehicle for the promotion of its faith. Nativist suspicion of Roman Catholic motives was never far from the scene during these decades, and even nonnativists at times expressed discomfort with the blending of religious and economic objectives.[78] Like the rhetoric employed by the NCRLC, ACTU members articulated their ideology and intentions with a vocabulary that had special appeal to American sentiments. It is unlikely, however, that emphasis on democracy — an ideology that the Vatican had yet to embrace — was as much a self-conscious element of the ACTU's lexicon as it was an unconscious expression of the association membership's self-understanding of being fully "Americanized."

While union corruption was certainly important to the ACTU's activities, until the mid-1950s the association focused especially on communism as its bête noir. Reflecting the encyclicals, the ACTU saw communism as the Church's main competition for working-class allegiance. Association

75. Ward, "The Role of the Association of Catholic Trade Unionists in the Labor Movement," 83–84; *The Labor Leader,* January 3, 1938, 3.
76. Ward, "The Role of the Association of Catholic Trade Unionists in the Labor Movement," 83–84.
77. For examples of this rhetoric, see McKenna, "ACTU," 117–18.
78. "'Nation' Looks at ACTU: Misses Some Things: Fails to Understand Motives," *The Michigan Labor Leader,* January 17, 1941, 3.

members believed, like many Americans, that the success of the Communist Party in the labor movement meant that unions risked being used as an arm of the Soviet Union. Moreover, given the climate of the Cold War culture, ACTU activists feared that communist domination of unions would ultimately result in the failure of the labor movement in the United States. The accusation of guilt by association would be continually raised against union activists by those interests working against strong unions.[79]

If the Communist Party was "enemy number one" in the eyes of the ACTU, the ACTU was no less despised by the Communist Party. George Morris, a regular columnist for *The Daily Worker,* an official news organ of the Communist Party in the United States, called the ACTU a collection of "The Vatican's agents," seeking to spread Roman Catholic influence into organizations like the CIO, an influence that went well "beyond [the Vatican's] spiritual functions."[80] ACTU members were suspected by communists of sometimes going as far as trying to destroy unions. "Union-Busting was always viewed as a nasty business," Morris once wrote,

> but the business of using the cloth of the Catholic priesthood to cover up union-busting is even nastier. The Rev. Charles Owen Rice, chaplain of the Association of Catholic Trade Unionists in Pittsburgh, is our exhibit in this case. Writing in the Catholic publication, *Our Sunday Visitor,* which tops all others in national circulation, Father Rice offers a free correspondence course to priests on disrupting what he terms "Communist-led" unions. The key to the Rice union-busting formula is a campaign in the union to "get them (the officials) to sign non-Red affidavits." With an ACTU fifth column operation inside the union and the company's pressure from the outside, it is possible to decertify the progressive-led unions as bargaining agents, Rice argues.[81]

Morris's focus on Rice was not surprising, given Rice's reputation as a point man in the Catholic fight against communism. Later historians like

---

79. McKenna, "ACTU," 117.
80. George Morris, "ACTU Program at CIO Convention," *The Daily Worker,* November 29, 1948, found in FUA, Box 2, Folder 53, "Association of Catholic Trade Unionists, 1949–1967."
81. George Morris, "Using the Cloth to Hide Anti-Union Dagger," *The Daily Worker,* June 16, 1948, found in FUA, Box 2, Folder 53, "Association of Catholic Trade Unionists, 1949–1967."

Steve Rosswurm would characterize Rice, whose labor activism was inspired by his encounter with Dorothy Day, as typifying "the crusade mentality of [the Catholic] anticommunist struggle." Rooted in "a deeply embedded Manichean view of the world and the requisite pugnacious temperament, Rice spent years fighting Communists and other leftists," wrote Rosswurm in his account of the Catholic Church's role in driving the Communist Party out of the CIO.[82] In his own reminiscences more than forty years later, even Rice himself characterized his anticommunist activities as having used inflammatory rhetoric and questionable tactics while overstating the threat communism posed.[83]

Encounters with figures like Rev. Charles Owen Rice, as well as his own observations of ACTU strategies for discrediting Communist Party successes at the bargaining table, led communists like Morris to conclude in the pages of *The Daily Worker* that "the ACTU . . . operates on only one basic premise: that anything left wingers do, good or bad, must be denounced."[84] Accusations like this placed the ACTU on the defensive among those who saw the possibility of harmonious class relations—a central tenet of the Roman Catholic ideology—as fanciful. In the ACTU's defense, John Cort wrote in 1949: "It takes courage for a union man to stand up and remind his fellow workers that they have interests in common with their employers. . . . It takes courage to risk being called 'reactionary,' and 'company stooge.' It takes courage and a good union record so that you can be sure the label doesn't stick."[85]

Each communist attack on the ACTU invoked the specter of divisiveness, the one charge that opponents of the ACTU continually leveled against the movement. This charge was particularly distressing for ACTU members because the very strength of the union movement depended on unity in the face of pressures from management. Management could, and often did, exploit division between laborers in contract negotiations. A frequent refrain among critics of American unionism in particular was that unions worked against each other's interests by being focused on their own success rather than on the success of the laboring class as a

---

82. Heineman, *A Catholic New Deal*, 72; Rosswurm, "The Catholic Church and the Left-Led Unions," 130.

83. Charles Owen Rice, "Confessions of an Anti-Communist," *Labor History* 31 (Summer 1989); see also Higgins and Bole, *Organized Labor and the Church*, 59–60.

84. George Morris, "Views on Labor: ACTU Out on a Limb," *The Daily Worker*, n.d.; article found in FUA, Box 2, Folder 53, "Association of Catholic Trade Unionists, 1949–1967."

85. John C. Cort, "Can We Lick the Labor Problem?" *The Sign* 29 (November 1949): 35.

whole. Rhetorically, few accusations held as much potency as that of cultivating division among the unions.

Catholics in the ACTU inverted those criticisms and declared that it was the communists who were really guilty of trying to divide the unions. George Kelly, writing in *The Commonweal,* claimed that unlike the ACTU, "Communists seek to dominate the labor movement." More insidious still, this domination was carried out in "the cause of a foreign power," the Soviet Union. Kelly's use of the phrase "foreign power" must have been intentional, given the frequency with which those hostile to Catholicism accused its membership of dividing loyalties between the United States and a "foreign power," the Vatican. Kelly asserted that "the ACTU serves only the cause of justice. The Communists use immoral means to obtain an immoral end. By no stretch of the imagination can the ACTU be described in this way."[86] This reference to morality cut to the heart of the matter from the Catholic perspective. The social encyclicals had judged the communist goals to be immoral, and with this assumption, no comparison between Catholics and communists on the issue of divisiveness was legitimate in Catholic eyes.

Devotionalism and the Shaping of Catholic Hearts and Minds

While the branches of the ACTU dedicated most of their energy to being an active force for change in the labor movement, they also aimed at cultivating the devotional practices and spiritual development of their members. *Rerum Novarum* had stipulated that "workingmen's associations" were charged with paying "special and principal attention to piety and morality, and that their internal discipline must be directed precisely by these considerations; otherwise they entirely lose their special character, and come to be very little better than those societies which take no account of religion at all" (sec. 42). Many published articles by ACTU members echoed the sentiment that social reconstruction begins with individual, personal reformation.[87] This belief spawned a wide array of devotional practices and group events encouraged by the association among its members. These included communion breakfasts,

---

86. G. Kelly, "The ACTU and Its Critics," 302.
87. See also Ward, "The Role of the Association of Catholic Trade Unionists in the Labor Movement," 87; McKenna, "ACTU," 120; John C. Cort, "The Labor Movement: Ten Years," *The Commonweal* 46 (May 23, 1947): 143.

annual retreats and missions, special "novenas to the Holy Ghost immediately before Christ the Worker," and the daily recitation of prayer phrased to pay homage to the laboring Jesus.[88]

Some devotional events were well attended. The ACTU organized 2,500 union members for a Mass in New York's St. Patrick's Cathedral shortly after World War II memorializing "labor's heroic war dead."[89] Association-sponsored communion breakfasts drew large crowds well into the 1950s. Every breakfast, as well as each meeting and rally, began with a special prayer:

> Lord Jesus, Carpenter of Nazareth, you were a worker as I am, give to me and all the workers of the world the privilege to work as You did, so that everything we do may be for the benefit of our fellowmen and the greater glory of God the Father. Thy Kingdom come into the factories and into the shops, into our homes and into our streets. Give us this day our daily bread. May we receive it without envy or injustice. To us who labor and are heavily burdened send speedily the refreshment of Thy love. May we never sin against Thee. Show us Thy way to work, when it is done, we with all our fellow-workers rest in peace. Amen.[90]

In the words of a New York ACTU chaplain, association members "were ambassadors to Christ on the waterfront, in the union halls, and the picket lines, and in the court room."[91] Members reveled in recounting experiences in which the spiritual fruits of participation in the movement went beyond attending breakfasts and Masses. The first ACTU president, Martin Wersing, recalled the association's "influence in having people return to the fold," when he wrote of telephoning an old friend who had been active with Wersing in the union movement. This friend had become ill and had subsequently abandoned much of his union activity. During the phone call, Wersing's friend surprised him with the news that he "had just completed a mission and for the first

---

88. Ward, "The Role of the Association of Catholic Trade Unionists in the Labor Movement," 89.
89. Cort, "Nine Years of ACTU," 5.
90. Ward, "The Role of the Association of Catholic Trade Unionists in the Labor Movement," 88–89.
91. Ibid., 89; from *The Labor Leader*, February 28, 1942, 4.

time in more than twenty years he was about to receive Communion." The clincher was that Wersing's friend gave "full credit for his return to grace and to his association with ACTU members in his union." Wersing added that he "could not even begin to add up the number of actual situations such as this" that he had experienced during his years with the ACTU.[92]

In the Articles of Federation for ACTU branches, all chapters were required to have each of its members sign a pledge: "I hereby pledge to abide by all the teachings and practices of my Catholic faith, including those teachings expressed in the social Encyclicals of Leo XIII, Pius XI, and Pius XII in their entirety. I pledge to do my utmost to oppose Fascists, Communists, Nazis, and racketeers and their philosophies and adherents." The pledge placed members in the position of needing to make a public commitment to their religion, beyond their association with co-unionists attempting to promote the rights of labor. The articles went further in calling for members to engage in each of the following "spiritual activities . . . in so far as possible":

I. Corporate communions quarterly if possible, but at least annually.
II. Annual Retreat—days of recollection.
III. Membership in Parish Societies.
IV. Annual ACTU Novenas to the Holy Ghost immediately before Pentecost.
V. City-wide monthly Holy Hours.
VI. Personal devotion to the Holy Ghost daily.
VII. Daily recitation of the Prayer to Christ the Worker.
VIII. Prayer "Come Holy Ghost" to be said at the beginning of all ACTU meetings, rallies, classes, and conventions before the prayer to Christ the Worker.[93]

Oaths, devotional activities, public recounting of conversion experiences or returns to "the fold," along with continued reference to the teachings of the popes, all served to invest the activities of the Association of Catholic Trade Unionists and its members with a sanctified status. Labor, the struggles of the union movement, the contests for authority

92. Ibid., 90.
93. "Articles of Federation of the ACTU," FUA, Box 2, Folder 53, "The Association of Catholic Trade Unionists, 1949–1967."

with communists and corrupt union bosses—these arenas and others like them came to be seen as sacred ground where the loyal servants of the Roman Catholic Church carried out their mission to transform the world and Christianize the social order. In this way, the ideology of *Rerum Novarum* and *Quadragesimo Anno* was reconstituted in the activities of the ACTU in a manner that reflected the particular interests of the movement.

The Fate of the ACTU

By the mid-1950s, the ACTU's status began to decline, sparked by several causes, including internal divisions arising between chapters. In the fall of 1956, the Detroit branch of the ACTU withdrew from the national ACTU over a conflict about the extent to which the organization should take specific stands with respect to union policy. The Detroit ACTU concluded, in contrast to other ACTU groups—especially New York—that the job of the association was to instill and promote Catholic principles among its members, while leaving individual unionists to decide for themselves how to cast their votes at union meetings. "The very act of taking an official ACTU position," they argued, "would be an attempt to serve notice to the world that ACTU members hold that viewpoint. But it wouldn't necessarily be true."[94] Because each individual had to be comfortable with his or her vote, it was beyond the scope of the ACTU to dictate these positions to its members.

John Cort, a leader of the New York ACTU, took issue with Detroit's position in the months leading up to the schism:

> How can anyone maintain that an organization like ours—a lay organization in the field of social actions—can avoid, or should avoid, taking action, taking stands on questions that involve violations of the Catholic social teachings which we profess to be promoting? ... It is possible for us to confuse our own opinions with the teaching of the Church. It is not always easy to distinguish basic doctrine from interpretation, or appreciation of doctrine. ... But it does not therefore follow that an organization

---

94. William A. Ryan, "Detroit ACTU Explains Its Decision," *The Wage Earner*, October 1956, 1.

of Catholic laymen should sit there like three monkeys with hands over eyes, ears and mouth, refusing to "see no injustice, hear no injustice, protest no injustice."[95]

But Cort and others were missing the point, wrote Detroit's William A. Ryan. The purpose of instilling Catholic social principles in the workers was so that these workers would themselves translate those principles into action. Cort, Ryan argued, "persists in the idea that the only type of action is a majority vote taken at an ACTU meeting." On the contrary, the only actions that counted were those of the members trusted to apply Church teachings, according to their own consciences, within their individual unions.[96]

While public breakups like the Detroit schism stymied the momentum of the ACTU (and internal division had been a part of the movement from the beginning), some scholars have alleged one cause of its demise above all others: the ACTU's obsession with stifling communism among the working classes.[97] The most comprehensive example of this claim was seen in the 1981 book by Douglas Seaton, *Catholics and Radicals*, and the sentiment has been echoed in the work of scholars like Steve Rosswurm.[98] Seaton argued that the ACTU was organized with the express intention of fighting communism in the CIO, just as, he argued, the Catholic Knights of Labor had formed to fight communism in the AFL. While the ACTU had broad-based support of unionism as its main objective in its first few years, over time the association developed a myopic fixation with fighting communism "by any means necessary."[99] Seaton's research neglects the reality that the membership continued to grow after the communist purge in the CIO and that ACTU members were deeply engaged long after. More important, there is ample data illustrating ACTU concerns with a wide range of topics not directly related to communism.

While Seaton can be faulted for overstating his case, there is no doubt that the decline of communism in the unions did affect the long-term growth of the ACTU. As early as 1948, Philip Carey was commenting

---

95. John C. Cort, "Should the ACTU Stop Acting?" *The Labor Leader*, September 1956.
96. W. Ryan, "Detroit ACTU Explains Its Decision," 11.
97. Higgins and Bole, *Organized Labor and the Church*, 58–61.
98. Seaton, *Catholics and Radicals*; Rosswurm, "The Catholic Church and the Left-Led Unions."
99. Seaton, *Catholics and Radicals*, esp. 222.

privately on his perception that the impact of having "the CP [Communist Party] difficulty somewhat settled" had damaged the Detroit ACTU. "There is no challenge that will bring the men to it," he wrote.[100] John Cort felt compelled to remind association members in 1949 that the problems labor faced went well beyond communism. "Suppose that Msgr. Fulton Sheen converted all but the most hopeless Communists and that the earth opened up and swallowed the remainder leaving no trace," Cort wrote, "would that solve our problems? To hear most of our orators and politicians, to read some of our publications, you would certainly think so." While free enterprise had done many good things for the nation, the United States was "also a country where in spite of initiative, knowhow, and resources we still don't know how to keep all our men working, even though the world, and many of our own people, are cold and hungry for what we can produce."[101] Five years later, Cort revealed his own sense of frustration that the ACTU emphasis on ridding unions of communists had led to a "smugness and complacency in the labor movement" as a result of its success. The effort now needed to be directed against the maintenance of the "status quo."[102]

One potential cause for the demise of the ACTU that has not been explored, to the best of my knowledge, has to do with the changing character of organized labor itself. During the 1950s, labor unions grew substantially. With this growth came a burgeoning bureaucracy that required centralized control. Labor policies beginning in World War II sinificantly affected this pattern by bringing together labor leaders, corporate executives, and government officials to craft an organized response to the war involving carefully regulated production as well as a cessation of labor hostilities. The nationalization of the labor movement had profound consequences for the movement's status, but with time, "the tendency to settle major disputes on a national basis became almost habitual." The result was that "labor policy became a part of national policy, far removed from the shop and the control of members."[103]

The ACTU was not designed to make its impact under these circumstances. The association's philosophy—inspired by the principle of subsidiarity—and its aim to affect the trade-union movement in the manner

---

100. Philip A. Carey, letter to R. McKeon, S.J., n.d., FUA, Box 1, Folder 53, "Association of Catholic Trade Unionists, 1949–1967."
101. Cort, "Can We Lick the Labor Problem?" 32–33.
102. Cort, "Side by Side with the Unions," 552–54.
103. Mowry and Brownell, *The Urban Nation*, 170–71.

that leaven affects dough became decreasingly effective as labor became more bureaucratic and centralized, the ACTU had thrived on being highly personalized, and it emphasized the importance of transforming the ideology of unionists in small groups with the hopes that these unionists would spread the ACTU message to a larger audience. But unionism in the United States, especially after the merger of the AFL with the CIO, appears to have become less responsive to its rank-and-file as a starting point for change, leaving power in the hands of an ever-diminishing few. In all likelihood, this dramatic transformation in the method and structure of the labor movement played a major role in the marginalization and decline of the ACTU.

The end of the 1950s brought with it a downward spiral for the ACTU. In the words of the outgoing New York ACTU president, Daniel Schulder, in December 1962:

> It is an obvious fact that the ACTU, over the past two years, has not prospered. We have declined in membership and effectiveness. We have failed to continue the ACTU educational programs and have exerted marginal influence on the course of the labor movement in New York City. It is only right that the responsibility must fall, in large measure, upon me as President during most of this period. . . . By all rights, we should have been destroyed long ago. . . . By all rights we should have been financially destroyed, but we have survived. We have survived the assaults from within and without. But the last and greatest assault has been the apathy of our organization. It has been an apathy of fatigue and distaste over the political fights of the recent past. It has been an apathy produced by our lack of an integral approach to the problems of workers and their unions, that exists today. It is symptomatic of the spiritual and emotional aridity that besets all groups when they no longer seem to be able to accept the challenges that face them.[104]

The ACTU continued to exist, despite fifteen years of decreasing membership rolls, until 1973. Where Catholic distributists in the NCRLC and the Catholic Worker viewed urban and industrial life as antithetical to the life

---

104. Daniel Schulder, President, ACTU Newsletter (December 1962), FUA, Box 2, Folder 53, "Association of Catholic Trade Unionists, 1949–1967."

of the spirit, ACTU members sought to sanctify labor in these contexts. In their labor schools, devotional meetings, and conventions, the association reconstituted the ideology of *Rerum Novarum* and *Quadragesimo Anno* to suit their circumstances. They defended private property as a natural right, with all the concomitant caveats regarding its "proper" use. They promoted labor unions as a natural form of human association in which individuals came together as a buffer against the competing forces of government and capital. Discussions regarding wages centered on the notion of "justice" and reflected the encyclical's view that earnings should be adequate to support a single wage earner (typically a male) charged with supporting a family. Appealing to the principle of subsidiarity, the ACTU patterned its own organization and operations in a manner that utilized the metaphor of "leaven," as its members cultivated change from the bottom up. Even the national president of the ACTU was limited in influence to planning national conventions and promoting the association's goals at a national level, with no recourse to dictating policy to local ACTU chapters. In fact, attempts to centralize the movement, typically spearheaded by the New York chapter, were continually rejected, reflecting the grassroots style that the organization had worked to cultivate.[105]

The ACTU's emphasis on class harmony put it in direct conflict with communists in the union movement. While members recognized class difference, conflict between the classes was not seen as the inevitable result of a dialectic trajectory of history. Instead, reflecting the encyclicals, class conflict was blamed on an immoral ideology that developed once a free market replaced human dignity as the measure for business decisions in the minds of those who owned productive capital. Only the failure to recognize their moral duties to one another kept labor and management from seeing their shared interests and cooperating. Recognizing this, of course, would be spurred on by adopting a common mythology resting in the theology of the Roman Catholic Church.

The Young Christian Workers

The Association of Catholic Trade Unionists represented one of several attempts to sanctify the industrial workplace. Another Catholic organization, with different roots and its own distinctive strategies, was the

---

105. George G. Higgins, "Letter: Response to the ACTU and Its Critics," *The Commonweal* 49 (January 21, 1949): 374–75.

Young Christian Workers (YCW). Where agrarian distributist Catholics saw urban industrial life as beyond redemption and necessitating a profound reorientation toward traditional rural self-sufficiency, the YCW joined the ACTU in attempting to sanctify the new industrial order. Utilizing language and symbols culled from the social encyclicals, the YCW fashioned an outline of a Christian industrialism tailored to fit the needs of a wider audience than the ACTU had spoken to: America's Roman Catholic youth. Like the ACTU, the YCW saw the tone and content of its message shift with the changing perceptions of the American economy until Vatican II.

The YCW in the United States descended from the European Jocist movement. Jocism was founded by Canon Joseph Cardijn in the mid-1920s, the son of a mineworker near Brussels whose death Cardijn blamed on the harsh conditions of his labor. When Cardijn was ordained to the priesthood, he was greeted by many of his friends at home as a traitor to the working class. Even after *Rerum Novarum* in 1891, the Church was still popularly perceived as being aligned with the aristocracy in Europe. The poor treatment he received at the hands of his old friends, coupled with the deteriorating health of his father, inspired Cardijn to devote his life to reconciling his Church with the industrial workers of the world.[106]

From early in his tenure as a priest, Cardijn tried to familiarize young people with the teachings of Leo XIII, recognizing that within a short time of leaving their Catholic schools for the factories of a rapidly industrializing Belgium they would lose contact with the Church.[107] His efforts met with little success. During World War I, Cardijn was charged by the German occupiers of Belgium with communicating with the Allies and was sentenced to prison. In a twist of fate, his time in prison allowed him to plan his apostolate to the working classes. On his release at the war's end, he was appointed the director of social work on behalf of the Belgian hierarchy, and his program was enacted.[108]

The Jeunesse Ouvriere Catholique (JOC), known as Jocism, became one of the premier strands of the Catholic Action movement initiated in

---

106. M. J. Smith, O.M.I., "The Young Christian Workers Movement: I," *Social Justice Review* 40 (January 1948): 295; "Founder of Jocism," *The Catholic Mind* 47 (May 1949): 292–93.

107. M. Smith, "The Young Christian Workers Movement: I," 295; "From Other Lands," *Orate Fratres* 17 (September 5, 1943): 456.

108. "Founder of Jocism," 295.

the 1920s by Pius XI. Catholic Action attempted to energize the laity in the promotion of the Church's mission. Cardijn's own principles were closely aligned with those of Pius XI well before *Quadragesimo Anno* had been penned. Both were committed to expanding the Catholic hold on the working classes at a time when technological changes and economic turmoil placed an unusually heavy burden on victims of rapid industrialization. In later years, both Pius XI and his successor, Pius XII, pointed to Jocism as a jewel in the crown of Catholic Action. The movement spread throughout Europe in the 1930s and 1940s. Even during World War II, Jocism managed to increase its membership among Catholic youth in occupied countries, including France.[109]

While the earliest attempts to establish Jocism in the United States can be traced to 1938, American Jocism did not begin in earnest until 1947 with the formation of the Young Christian Workers. Over the next decade and a half, the YCW would develop a distinctly American style. The class consciousness of Europe, so conducive to spreading the Jocist message of the dignity of labor, was not as firmly rooted in the United States and required a degree of adaptation on the part of the movement's American promoters. By the time the YCW peaked in the late 1950s, it had nearly three thousand members nationwide with strong, independent branches as far apart as Brooklyn, San Francisco, and Tulsa.[110]

Though established in cities across the country, the YCW was headquartered in Chicago, the home of Rev. Reynold Hillenbrand, the most influential advocate of the movement in the pre–Vatican II years. Ordained in 1929, Hillenbrand had a significant impact on the social thought of many Catholic priests while serving as the rector of St. Mary of the Lake Seminary in suburban Chicago from 1936 to 1944. George Higgins recalled Hillenbrand as having "ushered in an ecclesiastical New Deal" in the seminary by exposing the traditionally sheltered seminarians to opportunities for social action that existed at the time. He was known as a "papalist," which in that time period was synonymous with being a social activist.[111] Frustrated by what he sensed to be a gap between the theological preparation of seminarians and the encyclical teachings of the popes—with the latter being considered by some as occupying

---

109. M. Smith, "The Young Christian Workers Movement: I," 296; "JOC Survives in France," *America*, October 14, 1944, 22.

110. Mary Irene Zotti, *A Time of Awakening: The Young Christian Worker Story in the United States, 1938 to 1970* (Chicago: Loyola University Press, 1991), 4, 228.

111. Higgins and Bole, *Organized Labor and the Church*, 19–21.

a separate theological category of less importance than more traditional teachings—Hillenbrand accused seminaries of minimalizing papal teachings. This, he said in 1952, was "a practice no longer admissible since Pius XII . . . made clear the necessity of accepting the encyclical teaching[s]." The separate and unequal approach bred a lack of familiarity with papal teaching among American priests and, consequently, the American laity.[112]

"Economic life [was] the layman's field," wrote Hillenbrand, and as such it was all the more imperative that the laity be familiarized with the papal teachings on social justice and be organized to meet the demands that social justice brought with it. The prime object of his derision was the "Sunday Catholic employer" and the "Sunday Catholic worker": the former was antagonistic to labor unions, while the latter was unwilling to join them. The antidote to Sunday Catholicism was education and organization, enabling the laity to develop its own "priestly action." In an obvious attempt to shame his fellow clergy into more strenuous efforts to organize the laity, he wrote that Catholics needed to "restore what the Protestants always kept—participation."[113]

Beneath the banner of Catholic Action was a wide range of specialized Catholic Action forms dealing with narrow issues and audiences. Where the Young Christian Students organization was designed to imbue students with the principles of Roman Catholic life, and the Christian Family Movement was geared toward married couples and families, the YCW specialized in the apostolate of Catholics in the workplace. Yet this specialization extended to the internal structure of the YCW as well. Factory workers were grouped with factory workers, white-collar workers with white-collar workers, and in its early stages in the United States, men and women were grouped separately. They believed that "it would be ridiculous to have a group of business or office men attempt to better the conditions of workers in a factory. They would know nothing about the problems of workers in a factory."[114] Not only were YCW members subdivided into these distinct categories, but the group's message was tailored to suit the specific needs of the workers being

112. Reynold Hillenbrand, "The Priesthood and the World," *Worship* 26 (January 1952): 49–51.
113. Ibid., 52, 56–57.
114. M. J. Smith, O.M.I., "The Young Christian Workers Movement: II," *Social Justice Review* 40 (February 1948): 333.

addressed.[115] While this strategy was in keeping with a reading of subsidiarity that privileged smaller social units over larger ones, it also stood in tension with the metaphor of an organic economic order in which all social units were interdependent.

Observe, Judge, and Act

The YCW method stemmed from a three-stage plan developed by Canon Cardijn himself: observation, judgment, and action. YCW meetings began by posing a problem. Members made observations regarding the problem between meetings. *Observation* would be followed by *judgment* as to what caused the problem and what could be done to solve the problem in light of Catholic teaching. Finally, YCW participants were asked to take *action* to address the problem based on their judgment. While some problems were clearly too large to address adequately by a small group of devoted Catholic activists (like racism in the workplace, for instance), it was not necessary that the entire problem be solved as a result of the action taken. What was important was that the young worker took it on himself or herself to act in some way, "no matter how small or insignificant that action may be."[116]

The immediate goal was to instill a sense of purpose among the young lay participants in the movement and a commitment toward working to solve problems in their working lives as they arose.[117] Underlying this piecemeal approach, one can also see the centrality of fortifying the authority of the Roman Catholic Church, as was seen in the social encyclicals themselves. In the repetitive linkage of addressing even the most mundane workplace issues to the teachings of the Church, Roman Catholicism assumed the role of authorizing agent for decisions made in everyday work life. The categorical distinctions made by Hillenbrand's "Sunday Catholics" between religious life and life in "the real world" evaporated and were replaced by a sense of the Church's significant role in all things. As one YCW promoter put it: "Not so long ago we labored $50 or $60 or $80 a week, with no thought of what our work should be,

---

115. Hillenbrand, "The Priesthood and the World," 54.
116. John C. Cort, "From Small Groups a Big Movement," *The Commonweal* 60 (May 7, 1954): 116.
117. For more on the YCW method, see the chapter titled "Observe, Judge, and Act," in Zotti, *A Time of Awakening*, 45–71.

no idea that we were cooperating with our Lord in the re-creation of the world. We never realized that we can offer every moment of our work to God as a prayer. Now the most humble and menial job can have a religious and apostolic meaning."[118]

Much like the ACTU's self-understanding as leaven in a large labor movement dedicated to solving problems one small step at a time, the YCW approached all of its work with this philosophy and even structured its organization accordingly in the United States and Europe. The establishment of each YCW chapter began with recruiting a handful of people to lead the *cells* within the YCW. Cells were simply small groups of young workers who met regularly to observe, judge, and act on the problems they faced. Leaders would be responsible for helping to develop the sense of apostolic mission among those within her or his cell.[119] These cells were small, rarely exceeding twelve people. One organizer of the YCW, an Australian named Paul McGuire, described the cells as analogues to the cells of the mystical body of Christ. As a human cell divided when it grew, so too would a cell within the YCW movement, ensuring that issues were handled on a very personal level for each of the members involved and allowing for maximum participation of each member.[120] As John Cort noted in *The Commonweal*, the structure of the YCW cut against the grain.

> The small group is not a form of organization that immediately appeals to the American spirit. The American spirit is expansive and goes for the big meeting, with the dynamic speaker and a lively discussion on the floor, shared in by maybe five extroverts who have had previous experience in public speaking themselves. This is climaxed by the passage of a resounding resolution that gives the faithful the illusion of sweeping all the filthy books off the drugstore counters, or all the Communists into the sea, or all the good Irish Catholics into public office.[121]

It was precisely this impersonal organizational structure Cort was satirizing that the YCW wanted to avoid by implementing their system of

118. Billy Hough, "Chat with YCW Chaplains," *Apostolate* 2 (Spring 1955): 7.
119. Edward Hogan, "The First Ten Years," *Apostolate* 5 (Summer 1958): 3.
120. Zotti, *A Time of Awakening*, 10–11.
121. Cort, "From Small Groups a Big Movement," 116.

small cells. At the same time, the method rang true with their understanding of subsidiarity.[122]

To say that the YCW had a unified and detailed agenda would be an exaggeration, because each cell had its own dynamics and developed according to its own fashion. A more accurate characterization would note that YCW cells attempted to begin addressing the problems of the workers from the same set of premises. These premises were outlined in a succinct "Manifesto of the Young Christian Worker," approved by the 450 delegates to an international convention of the YCW at Brussels in September 1950. Not surprising, the manifesto closely reflected the principles elucidated in *Rerum Novarum* and *Quadragesimo Anno*.[123]

Beginning with a nod to the broader Catholic mythology, the manifesto began by noting that all action taken on behalf of the worker must be done with the understanding that the human being "has an eminent and inviolable dignity" springing from a relationship with God. It is the preeminent mission of the worker to nurture the family and community through which the human personality may fulfill its potential. With this in mind, the YCW made each individual worker responsible for the "de-proletarianization" of society. Where the Marxist envisioned an inevitable revolution, the YCW held that de-proletarianization was possible through education, professional training, decent housing, good working conditions, a just wage, and a right to a family life. These elements of economic security depended on savings and the private ownership of homes.[124] Parting company with the NCRLC, the YCW did not emphasize agricultural self-sufficiency and extended the importance of home ownership to the urban dweller as well.

Echoing the encyclicals, the manifesto announced that those who labored had the "right to work which—instead of making [the worker] a slave to machines and to capital—will free him from the proletarian complex." This demanded the "regulation of mechanized work—the production line, time studies, etc.—and of every method of work which destroys the sense of personal responsibility." Moreover, these goals would be accomplished through unions and professional associations

122. Peter Foote, "Evolution of YCW: Notes on the Chicago Experience," *Apostolate* 7 (Spring 1960): 35.
123. "Manifesto of the Young Christian Worker," *The Catholic Mind* 49 (July 1951): 462–64.
124. Ibid.

that prepared workers "for an active participation in the administration of enterprises and professions."[125]

Similar to the manner in which the encyclicals were built around a Catholic conception of the family, the YCW saw family life as central to promoting the dignity of the worker and devoted nearly a third of its manifesto to outlining this role. Issues such as "promiscuity at work and during leisure time," as well as the "pornographic press," were obstacles to maintaining healthy families. So too was the blurring of distinctive gender roles in the workplace and at home. While the working woman was entitled to the basic economic and cultural necessities required for men, these were seen as a means of providing her with the support needed to fulfill her "personal mission as a wife, as a fiancée, as a future mother," and as an "educator for a new generation of workers."[126] In this way the Catholic organic metaphor for society was satisfied as the pieces of the social order were cast to fit their distinctive but limited roles for the good of the whole. Much as *Quadragesimo Anno* refashioned the principles of *Rerum Novarum* to suit the circumstances of a later generation, the YCW manifesto distilled the principles of the encyclicals to suit the circumstances of its audience. In this way, the text provided the organization with the framework necessary to guide the judgments and actions of its members while also shaping the cognitive prism through which observations would be made.

The development of strong cells within the YCW depended on the formation of leaders within the organization. The goal of the cells was "to influence all through a comparatively small elite group," according to Canon Cardijn. They applied the same method when it came to developing the individual cells themselves. Leadership formation was the "most important task" in cell creation, and a 1957 leadership training program required that leaders be trained to develop a sense of union with the Church, to form "supernatural" lives of their own in union with Christ, to understand Church doctrine, and most important, to take *action* to meet needs of the day. Furthermore, leadership recruits received lessons that sounded like the curriculum of an informal MBA program, focusing on such things as advertising, public speaking, counseling, leading discussion groups, and group dynamics. The training course even

---

125. Ibid., 462–63.
126. Ibid., 463.

focused on the need to understand labor unions in order to be effective within them and on developing political savvy.[127]

Getting young workers to come to YCW meetings was the greatest challenge for cell leaders. They promoted many "methods of winning young people through friendship."[128] Dolores Marino, a YCW leader in Milwaukee, emphasized the importance of adapting to one's "environment in every way except sin" as a means of making other young people comfortable with your presence and receptive to your ideas. YCW leaders would continue to socialize with their coworkers at taverns or diners, so that joining the YCW would not result in removing oneself from the daily lives of workers.[129] In colloquial terms, the goal of the YCW leader was to make participation in the group appear "cool." The editors of *Apostolate,* a YCW magazine published in Chicago, listed the personality traits of the ideal cell leader. In addition to generosity, honesty, and a sense of humor, the YCW leader was "not a 'square,'" enjoyed sports, and did not give the outward impression of being devoutly religious, although "deep down he is."[130] The defensiveness and alienation which Canon Cardijn himself must have felt when rejected by his childhood friends after his ordination seemed to have translated into a cautious but determined method for gaining the trust of young men and women. It also spoke to the boundaries that separated public and private religious life in America by the mid-twentieth century.

Hillenbrand and the YCW

Though each cell of the YCW in the United States developed in its own manner according to its own dynamics, the influence of the movement's leaders, especially Reynold Hillenbrand, was instrumental in setting the tone for the organization nationwide. In 1955 Hillenbrand spelled out a social program explicitly linked to the philosophies of the social encyclicals. The sanctity of private property and its wide distribution were necessary to "secure against the vicissitudes of life," as well as "to bring out the best in human nature." A just family wage for workers must

---

127. John Hayes, "Cardijn in the World," *Apostolate* 4 (Spring 1957): 23–24; "YCW Training Course," *Apostolate* 4 (Spring 1957): 18–19.
128. Ibid., 19.
129. Dolores Marino, "Y.C.W. in Our Factory," *Apostolate* 2 (Winter 1954): 20–26.
130. "A Leader Should Be—" is inserted at the end of Marino's article (ibid., 26).

meet Pius XI's standard of "not just a sufficiency but an *ample* sufficiency." "Ample," wrote Hillenbrand, meant "enough to supply cultural advantages, recreational advantages, educational expenses, medical supplies," and things of that nature.[131] His elaboration on the term "ample" was a bit more generous than Pius XI's own words on the subject. Pius XI had written that "ample sufficiency" was needed for workers so that they do not

> become slack in their work, for a man is born to labor as a bird to fly, but that by thrift they may increase their possessions and by prudent management of the same may be enabled to bear the family burden with greater ease and security, being freed from that hand-to-mouth uncertainty which is the lot of the proletarian. Thus they will not only be in the position to support life's changing fortunes, but will also have the reassuring confidence that when their lives are ended, some little provision will remain for those they leave behind. (*QA* sec. 61)

Hillenbrand's insistence on a guaranteed family wage extended to supporting beefed-up minimum wage standards and the need to address widespread violations of the law as well as the law's failure to cover all workers.[132]

Hillenbrand saw the application of the principle of subsidiarity with respect to government involvement in the economy as being "very simple." He wrote that "it was enunciated by Leo XIII, Pius XI, and Pius XII that the government should do the least possible in economic life." By Hillenbrand's reading, however, "the Popes have insisted . . . that the principle holds true only where there are no injustices, no inequities to remedy. If that is not true, the government must take measures. The Church does not, therefore, envision a government which is over-laden with economic responsibilities." Parenthetically, Hillenbrand asked, "why for instance, do we have to have a law describing the amount of washing and toilet facilities in places of work. It degrades the majesty of the government to have to descend to such small details. And yet the government has to do it, because sometimes no one else will see to it."[133]

131. Reynold Hillenbrand, "5 Point Social Program," *Apostolate* 3 (Winter 1955): 11–24, esp. 13–14, 17.
132. Ibid., 18.
133. Ibid., 21.

This final sentence revealed his take on subsidiarity's application to government involvement in the transformation of economic life more clearly than in any of his previous writings.

While "the Church wants people to organize—employers into trade associations, employees into labor unions," Hillenbrand noted, he stressed labor unions because "without labor organizations, workers are weak. With them they have some power—the power of negotiation, the power of striking if necessary." He felt that this natural right had been threatened by congressional passage of the Taft-Hartley law, a "ghastly" example of "a law which makes the vindication and implementation of that human right, so strongly defended by the Church, much more difficult."[134]

Though never directly involved in unions themselves, the YCW actively promoted them among their members. They were "seen as the primary means of improving working conditions" among YCW members, and encouraging unions became a staple of cell programs early on. With Hillenbrand's influence, the YCW renewed their commitment to union organizing in the mid-1950s.[135] This effort was designed, in part, to counteract communism. Communists succeeded, Hillenbrand argued, because they dealt with real issues in a substantive manner. "Communism has had its appeal for only one reason: because it presents itself as a solution to the economic problem, the industrial problem, the problem of the employer and worker; because it sets itself to right the injustice in the whole field of labor. As Pius XI says there is something messianic about Communism. It is redemptive. It proposes to redeem those who are economically distraught." Needless to say, Hillenbrand saw it as a false solution and offered instead his reading of Leo XIII and Pius XI.[136]

YCW leader Dolores Marino's reflections of her own experience at a factory in Wisconsin underscored the perceived problem. When the state of Wisconsin attempted to limit compensation for hearing loss resulting from working conditions only to those who were declared totally deaf, the only union that protested was the communist-dominated union of the United Electrical Workers. "Where were the Christians who love one another?" she asked. Her first union meeting was run by a rumored communist, and the communist influence on the union resulted in its

---

134. Ibid., 20.
135. Zotti, *A Time of Awakening*, 134; Mary Lou Mangan, "YCW Program," *Apostolate* 3 (Fall 1956): 15–17.
136. Hillenbrand, "5 Point Social Program," 11–14.

"continually widening the gap between labor and management" through the rhetoric of its leaders who taught the membership "to hate our employers." The YCW was necessary, Marino pleaded, if workers wanted to maintain unions while stripping away the Marxist vestiges of class antagonism, an ideology in direct opposition to that of the Church.[137]

Marino exemplified YCW members who took it on themselves to apply the organization's teachings to her own participation in a union. Despite no official affiliation with unions, the YCW joined other Catholic labor organizations—including the Council on Working Life in Chicago (formerly the Chicago Catholic Labor Alliance) and the Catholic Labor Alliance in Detroit, both notable for their rejection of the ACTU tactic of taking official positions on specific union policies—to educate workers about the importance of union membership. In San Francisco, the YCW even organized one of the earliest Catholic labor schools on the West Coast, promoting the rights and responsibilities of labor unions based on the lessons of the encyclicals. Dozens of former YCW members went on to become prominent labor leaders on their own.[138]

The Fate of the YCW

It is difficult to assess the impact the YCW had on the working lives of young Roman Catholics in the United States, though the results of a survey published in Mary Zotti's study of the movement, *A Time of Awakening*, make it clear that the group made a lasting impression on many of its participants. Yet even at its peak membership of 3,000 in 1957, only 180 of the total 16,000 Roman Catholic parishes in the United States had branches of the YCW. This ratio appears even more stark when considering that in the same year, out of 49,000 priests, only 180 had committed to being YCW chaplains.[139] Despite regular appeals for clerical support appearing in YCW publications, few priests responded to the call. It was no coincidence, then, that the decline of the YCW was linked to the deterioration of Reynold Hillenbrand's health and his growing inability to keep up with the needs of the specialized youth movement. Zotti also pointed out that by the end of the 1950s, emphasis on

---

137. Marino, "Y.C.W. in Our Factory," 22–26.
138. Zotti, *A Time of Awakening*, 135–36.
139. Ibid., 135–40.

labor issues gave way to "the civil rights movement and action on other urban problems."[140]

The organization's structure appears to have been another reason for the YCW's decline. Cell meetings were built around issues known as "inquiries." The inquiry was a question or subject that the members of the cell were expected to approach through the observe, judge, and act method. These inquiries might involve the obstacles to forming labor unions, personal morality in the workplace, or developing the foundations for individual economic security. The national board of the YCW would develop inquiries around particular annual themes; however, these inquiries sometimes ran the risk of limiting the possibilities for unbiased observation by the "slanting of questions and loading of quotations." Priest and sociologist Andrew Greeley, who was active in the Chicago YCW, warned that preparation of inquiries by a national board far removed from the social situations of cells in other parts of the country could lead to ineffective meetings and the stifling of local autonomy. For instance, an inquiry on race relations in the workplace designed by Chicago members might result in a very different set of observations and actions by a cell in Memphis or New Orleans than the national board members had intended.

In this criticism, Greeley was getting at the heart of an issue that was coming to a boil within the Roman Catholic Church by 1959 and would be addressed directly in the Second Vatican Council. As Greeley phrased it, "the question is to what extent are we willing to let the democratic processes work in the movements, to what extent are we willing to let people develop in their own fashion instead of forcing them to develop into our preconceived patterns."[141] The direction the YCW should take and the extent to which that direction should be the result of the free choice of the individual cells were concerns that led to the disillusionment of some YCW members and perhaps to the eventual disbanding of the YCW itself.

American attitudes toward class, coupled with an apparent ambiguity in the American YCW's sense of mission as it evolved in the 1950s, also contributed to the movement's decline. As noted earlier, the YCW inherited a mission from its European Jocist forebears to come to the

---

140. See Hough, "Chat with YCW Chaplains," 4–8; Zotti, *A Time of Awakening*, 272–73.
141. Andrew Greeley, "The Problem Approach to Social Inquiry," *Apostolate* 6 (Spring 1959): 2–5.

aid of the working classes and win them back for the Roman Catholic Church. Though this stated aim never changed, the very conception of "working-class" Americans became increasingly problematic for some in the post–World War II period. Certainly the Cold War contributed to a new and intense effort to imagine the United States as populated by a nearly all-consuming middle class. Among Catholics especially, the improved economic and social status after World War II, fueled by the GI Bill and a new college-educated generation of Catholics, created a transformation of consciousness. As historian Jay Dolan put it, "Catholics entered the 1950s confident about their place in American society. Being Catholic was indeed compatible with being American."[142] Being "working class" was less likely to be seen as a badge of honor, a mentality associated with the "ghettoistic" mind-set of many American Catholics but was instead seen as a burden. When Catholics finally had the opportunity to gain their piece of the proverbial pie, many lost interest in those things that had marked their status as industrial laborers—a trend that reached even to those who continued to work on the lines in factories.

The YCW was placed in the position of having to conform its rhetoric to its actual makeup in the 1950s. A 1956 survey showed that in Chicago itself, only one-third of the group's membership was composed of "blue-collar" workers while the remainder wore the "white collar." In fact, almost one-quarter of the Chicago membership was made up of college graduates by 1956, a large portion by the standards of the day.[143] The trend was the same nationwide, as membership reflected the beginnings of America's own transformation from an industrial economy to a technological and service economy.[144]

This transformation within the YCW was visible to many as they were moving through it, and it did not go by uncontested. A 1958 article in the YCW's flagship magazine written by a California priest, Keith Kennedy, expressed grave concern with the changes taking place within the organization. Kennedy began by pointing out that while the concept of an "extensive *middle class* is a truth . . . it becomes a truism if one overlooks that flanking that broad sweep to one side is a very definite class of the wealthy, and to the other a definite and extensive area inhabited

---

142. J. Dolan, *The American Catholic Experience*, 417.
143. Foote, "Evolution of the YCW," 29–30.
144. Zotti, *A Time of Awakening*, 139.

by the less-than-middle class." For this reason, Kennedy balked at the YCW's abandoning its emphasis on a "work-centered" movement. To say that working-class consciousness in the United States was not the same as it was in Europe did not mean that there were "no workers' problems nor worker mentality here," Kennedy insisted: "Their difference does not conclude to their non existence." He produced an elaborate list of problems still facing American workers ranging from "right-to-work" legislation to the bracero program importing Mexican farm laborers to keep labor costs down. The general prosperity that appeared to have come to the nation rendered the young worker

> gloriously indifferent to his own problems, to his union, to whatever might bring down the curtain on the illusion of security given by the jingling of a few coins in his pocket. It's the great democracy of the dollar. There is no class consciousness here because any worker (with the right color skin, of course) can go anywhere that the very wealthy go, provided, naturally, that he is able to pay his way, even if he happens to be paying through the nose. Even his solidarity with other workers is a thing vaguely sensed, seldom expressed. It is this indifference that has been and remains the greatest obstacle to the YCW in the USA. It became a very tangible and cogent reality to me recently when the best leader prospect I have come across in years, in spite of every effort to enlist him, countered with, "Yes, Father, I see that all of these problems exist, but I'm just not interested in doing anything about them."[145]

Beyond the decline of class consciousness, the other most commonly cited culprit for the lost sense of mission was the decision to have coeducational cells by the mid-1950s. It is difficult to know if the decision itself sprang from a sense that the momentum of the organization was at risk. YCW leaders admitted that "mixing" was a conscious attempt to bolster membership by playing on the "natural desires" of young men and women to socialize with one another.[146] Critics like Kennedy, however, charged that this led to a "boy-meets-girl" mentality within the organization and ultimately to a lack of commitment to the mission and

---

145. Keith Kennedy, "YCW: A Worker's Apostolate?" *Apostolate* 5 (Spring 1958): 15–18.
146. Foote, "Evolution of the YCW," 30; Zotti, *A Time of Awakening*, 148.

a superficial attachment to the YCW.[147] Confirmation of those suspicions could be found in the very titles of sessions at the 1958 YCW Convention in Indiana: "How to Know You Are in Love," "How to Choose a Marriage Partner," and "The Single Life." Sessions like these suggest that by the end of the decade, the YCW was as much a social club as an organization committed to addressing the needs of the working class.

Despite the YCW's decline, there can be no doubt that the American YCW and its European Jocist predecessors took as their starting point the ideology of the Church as expressed in the papal encyclicals. Armed with a common rhetoric and a set of general principles, the YCW, like the ACTU, attempted to infuse the authority of Roman Catholicism within the daily lives of working men and women. Even the most menial industrial jobs, thought by fellow Catholics in the NCRLC and Catholic Worker movement to be irredeemably dehumanizing, were targeted for sanctification. Though the YCW was not satisfied with the working conditions many Americans faced, its goal was not the creation of a rural peasantry and an economic restructuring along medieval agrarian lines. "The Young Christian Worker movement differs radically with the Distributists in so far as Canon Cardijn has always emphasized that the YCW does not set out to rescue young workers from their environment (send them to the country)," wrote one YCW member, "but on the contrary to train the young workers to transform their everyday environment of work, leisure and family life and make it Christian."[148] For the YCW, science and technology were seen as products of God's own creativity. As a 1959 article in *Apostolate* put it: "We cannot make the world holy by washing our hands in innocence of the world. We can make the world holy only by penetrating the world. We can make the world holy only by entering the world."[149] By the end of the 1950s, urban industrialism had so transformed the American landscape that this commentator associated rural living as an escape from "the world," a notion that would have sounded bizarre half a century earlier.

The YCW made sense of the encyclical mythology in largely the same manner as the ACTU and the SAD, despite catering to a different—though

---

147. Kennedy, "YCW: A Worker's Apostolate?" 19; see also Zotti, *A Time of Awakening*, 147–54.

148. Paul T. Harris, "Communications: 'Obituary for Distributism,'" *The Commonweal* 61 (February 11, 1955): 505.

149. Philip Sharper, "The Catholic Layman and the Theology of Work," *Apostolate* 6 (Summer 1959): 18, 22.

sometimes overlapping—audience. Moreover, they often utilized the same discursive strategies to garner support. The sanctity of private property, the compatibility of class interests, the centrality of the family complete with divinely consigned gender roles, the principles of a living "family" wage, and the natural right to unions were all part and parcel of the YCW program as much as that of the ACTU and the SAD. The YCW and ACTU both believed themselves to be in compliance with the principle of subsidiarity in their "bottom-up" structure, though perhaps as a result of greater clerical influence, the YCW tended to be more of an advocate for government economic planning like the SAD, while the ACTU tended to rely more on the power of the bargaining table. Unlike the distributists, these groups saw the industrial world as fertile ground for sanctification. Sanctification would take place as labor and management both recognized the wisdom and authority of the Roman Catholic plan for a just social order and conformed to its vision accordingly.

(4)

Sanctifying American Capitalism

For all the differences between Catholic rural lifers and those who sought to sanctify the industrial order, they were bound by a common suspicion of capitalism and its consequences. They took solace in the encyclical denunciations of the laissez-faire mentality, a mentality that they believed was all too pervasive among the social elites who benefited most from the American economic system. Appeals to a free market were wrongly used to justify what they took to be the commodification of labor and the degradation of the dignity of workers. In the words of the Benedictine and renowned liturgical reformer Virgil Michel in 1938, "are there not many Catholics among us today who would balk at the statement that the whole capitalistic system is doomed, and that it must go if there is to be anything like a Catholic revival? Capitalism is finished! Can any intelligent person doubt it?"[1]

Even the Catholic Worker movement—with its anarcho-distributist philosophy's suspicion of state intrusion into the affairs of smaller social units—was motivated in its suspicion of the state by precisely the opposite reasoning used by capitalists. For instance, Dorothy Day and the Catholic Worker opposed Social Security legislation, not because it violated the principles of a free market and overextended state influence, as some capitalists argued, but rather because they feared that it would prolong the capitalist system by providing the working classes just enough comfort to be content with their servitude.[2] Even though appeals for radical transformation became significantly less frequent by the late 1950s, there remained a sense among those we have discussed in the previous

---

1. Virgil Michel, "What Is Capitalism?" *The Commonweal* 28 (April 29, 1938): 6.
2. Joseph M. Becker, "Who Are Opposed to Social Security?" *America*, May 15, 1948,

chapters that some substantive structural changes were necessary if the American social order was to be authentically Christian.

But for others, the American capitalist system provided the surest route toward a society built on justice. Catholic supporters of capitalism were typically called "conservatives." As historian Philip Gleason has noted, classifying Catholic social thought of any stripe as "liberal" or "conservative" poses problems. "The vagueness of the terms themselves and the simplistic way they are usually employed," wrote Gleason, are destined to make their usage problematic. To illustrate this point, one need look no further than Gleason's own use of these terms as he tried to characterize the attitude of German-American Catholics in the late nineteenth and early twentieth centuries. In that context, he described liberals as those who "took a more optimistic view of the relationship of the Catholic church to American culture," while conservatives "had reservations about the easy compatibility of Catholicism and the American spirit."[3] By the time we arrive at the middle of the twentieth century, these descriptions could have easily been reversed when speaking of Catholic attitudes toward capitalism in the United States. It was the conservatives who possessed a "more optimistic view" of American capitalist culture's compatibility with the Catholic ethos, while liberals remained suspicious of the economic order.

The Bolshevik Revolution, the Great Depression, the rise of fascist totalitarianism, the New Deal, and World War II had all done much to redraw the ideological maps of Catholics in the United States. In the economic realm, the term "conservative" came to refer to those who were suspicious of the encroaching power of the state set forth in the New Deal reforms. With an eye directed at ascendant socialist movements in Europe and the rise of the Soviet Union, FDR's reforms were deemed indicative of a growing trend toward collectivization and an abandonment of the market economy that had dominated the American scene since its founding. The warnings of Leo XIII and Pius XI regarding socialism's incompatibility with a Catholic economic order informed their suspicions as the line between socialism and the new economic reforms seemed ambiguous to some.[4]

In the generation before Vatican II, the voices of Catholic economic

---

3. Philip Gleason, *The Conservative Reformers: German-American Catholics and the Social Order* (Notre Dame, Ind.: University of Notre Dame Press, 1968), 4, 30–31.

4. David J. O'Brien, *American Catholics and Social Reform: The New Deal Years* (New York: Oxford University Press, 1968), 58.

conservatives among both the hierarchy and the laity were a minority. Memories of the Great Depression, and more important, of the loosely regulated capitalism that precipitated the economic despair, remained prominent in the Catholic mind. The Catholic exodus from the lower tiers of the American economic ladder had just begun in earnest, and their alliance with Roosevelt's Democratic Party had yet to be severely tested.

This chapter, however, examines those Catholics whose sympathies rested with market capitalist principles as a means of preserving liberty while staving off the encroachments of the state. Not surprising, they were bound to their "liberal" interlocutors by a common mythology, grounded in natural-law theology and articulated in *Rerum Novarum* and *Quadragesimo Anno*. They were every bit as likely to appeal to the encyclical tradition to authorize their view of the world, yet that view was frequently in sharp contrast with that of other Catholics pointing to the same texts for authority. By the 1950s, the voices of Catholics publicly defending American capitalism began to increase in number and intensity as confidence in the nation's economy expanded over the course of the decade. The Cold War intensified America's consciousness of itself as a "Capitalist country" in a dialectical relationship to the communist Soviet Union. Defending capitalism came to be seen by some as an act of patriotism—much like defending democracy had been since the American Revolution—and in a manner that would have seemed odd only decades earlier.

Of course, this shift was not inevitable. As historian Elizabeth Fones-Wolf has documented, a concerted effort by well-funded organizations like the National Association of Manufacturers and the Chamber of Commerce of the United States had begun, as early as the late 1930s, to undermine support for the New Deal; extol the virtues of competition in industry, wages, and prices; create organized opposition to government taxation; and link labor unions in the public mind to organized crime and socialism.[5] Among some Catholics, the message seemed to resonate. Inspired by an article in the *Saturday Evening Post,* the conservative Catholic periodical *Ave Maria* declared in 1951 that "no matter what the Lefties may say . . . no American should be ashamed" of capitalism. "Even in its imperfect state, capitalism has bestowed . . . great

---

5. See Elizabeth Fones-Wolf, *Selling Free Enterprise: The Business Assault on Labor and Liberalism, 1945–1960* (Urbana: University of Illinois Press, 1994).

gifts upon Americans," while the Soviet system produced nothing but "poverty and serfdom."[6] This sort of rhetoric became increasingly common as the decade wore on.

Defining Capitalism

How capitalism was defined had a profound impact on how acceptable it was to the American Catholic. Yet defining the term was at the heart of the problem for both its supporters and detractors. Capitalism could be defined so innocuously that virtually all Americans would be counted as supporting it, or it could be defined in such a way that it would be nearly impossible to recognize as existing anywhere in the world. This point was illustrated by J. H. Schackmann's 1939 article in *Catholic World*. In an informal survey, Schackmann asked a number of educated Catholics with whom he was acquainted, "in the sense in which *you* understand the word, do *you* think a Catholic is committed by the official teaching of his Church to defend and maintain the Capitalist system?" To this question, 75 percent answered "yes," 20 percent were unsure, and only 5 percent answered "no." Of course, there was nothing scientific about the survey and it was likely to have been substantially influenced by the social circles in which Schackmann circulated, but Schackmann himself pointed out the greatest limitation of his data: he had no way of knowing what his respondents understood the term "capitalism" to mean. The fact that the respondents frequently asked for Schackmann's clarification of what he meant by the term served to drive this point home.[7]

Dictionary definitions were a common place to turn for both defenders and detractors of capitalism. Capitalist critic Virgil Michel cited the fourteenth edition of the *Encyclopedia Britannica* as saying that capitalism was "the world-wide system of organizing production and trade by private enterprise free to seek profit and fortune by employing for wages the mass of human labor." This was followed, however, by a rejoinder in the text that "there is no satisfactory definition for the term."[8] Schackmann also cited dictionary definitions. *The New Standard Dictionary*

---

6. "Record of Capitalism," *Ave Maria* 73 (June 23, 1951): 772–73.
7. J. H. Schackmann, "Are Catholics Committed to Capitalism?" *Catholic World* 148 (January 1939): 423, emphasis in original.
8. Michel, "What Is Capitalism?" 6.

listed three meanings for capitalism: "(1) a system that favors the *concentration* of capital in the hands of a few; (2) the power and influence of *concentrated* capital; and (3) the possession of capital." He followed these with several definitions from *Webster's International Dictionary,* including "(1) the state of having capital; (2) the possession of capital; (3) an economic system in which capital or Capitalists play the principal part; (4) the *concentration* of capital; and (5) the power and influence of capital, *as when in the hands of a few.*"[9] If dictionaries reflected popular uses of the term accurately, clearly one's sentiments toward capitalism were likely to be profoundly influenced by which definition one imagined. Virgil Michel went beyond dictionaries to cite intellectual authorities with frequency, including Catholic writers like Paul Jostock, economist Goetz Briefs, and the director of the Central-Verein, Frederick P. Kenkel. The definition that came closest to reflecting Michel's own ideology was that of English distributist Hilaire Belloc, who defined capitalism as "a system under which wealth is produced by a mass of citizens politically free, but dispossessed, and these working for the profit of a far smaller number of effective owners and controllers of the means of production."[10]

Michel's citation of the famed German sociologist Max Weber's definition of capitalistic action as that which is "'adapted to the systematic utilization of goods or personal services as a means of acquisition' in such a way that the accumulated capital is increased" brings to light another factor in the Catholic attitude toward capitalism: its association with Protestantism. Weber's famed book *The Protestant Ethic and the Spirit of Capitalism* lent fuel to the flame of many Catholic critics of capitalism who traced the roots of individualism, materialism, and the laissez-faire spirit directly to Luther and the Protestant reformers — a strategy employed in the encyclicals themselves. For some Catholics, especially those hostile to capitalism, the fate of that economic order was tied directly to the fate of Protestantism.[11]

9. Schackmann, "Are Catholics Committed to Capitalism?" 424, emphasis in Schackmann and not from the dictionaries he cited.
10. Michel, "What Is Capitalism?" 7–8; cites Hilaire Belloc in *G. K.'s Weekly,* December 2, 1937, 212.
11. Michel noted that an address delivered at the Chicago Theological Seminary on "Protestantism and the Present World Situation" argued that "traditional Protestantism 'can continue to exist only if it succeeds in undergoing a fundamental change; a change that will destroy it as Protestantism.'" From this statement, Michel drew what appeared to him to be a logical corollary that "regardless of whether this [statement on Protestantism] is true or not, it gives us a good clue as to the real situation of present capitalism: Capitalism is so

Conservative Catholic definitions of capitalism rarely focused on the concentration of wealth or the profit motive but instead on the right to private property—a right firmly fixed in *Rerum Novarum* and *Quadragesimo Anno*. "Capitalism can mean but one thing," wrote one defender of the system, "i.e., the right of ownership of private property legally acquired, and the right to use it for one's own or others' comfort or benefit." On the surface, at least, no informed Catholic could argue that a capitalism so defined was objectionable in the Church's eyes. Conservatives were also apt to equate capitalism with the fruits of its production. One editorial in *Ave Maria* noted that "the Detroit assembly line makes it possible for Americans, representing only 7 per cent of the world's population, to own more than 75 per cent of the world's automobiles. That's capitalism!" The Jesuit economist Bernard W. Dempsey went as far as arguing that "there is no such thing as capitalism. The word is incapable of scientific definition: it exists only in the Marxist dream world," where it meant, in Dempsey's reading of Marx, "any system of social economy which tolerated private property."[12]

At least since Augustine's *City of God*, which drew a Platonically informed line between the heavenly Church and the earthly Church, Christians have depended on distinctions that separate "accidents" from "essences" as a means of protecting cherished institutions from bearing the stains of their worst elements. As such, many conservatives drew a sharp distinction between the "spirit" of the capital*ists* themselves and the "organization" of capital*ism*. While the spirit of capitalists often "makes gain the end of society," the root cause of this deviation from the divine will could be found in the inherently sinful nature of human beings. Thus, the problem was our failure to recognize and act on human dignity, not the division of ownership between capital and labor. It was this distinction that one Catholic author was trying to make when he wrote: "Capitalism in itself is a good system. It is based upon the idea of property, and a man needs property if he is to grow and find happiness in life. But capitalism, historically, has for centuries been perverted, especially by the all pervasive role of money." Human greed destroyed an otherwise good thing. Still, "if American Capitalism is to be condemned

---

doomed to extinction that it can continue to exist only in so far as it ceases to be capitalism." See "What Is Capitalism?" 8.

12. Thomas F. Daly, "Letter to the Editor: What Is Capitalism?" *The Commonweal* 28 (June 10, 1938): 185; "Record of Capitalism," 36; Bernard W. Dempsey, S.J., ". . . But Don't Call it Capitalism," *Social Order* 4 (May 1954): 208, 203.

because of the misconduct of a few businessmen," said one Catholic economist, "one has to condemn the Church because there have been and are bad clergymen and one has to condemn all unions because of the existence of some racketeers and criminals in the labor movement."[13]

By the 1950s, many who were sympathetic to the American capitalist system sought to rename it altogether in order to strip it of its post–Great Depression negative connotations. In the intervening years, these conservatives argued that the nature of capitalism in America had changed sufficiently so that it was no longer recognizable in the anti-capitalist rhetoric of earlier years. In 1951 William Nichols, the editor of a weekly magazine supplement included in many Sunday newspapers, wrote an article titled "Wanted: A New Name for Capitalism." Nichols characterized the American economic system as "imperfect but always improving, and always capable of further improvement—where men move forward together, working together, building together, producing always more and more, and sharing the rewards of their increased production." He suggested a few possibilities, including "'the new capitalism,' 'democratic capitalism,' 'economic democracy,' 'productivism,'" and others, but solicited his readers to send in their own suggestions. Over fifteen thousand suggestions arrived, and by the mid-1950s the expression "people's capitalism" had come into vogue. This new enthusiasm for American capitalism was compounded by the publication of Peter Drucker's *New Society*, Frederick Lewis Allen's *Big Change*, and *U.S.A.: The Permanent Revolution*, published by the editors of *Fortune* magazine. Each of these studies "related a similar story: In the United States we have never had it so good."[14]

Catholics and Capitalism

This national trend was mirrored in Catholic circles as well. Jesuit Richard McKeon argued in the pages of *Social Order* in 1953 that "present-day

---

13. D. Marshall, "The Church and Capitalism," *Catholic World* 146 (November 1937): 178; C. J. Eustace, "Which Leviathan—Big Business or the State?" *Catholic World* 166 (February 1948): 441–46; "People's Capitalism," speech by Rev. Edward Keller, C.S.C., delivered before "The Friday Morning Club luncheon meeting on Friday, May 2, Los Angeles, California," no year given, though it appears to have been in the 1950s, University of Notre Dame Archives (hereafter UNDA), Notre Dame, Indiana, Rev. Edward Keller Files, AC 837, Box 2, Folder: "CKEL Lectures Given by Keller Around the Country."

14. Douglas T. Miller and Marion Nowak, *The Fifties: The Way We Really Were* (Garden City, N.Y.: Doubleday, 1977), 106–7, 112.

American capitalism differs considerably from the economic liberalism which characterized most of our industrial activity throughout the nineteenth century." The capitalism that critics attack "is not the capitalism which for the past twenty or more years has been evolving in the United States." Unlike some pro-capitalists, McKeon credited the reforms that followed the Great Depression with ushering in the new and improved capitalist system. His own definition of capitalism, one that he referred to as "fairly satisfactory," focused on property rights. It was a system "wherein private wealth is reserved and used for further production." Thus, echoing the encyclicals, because we have a natural right to private property, "Capitalism in itself, when it fulfills the duties of justice and charity, is good."[15]

McKeon's article included a two-page spread with side-by-side columns illustrating the differences between "Old Capitalism" and "New Capitalism." At the top of the list, under the heading "General Characteristics," McKeon attributed "divorce from morality and ethics" to old capitalism, while crediting the new capitalism with having "moral principles emphasized." "Excessive individualism" of the old capitalism played foil to the "growing social consciousness" of the new, while "Wall Street, a symbol of power" was set against "Main Street, symbol of power." This structure of illustrating the disparity between past and present continued under the headings of "Management," "Labor," "Distribution of Wealth," and "Government." Only under the category of "Government" did the new fail to improve on the old. Government under the old system was plagued by "frequently extensive corruption" and "powerful lobbies for economic interests." Yet, by 1953, all McKeon could say about government in the new capitalism was that "corruption continues" and "lobbies continue." Clearly much had changed in the previous two decades, particularly in the area of regulatory reform, which McKeon noted. Still, one did not need to be a hardened skeptic to question McKeon's assertion that in America's new capitalism, "dignity [was] recognized" and "just wages" had been achieved. While acknowledging more work needed to be done, and questioning Peter Drucker's thesis of the "Permanent Revolution" for its apparent blindness to several sectors of the economy, his article brimmed with optimism that the current

---

15. Richard M. McKeon, S.J., "New Capitalism vs. Old," *Social Order* 3 (March 1953): 99–100.

system would evolve into something similar to "the ideal, from a Christian point of view."¹⁶

McKeon was not alone. In 1949, Ralph Gorman, editor of *The Sign*, declared that "nothing is further from the truth" than the Catholic canonization of the American "free enterprise" system. But by 1956, his editorial page announced that the United States "seems to be achieving a new capitalism. The old idea of class struggle and exploitation is yielding to an increasing sense of social responsibility." He concluded, "we may well be at a turning-point of history." The change in tone was clear. Catholics sympathetic to capitalism began to focus, fittingly, on how to "sell" capitalism. The task of the Catholic capitalist was to "package it a bit more invitingly," wrote one commentator in the pages of a Catholic monthly. This required an emphasis on the spiritual and social nature of capitalism rather than an exclusive view toward production and efficiency.¹⁷

Arnold F. McKee echoed these sentiments in a 1956 article in *Social Order*. McKee deemed "the great propaganda campaign" to sell "The New Good Capitalism" a failure. Branding with the phrases "'Dynamic Capitalism' and 'People's Capitalism' have all failed to sell the product." The reason, McKee believed, was the failure to deal with economics in the social and moral realm, the realm in which Catholic teaching had placed it. It was necessary to stress how the American system, though imperfect, was able to "broadly conform to the requirements of human nature and dignity and to the purpose and ends of the economy as part of society," that of "leading a fully human life." Even the communists understood the importance of contextualizing economics in the realm of social ethics, McKee charged, and this was precisely the reason for their success. American capitalism produced those things that "reflect and manifest, albeit imperfectly, social justice: and it is the principles of this that America should be urging on the world, not some ill-understood and ill-fitting doctrine of capitalism" that focused solely on widespread stock ownership or increased productivity.¹⁸

---

16. Ibid., 100–102.
17. Ralph Gorman, C.P., "Capitalism Canonized?" *The Sign* 29 (December 1949): 6; "A New Capitalism in the Making?" *The Sign* 36 (October 1956): 12; Peter Land, "Capitalism: Toward a Humane Economic Order," *Social Order* 1 (November 1951): 421.
18. Arnold F. McKee, "Selling American Capitalism: A Conspicuous Failure," *Social Order* 6 (November 1956): 411–14.

Defending American Capitalism

As these examples have illustrated, defining capitalism and determining which elements of capitalism were worth preserving and promoting proved a difficult task. Both sympathizers and critics of the system were constantly forced to clarify their terms before making arguments in favor of or in opposition to capitalism. As one commentator bemoaned, "unfortunately words are defined by usage rather than committees and guillotining a word editorially does not kill it. It goes on being used."[19] Conservative Catholics were left with the term "capitalism" whether they liked it or not, and they sought to purge it of its negative connotations by arguing for its compatibility with Catholic social teaching. As with the rural lifers and urban industrialists we have already examined, certain elements of the encyclicals proved especially helpful to authorizing the conservatives' economic ideologies. The sanctity of private property, the natural harmony of class interests, and the principle of subsidiarity were the most frequently cited elements of the encyclical mythology invoked by Catholic conservatives seeking to sanctify the American system of capitalism.

John A. Dinneen, a Jesuit professor of philosophy at St. Peter's College in New Jersey, was one Catholic seeking to resurrect the idea of capitalism from the beating it had taken in earlier decades. Dinneen preferred the term "market economy," provided that it was not understood "in any exaggerated liberalistic sense" associated with the nineteenth-century Manchesterians. A frequent contributor to Catholic periodicals, Dinneen's 1955 piece in *The Catholic World*, "'Capitalism' and Capitalism," distinguished the "economic system in which capital and labor for production are provided by different people" from the *abuses* of that system that Dinneen believed were endemic to the human condition. When properly ordered—free from excessive state intervention as well as monopolies—the market economy was "true democracy in action," enabling consumer control "from the production manager to the housewife." In contrast, Dinneen described a "coercive economy" characterized by collectivism and posing a "mortal danger" to the capitalistic West. The Church condemned the collectivism Dinneen described and moreover "has indeed been an ardent supporter of capitalism in its essential

---

19. John C. Cort, "Capitalism: Debates and Definitions," *The Commonweal* 61 (November 26, 1954): 221; cites Thomas P. Neill, "Liberalism," *Social Order* 4 (1954).

structure, recognizing that it is based upon man's natural right to private property." He tempered his assertion with the reminder that this approbation did not extend to a "false concept of private property," presumably one devoid of its social function. It was "'laissez faire' and 'economic liberalism'" that the Church condemned and not the *essentials* of the system. Relying on the separation of essence from accidents, "the abuses and injustices accompanying" capitalism had to be distinguished from its structure.[20]

Dinneen's outlook reflected a tendency described by historian William Leach to associate democracy with a wide choice of consumer products, thereby rendering the American people equal insofar as they were given an equal right to choose commodities. Utilizing an increasingly common parallel that harmonized the capitalistic and democratic systems, the individual consumer "casts a vote" with purchases. "Thus, if the manufacturer finds the price of rubber or cotton too high," Dinneen argued, "he will turn to synthetic substitutes; if the housewife is unable to include butter on the family budget, she will buy more oleomargarine." As capitalism was essential for democracy, it also deserved the credit for sustaining our large population, our technological progress, unprecedented wealth, and even the success of the Catholic school system. Capitalism, Dinneen believed, had "brought about the condition and leisure necessary for political, cultural, *and religious progress*. It has put within reach of the American people as a whole that minimum of material abundance which is necessary for the practice of virtue." All of these points were forgotten by "so-called reformers" caught up in their "frantic outcries" against the system.[21]

"The Path of the Church is clear," wrote Dinneen. "It steers between the Scylla and Charybdis, between the system denying the right to consumptive goods and/or the means of production and the exaggerated form of capitalism which recognizes unlimited right over property without any subordination to the common good." Steering between the two required being directed toward two bedrock principles of the Church: the natural right to private property and the principle of subsidiarity.

---

20. John A. Dinneen, S.J., "'Capitalism' and Capitalism," *The Catholic World* 180 (January 1955): 293–97; for more on Dinneen, see Patrick Allitt, *Catholic Intellectuals and Conservative Politics in America, 1950–1985* (Ithaca, N.Y.: Cornell University Press, 1993), 72.

21. William Leach, *Land of Desire: Merchants, Power, and the Rise of American Culture* (New York: Pantheon Books, 1993); Dinneen, "'Capitalism' and Capitalism," 294–95, emphasis added.

"It is wrong," explained Dinneen, "for any society to perform a function which the individual can perform or for a larger society to perform a function which a smaller society can perform." Though he omitted the statement Pius XI used to introduce his discussion of subsidiarity in *Quadragesimo Anno*—that "much that was formerly done by small bodies can nowadays be accomplished only by large organizations" (sec. 79)—Dinneen acknowledged that there was a need for economically based social reforms both in the United States and abroad. Those reforms, however, could only be successfully carried out within the structure of capitalism, not collectivism. Though the economy of his day had admittedly produced too great a concentration of wealth, the solution was not "state intervention and the wholesale nationalization of the means of production. . . . Such a step would only lead to greater tyranny."[22]

Another requirement for restoring economic justice involved labor's recognizing its common interests with management. "After all," wrote Dinneen, the worker "is a co-principle of market economy, and the natural partner of management. With initial difficulties settled, employer and employee could develop a permanent spirit of collaboration and harmony, recognizing the great number of interests common to each." His statement reflected the encyclical teaching that class antagonism was a violation of nature, while at the same time implicitly accepting the social hierarchy of the capitalist system—though distinguished from the fixed social hierarchy of Europe in the potential for mobility within the system. Among his practical solutions to building bridges between labor and management, Dinneen suggested profit-sharing plans; increased benefits, including life and health insurance; and greater labor participation in some management decisions. Running counter to the optimism, however, he concluded his defense of capitalism with a veiled warning:

> With the Communist cancer spreading throughout the globe, it is imperative that Mr. Average American grasp the nature and the worth of a democratic economic system, of ordered market economy based on the right to private property. Certain reforms, to be sure, are necessary in modern industrial society, and we have tried to indicate a few. But the signs for the future of the American market economy, at least, are bright. We have come

22. Dinneen, "'Capitalism' and Capitalism," 295–96.

a long way from the wild and woolly days of unscrupulous nineteenth-century financiers like Big Jim Fiske and Jay Gould. It seems impossible that we should witness a return of their unjust practices.... One thing ... cannot be overstressed ... only the democratic system of ordered market economy befits the dignity of man and it alone brings genuine prosperity.[23]

The Texas conservative Francis Graham Wilson, an Episcopalian convert to Roman Catholicism in 1924, became a prominent voice during the Cold War years for a Catholic opportunity "to lead a conservative revival" in the United States. Such a revival was necessary to stem the tide of revolutionary liberalism, and Catholicism was best suited to lead it because of its compatibility with what he understood to be the five central tenets of conservative thought: "First, that there is an intelligible pattern in history, not a mere succession of intrinsically unrelated events; second, that human nature is imperfect and corruptible; third, that 'there is a moral order in the universe in which man participates and from which he can derive canons of principles of political judgment'; fourth, that government must be closely circumscribed; and fifth, that private property is the foundation of civilization."[24] Wilson found each of these principles within the body of Catholic theology and social thought. Moreover, Catholicism possessed a natural antipathy to revolutionary liberalism and utopian movements, which had historically appealed "for the destruction of the Great Tradition of Institutional Christianity and Christian Philosophy." Ironically, these movements were stripping away the very measures necessary for judging their success, because, as T. S. Eliot remarked, any tradition "must be associated with an orthodoxy by which it can be judged." While modern Catholics may not have been willing to defend the status quo of the ancien regime, there remained a philosophical grounding in orthodoxy and natural law that rendered revolutionary liberalism anathema to the Church. That, coupled with Catholic understanding of human nature and original sin, eschewed the possibility of utopian idealism and made the Church comfortable allies with conservatism.[25]

23. Ibid., 296–97.
24. Allitt, *Catholic Intellectuals and Conservative Politics in America*, 58, 49; quotes Francis Graham Wilson, *The Case for Conservatism* (Seattle: University of Washington Press, 1951), 12.
25. Francis G. Wilson, "Catholics and the 'New Conservatism,'" *Social Order* 6 (June 1956): 247–51.

On the economic front, Wilson believed that the encyclicals—"often universal and timeless in import"—armed Catholics with an understanding of natural law. His exegesis of the texts led him to conclude that freedom for persons in both the political and economic order was at their core. While judging any economic order had to take into consideration the particular conditions of that society, the ultimate "test of legitimacy of an economic order would be its fulfillment of primary moral conditions. It might seem, then, that a Catholic conservative may defend capitalism on the ground that it provides the conditions of a possible Christian life." Though the encyclicals elucidated the natural rights to which a person is entitled, including the right to private property, to "a living or a frugal wage," to unionize and freely associate, these rights did not mean "that a Catholic may claim a revolutionary realization of these goals." Rather, Wilson explained, these were "objectives for the long run." While a person may have a right under natural law, "wisdom and prudence may indicate the conditions and the extent to which it may be claimed in the actualities of politics." After all, he argued, we have "an obligation to obey the state, which is, perhaps, another way of saying that we do not have a right to a personal utopia."[26]

The term "prudence" made its way into Wilson's argument with some frequency. "The prudential argument for the free market economy," wrote Wilson, "is that it gives more effectively to the citizen the rights he might claim in an absolute sense in a perfect realization of a Catholic society." Central to the preservation of these rights, the free market system "or some form of capitalism" has provided "a basic economic protection of the family"—a message harkening back to *Rerum Novarum* and *Quadragesimo Anno*, which understood the family to be the primary social unit, the preservation of which all political, social, and economic order was to be judged by. The "Neo-Capitalism" of America's 1950s, so called because of "its assumption of many social responsibilities to workers and its support of the military activity of the modern state," was far removed from the laissez-faire economies that the popes had derided. The American capitalist system's protection of the fundamental necessities for the fulfillment of the human personality, as understood through natural law, made for "an easy adjustment of the Catholic conscience to American society."[27]

26. Ibid., 250–51.
27. Ibid., 251–53.

Ferdinand Falque

Where Dinneen and Wilson were sometimes giddy in their praise of American capitalism, seeking to appeal to a broad range of Catholic readers, Rev. Ferdinand Falque was a strident combatant of all things liberal. Falque was a former faculty member of St. Thomas College in St. Paul, Minnesota, and a pastor in Staples, Minnesota, a depressed railroad town. By his own account, he was raised in a poor family of nine children in Wisconsin, his father an employee of the Northwestern railroad. The decaying status of the railroad worker in Staples mirrored a trend nationwide, precipitated largely by the mass production of the automobile and the increasing popularity of the airplane.[28] In Falque's view, however, the responsibility lay squarely on labor unions and government handouts.[29]

The National Association of Manufacturers (NAM) was the most influential voice in promoting the principles of a free-market economy and served as the mouthpiece for the ownership and management class. Falque was frequently published in the pages of the NAM's periodicals and pamphlets, and he even participated in the lobbying group's radio broadcasts. Falque's tracts were also published by a conservative foundation owned by a Roman Catholic, Arthur L. Conrad, who served as the foundation's president.[30] No doubt Falque's unabashedly polemical style served the interests of both the NAM and Conrad's foundation, as he made no efforts to hide his contempt for union leaders and "materialistic liberal[s]," whom he pictured as out-of-touch intellectuals living in ivory towers and glorying "in the appellation of 'egg head.'"[31]

Another favorite nemesis of Falque's was the Social Action Department of the National Catholic Welfare Conference. Falque came to the

---

28. By 1930, railroad capacity had dropped nearly 70 percent from the previous decade as a result of the automobile. See Joel Dinerstein, *Swinging the Machine: Modernity, Technology, and African American Culture Between the Wars* (Amherst: University of Massachusetts Press, 2003), 150; cites "Fortune Round Table—Transportation Policy and Railroads," *Fortune*, August 1939, 50.

29. Letter from Rev. Ferdinand C. Falque to Msgr. George G. Higgins, August 1, 1954, The American Catholic History Research Center and University Archives (hereafter ACUA), Catholic University of America, Washington, D.C., Box 32 (Ferdinand C. Falque Folder), George Gilmary Higgins Papers.

30. ACUA, Box 32 (Ferdinand C. Falque Folder), George Gilmary Higgins Papers. One radio appearance on a NAM broadcast took place on an ABC radio program called *It's YOUR Business*, September 22, 1956.

31. Rev. Ferdinand C. Falque, "Liberalism 'in the Guise of Uplift,'" *Homiletic and Pastoral Review* 57 (January 1957): 327.

attention of the then assistant director of the SAD, George Higgins, with a 1954 article appearing in *Pastoral Life,* a periodical designed for priests. In "The Theology of Work," Falque declared that "the solutions of the ills of modern society are all theological," and they involved, first, recognizing original sin. "Modern liberalism," he wrote, "has been in error and it has been begetting a world of chaos" as a result of separating the concepts of love and work from "their essential element, pain." Pain was sanctifying, and without it, "work has no redemption," just as "without the Cross love is the fuzziest of all concepts." The modern labor movement and advocates of "social justice" were guilty of regarding "work as an evil, instead of regarding it as a means of overcoming evil" through its nobility. "Social Justice," he opined, "often means little more to labor reformers, than getting more for doing less." In fact, capitalists in the ranks of management had been afflicted with this non-Christian materialism, leading to the abuse of the capitalist system—"a system compatible with Christian virtue in its basic principles, but gone hogwild in the 'liberal' view of mankind." Of most concern was the fact that

> high and holy Catholic doctrines like that of Christ's Mystical Body is made to serve arguments for cooperatives, based on materialism, greed and bureaucracy. The dignity of work, is expounded as the nobility of picketing. You can find it all in a dozen avant garde Catholic periodicals of more or less doubtful authorization calling themselves "liberal" or "worker" organs. They are heavily sprinkled with quotations from Papal Encyclicals, but check deeper these same Encyclicals and you will find them completely at variance with the "liberals." Catholics with a Catholic instinct, fortunately have not been misled in great numbers.[32]

Higgins responded to Falque's article in his syndicated column, The Yardstick, by calling the article an "unrestrained indictment of the American labor movement" and "the most sweeping thing of its kind we have ever read in a Catholic publication." The accusations, Higgins claimed, were too generalized to allow for rebuttal. "With the exception of poor St. Joseph, no individual or organization is mentioned by name. . . . On

---

32. Rev. Ferdinand C. Falque, "The Theology of Work," *Pastoral Life,* May–June 1954, 23–26; George G. Higgins, "Merits Condemnation," The Yardstick, June 7, 1954, found in ACUA, Box 32 (Ferdinand C. Falque Folder), George Gilmary Higgins Papers.

the one hand, he seems to be saying that St. Joseph, were he living in twentieth century America, would be opposed to the letter and the spirit of the social encyclicals."[33]

Falque's article struck a nerve. Higgins received dozens of letters from conservatives echoing Falque's sentiments and defending his claims. Shortly thereafter, Higgins and Falque began exchanging letters, beginning with Falque's reply to the Yardstick column that had addressed his article. "Your leftish knack of twisting what I wrote then attacking it sanctimoniously, leads me to believe you are not in good faith," wrote Falque. "My article makes two points clear," he stressed. "It states that all social effort not based on the true Christian concept of work in light of the doctrine of Original sin is futile. It brings out the fact that modern labor reforms are for most part [sic] based on pagan concepts of work." And, in what appeared to Higgins to be a direct swipe not only at groups like the Catholic Labor Alliance and the ACTU, but also at the SAD itself, "it points out that quite a few self-styled labor movements in the Church, not the Church's official stand, are seeking to accept all the tenets of pagan social liberalism and merely apply Catholic doctrines to them."[34]

Higgins took a month to reply. "I am extremely sorry that my column has offended you so deeply," he wrote, "but frankly, Father, I cannot agree with you when you say that the column 'constitutes slander,' any more than I can agree with you when you say that I have 'twisted' the meaning of your article." Higgins accused Falque of an ad hominem attack when he used the word "leftish" to characterize his views: "No hard feelings, but I honestly think it would be better to approach the subject objectively instead of imputing motives or casting aspersions on one another's integrity." The remainder of the letter sought to illustrate that Falque's position was not as "clear" as Falque believed it was and attempted to press Falque on specifics as to what he believed would constitute justice. Did he oppose the forty-hour workweek? If not forty, how many hours did he advocate? What did Falque mean by "collectivism"? Was he using the term "in the accepted encyclical sense of the word, or ... giving it a specific meaning of [his] own?" Quoting Falque's words back to him, Higgins wrote, "in the last paragraph of your letter

---

33. Higgins, "Merits Condemnation."
34. Letter from Ferdinand Falque to Msgr. George G. Higgins, June 25, 1954, in ACUA, Box 32 (Ferdinand C. Falque Folder), George Gilmary Higgins Papers.

you state rather patronizingly that 'if this is all new and shocking to you, you are living in a very constrained fool's paradise.' I won't even try to answer that one. I will merely say as good naturedly as possible that I feel that at least I am in good company."[35]

Falque's response came in just two days. He expressed dismay that Higgins had attacked his article written for a "distinctively clerical magazine" in a syndicated column appearing in popular newspapers, assuring that most of Higgins's audience would never have the opportunity to actually read Falque's words. Then Falque began to get to the heart of the matter, his attitudes toward Higgins and the NCWC. "The flavor and tendencies of your column must have been of a leftish nature for a long time," Falque jabbed, "because I cannot tell you how many lay folk have written me that they made an effort to get my article because as they put it, 'if that column was against it, it must be really good.'" Falque was "not grieved or hurt by the controversy otherwise," for he had "lost faith and confidence in anything with the NCWC on it more than a decade ago, already." He clarified his point to say that this did not reflect a loss of confidence in the bishops themselves but rather only in the "mass of literature turned out by the bureaucracy, heavily tinged as it has been for years with a brand of uplift that can be turned to almost anything, Socialism and Communism included." His swipes at Higgins as a prominent representative of the NCWC continued:

> I certainly do not carry the Church on my shoulders and my attitude has been that its [sic] not my business. If it were I'd clean house quickly and staff the outfit [the NCWC] with fewer but better scholars. Its [sic] a commonplace among priests that somebody you studied with, who was always a bluff, usually blossoms into a great figure in the NCWC. During the last several administrations they even got close to Roosevelt etc. etc. I have known Bishops too who were glad to get them promoted there so as to be relieved at home. These are sordid realities, but it doesn't help to kid ourselves that they are not so.[36]

Correspondence between the two men was sporadic after 1954. After Falque delivered a controversial address to the seminarians at the

---

35. Letter from Msgr. George G. Higgins to F. C. Falque, July 30, 1954, in ACUA, Box 32 (Ferdinand C. Falque Folder), George Gilmary Higgins Papers.

36. Letter from Ferdinand Falque to George Higgins, August 1, 1954, in ACUA, Box 32 (Ferdinand C. Falque Folder), George Gilmary Higgins Papers.

Benedictine Saint John's University in Collegeville, Minnesota, he reappeared on the radar screen of the SAD. His address was on the liturgical reform movement, but it was significant in its connecting the impulses of that reform to those in the realm of economics. Both movements suffered from a common defect in the way they viewed the world: "On the valid truth that man is a social animal has been superimposed here the fallacy that man is a collective animal. The two are not the same, yet they have been confused." The attempt to make the laity active participants in the Mass and the collectivist impulse in economics ignored the truth that the value of cooperation was ultimately the sanctification of the individual. The individual had been forgotten, Falque warned, and subjugated to the group will. For social action to be authentically Catholic, it had to "arise from interior and very individualistic love." The individual layperson observing the Mass while engaged in personal prayer and reflection was a better reflection of the theology of the Church than the collective responses of the *missa recitata*. Making the leap to economic policy, Falque claimed that "it is not a mere coincidence that enthusiasm for the liturgical movement in the superficial and professional sense is strongly tied to collectivism and materialism in the social and economic spheres. A supernatural Marxism has been achieved. I should rather say a theological Marxism, under terms and slogans of the supernatural." In the wake of this theological Marxism, "we have [Vincent] Gieses of Fides fame, the John Cogleys and so many other *Commonweal* Catholics, the labor priests and their labor chatter, the alliance of the labor movement as it exists and has existed in the United States, based on purely pagan concepts of man and work, canonized by the Monsignor Ryans, the Bishop Haas's and the Monsignor Higginses."[37]

Though Falque's critiques of Higgins and others by name caused an uproar (one witness claimed that the written speech was mild compared to the off-the-cuff remarks Falque made), the most surprising aspect of the speech was the fact that it was delivered at Saint John's University, a center for liturgical reform, and directly attacked the university for its participation in the "theological Marxism" that Falque described. Higgins described his reaction as "one of sorrow rather than anger. I feel sorry for the poor fellow." Paul Marx, O.S.B., a faculty member who witnessed the speech, described Falque as a "strange man," "irrational,"

37. Ferdinand Falque, "Address to Seminarians at Saint John's University," March 1957, copy sent to Higgins by Paul Marx, O.S.B., March 26, 1957, in ACUA, Box 32 (Ferdinand C. Falque Folder), George Gilmary Higgins Papers.

and "not to be taken seriously." Higgins, in a memo to a colleague, hypothesized that Falque was "a little unbalanced," though following up with the aside: "I admire his peculiar kind of courage for lambasting the poor Benedictines at Collegeville right in their own backyard."[38]

Unbalanced or not, Falque's views challenged what had been emerging as the orthodoxy among Catholic activists for social reform. He was even willing to make his case in a conservative Protestant paper called *Christian Economics,* a rare ecumenical gesture for a conservative Roman Catholic priest in 1957. He compared Catholic liberals to the flawed advocates of the Protestant Social Gospel movement: "They have let themselves become ardent supporters of the 'welfare State' under the guise of Christian liberalism and a Christian concern for the betterment of society." While well-meaning, they "have been so taken up with what they call social justice as to forget that Society is but the multiplication of individuals and that justice is a virtue in persons." In doing so, both Protestants and Catholics of this stripe were guilty of "playing into the hands of philosophers and statesmen who hate Christianity and are out to destroy it, but getting every manner of Christian cooperation because they talk glibly of humanitarianism, one worldism, brotherhood, racial harmony, and the like." It was not long before Higgins openly chastised Falque for writing in a "Fundamentalist" Protestant publication "which regularly promotes a line of thought or point of view . . . which can hardly be classified as orthodox from the standpoint of Catholic teaching."[39]

The debate between Falque and Higgins is illustrative of a common dynamic that sets in when the participants in any disagreement share a common mythology. While personal invective is sometimes avoided, accusations that the sacred texts reflecting the mythology have been misread or misunderstood—in this case, the encyclicals—is common, followed by appeals to other authorities (such as bishops), followed by questions regarding one another's orthodoxy. The latter is often accompanied by associating one's opponent with individuals or groups that those who share the common mythology are likely to view with distaste

---

38. Ibid.; letter of Paul Marx, O.S.B., to George Higgins, March 27, 1957, in ACUA, Box 32 (Ferdinand C. Falque Folder), George Gilmary Higgins Papers; memorandum from George Higgins to Monsignor Carrol, March 29, 1957, in ACUA, Box 32 (Ferdinand C. Falque Folder), George Gilmary Higgins Papers.

39. Ferdinand Falque, "Misconceptions of Social Justice," *Christian Economics* (January 22, 1957), in ACUA, Box 32 (Ferdinand C. Falque Folder), George Gilmary Higgins Papers; Higgins's Yardstick response in ACUA, Box 32 (Ferdinand C. Falque Folder), George Gilmary Higgins Papers.

(Marxists or fundamentalists). In this case, Falque's lack of rhetorical discipline and penchant for attacking the jugular appeared to have served him poorly in contrast to Higgins's comparatively restrained criticisms.

Falque's worldview was not restricted to attacking liberals. He developed his own constructive approach to economics, or what he called a "moral capitalism." His outlook was premised on his faith in the eternal spirit. Christ taught that "we should not fear those who kill the body but rather fear those who kill the soul," Falque wrote. We could meet our material needs with proper spiritual development. Poverty and social dislocation were not a structural problem but a moral one that had to be met with charity. Liberal social reforms were based on the flawed belief in human perfectibility: "In the face of Christ this philosophy denies that the poor we shall always have with us." Because charity sprang from individual freedom, it was compatible with capitalism—the sort found precisely in the United States. "This is why," Falque argued, "a capitalism that was Christian, but possessing every human defection, could nevertheless produce and distribute countless material blessings and benefits for our age, when the best planned and protected materialistic regimentations cannot give their hungry millions bread." For Falque, the true Catholic was the true capitalist as well. Capitalism honored the individual, while liberal progressives believed "the only thing . . . higher than man [was] the crowd, the community, numbers." Like the capitalist, "the Catholic knows that man is not essentially perfectible. He knows that government, labor unions, co-operatives, education, religion, social uplift can all be vitiated and that they are often deviated from their true purposes into achieving exactly the opposites. This is because the true Catholic mind remains aware of original sin and its consequences."[40] In line with the entrepreneurial spirit, the true Catholic, like the capitalist, was "willing to take a chance on man just as God took a chance on him." This demanded giving individuals freedom. While the Catholic "knows that concerted brotherhood is the greatest force for good on earth," it had to be "engendered from free wills accepting and working for that which is good. This is not mechanistic brotherhood or mechanistic union; *it is a union engendered by charity.*"[41]

In a sense, Falque's work was an attempt to reorient the work of Leo XIII in *Rerum Novarum* to what he perceived as a new reality. Leo XIII's

---

40. Falque, "Liberalism 'in the Guise of Uplift,'" 325–27.
41. Ibid., 327, emphasis in original.

encyclical worked to counteract the pervasive view that the Church's focus on the spirit and an afterlife left it voiceless in the realm of the material world. *Rerum Novarum* sought to convince the world that the social and economic order was tied to the fate of the Church and sprang from the Church's saving mission. Therefore, the material conditions of humanity had profound moral implications that affected salvation and the soul. While Falque agreed with Leo XIII's position, it is clear he believed that misguided liberal Catholics had taken the significance of materiality too far in the intervening years at the cost of spirituality.

The High Priest of Capitalism

If Ferdinand Falque was the attack dog of pro-capitalist Catholics, Rev. Edward A. Keller was their statistician, if not their high priest, by the 1950s. Keller was the director of the Bureau of Economic Research at Notre Dame University and a well-connected Republican. He once claimed that the primary motive for his economic research was "to refute the economic arguments of the Communists and fellow-travelers in this country who surfaced after Roosevelt's recognition of the Soviet Union." After Herbert Hoover's defeat at the hands of Roosevelt, Keller became close friends with the former president and continued to hold the conviction that Hoover's policies would have brought the country out of the Depression much faster than the New Deal and that the Depression resulted simply from a business cycle that should be viewed as "a normal phase of modern industrial life."

At Hoover's recommendation, Keller worked with Cecil B. DeMille on a private report detailing alleged "Communist infiltration of the Motion Picture Industry" that set the stage for the "now-famous hearings of the UnAmerican Activities Committee." His friendship with DeMille continued throughout his lifetime. In the late 1960s, Keller described his participation in "a small group of anti-Communists who went as far back as the 1930's." DeMille, Hoover, and others were among the "little band" united by their fear of "world Communism," including "Joe Kennedy, Sr., George Sokolsky, Orlando Weber, B. E. Hutchinson (vice president of Chrysler Corp.) . . . Carrol Reece, J. B. Mathews," and a few others.[42]

42. "Oral History Interview with Edward Keller, C.S.C. (Regarding Herbert Hoover), 1969," UNDA, Rev. Edward Keller Files, A 837, CKEL Box 1: "'Edward Keller, CSC' Personal Papers," esp. 1, 19, 36, 50–52, 56; Edward Keller, "Previous Depressions," *Ave Maria* 42 (August 24, 1935): 225–30.

Keller provided a steady stream of arguments favoring the compatibility of capitalism with Catholic social teachings in the form of pamphlets, articles, and books.[43] To much of the left, Keller was viewed as a "reactionary," and on economic issues, "the right-wing spokesman."[44] His Bureau of Economic Research was rumored to be financed by pro-business organizations like the National Association of Manufacturers, and he certainly maintained ties with the NAM during his career.[45] Though some liberal characterizations painted him to be an extremist, compared to other figures like Falque his rhetoric was quite tame, preferring the power of statistics to impassioned polemics as a means of getting his message across. When possible, he worked to forge agreement with figures in the Church with whom he was ideologically opposed, as he did with his participation as a consultant to a committee dealing with the Industry Council Plan sponsored by the NCWC (a topic that will be addressed more thoroughly in Chapter 6).[46]

Unlike many Catholics involved in the rural life and labor movements who used the encyclicals to authorize criticisms of American economic practices, Keller argued that the "encyclicals do not condemn our economic system of free enterprise but instead give a strong moral foundation for such a system." As a result, "Catholics . . . rejoice as American

43. Allitt, *Catholic Intellectuals and Conservative Politics in America*, 71–72; Edward A. Keller, "Who Gets Our National Income?" *Catholic Digest* 12 (May 1948): 44.
44. Cort, "Capitalism: Debates and Definitions," 221–22.
45. Letter from a Fr. Bertrand, O.S.B. at Notre Dame to a Fr. Jerome, n.d., ACUA, Box 38 (Father Edward Keller's Correspondence Folder), George Gilmary Higgins Papers; see letter from B. E. Hutchinson to Edward Keller, June 19, 1957, with enclosed photograph of Keller at the NAM headquarters, UNDA, Rev. Edward Keller Files, A 837, CKEL Box 1: "'Edward Keller, CSC' Personal Papers," Folder: CKEL Correspondence 1954–60; see also letter from Victor E. Campbell, Director of Clergy-Industrial Relations at NAM, on NAM stationery, to Edward Keller, September 23, 1958. Keller was a representative to a conference sponsored by NAM on June 19, 1958, in Cleveland, Ohio, bringing religious leaders and business leaders into dialogue on the moral implications of social and economic problems. Found in UNDA, Rev. Edward Keller Files, A 837, CKEL Box 1: "'Edward Keller, CSC' Personal Papers," Folder: CKEL Talks, 1959–61. Fones-Wolf, *Selling Free Enterprise*, 264, notes Keller's meeting with NAM manager Noel Sargent before the publication of Keller's book on right-to-work laws, *The Case for Right-to-Work Laws—A Defense of Voluntary Unionism* (Chicago: The Heritage Foundation, 1956). She cites a letter from Noel Sargent to Mr. Harvey Frye et al., March 16, 1955, National Association of Manufacturers Records, Hagley Museum and Library, Wilmington, Delaware, Acc. 1141, Series I, Box 163.
46. The committee, working between 1950 and 1951, was made up of people like Benjamin Masse, Goetz Briefs, Raymond McGowan, George Higgins, and John F. Cronin. Keller was one of several consultants who helped craft a statement on the ICP. See UNDA, "Folder: Industrial Council Committee (National Catholic Welfare Conference) 1950–1951," in Rev. Edward Keller Files, A 837, CKEL Box 1: "'Edward Keller, CSC' Personal Papers."

citizens that their country welcomes rather than repels the advice of the Holy See on the moral problems that pervade our economic life." Those who disagreed failed to see the "real intent" of the encyclicals.[47]

A three part series in *Ave Maria*'s 1947 volume prefigured Keller's 1953 influential study, *Christianity and American Capitalism*, in its style and message. Not surprising, the right to private property was the starting point in Keller's defense of capitalism—a right, he stressed, that had been validated by the encyclicals. The "free enterprise" system of the United States withstood papal scrutiny, for Pius XI had defended "free competition" as "just and productive of good results." It was only the "'unlimited competition' and extreme '*laissez faire*' doctrines of the early English classical economists" that the Church condemned. Such an ideology had never dominated the American system that had always placed restriction on competition to protect its citizenry. The real leviathan Americans needed to fear was the encroachment of government. Contrary to popular wisdom, he argued, the New Deal had released "'big business' from anti-monopoly laws," including the Sherman Antitrust Act, with the passage of the National Industrial Recovery Act. Restrictions that had been in place to protect consumers were repealed. Moreover, the Clayton Antitrust Act of 1914 had provided unions with all the protection they needed, rendering the New Deal superfluous.[48]

A recurring theme in Keller's work was what he considered to be a misconception regarding wealth. Wealth was not a zero-sum game and was central to economic growth. "The encyclicals do not condemn large and superfluous income *per se*," Keller wrote, though he warned that the wealthy had "grave obligations" to provide charity for the poor and needy. But the wealth of the capitalists benefited the poor as well through reinvestment, either in their own businesses or through the purchase of stocks, bonds, and other ventures. These investments brought tools to the shops and factories that enhanced productivity, "not only increasing the opportunity of employment for the workers of the country, but at the same time, making possible an ever increasing standard of living for the workers." It was thanks to the rich, then, that the standard of living for the laboring classes in America was constantly improving.[49] In fact, the rich were not even getting their fair share of the national

---

47. Edward A. Keller, "The Church and Our Economic System: I," *Ave Maria* 65 (March 1, 1947): 263.
48. Ibid. 263–64.
49. Ibid., 263–65.

income. Based on a study by Keller's Bureau of Economic Research, America's wealthy received only 1 percent of the national income after taxes in 1944, compared to 11 percent in 1928. Not only did Keller use these statistics to dispel the belief that the rich were getting richer, but he warned that the trend was ominous. Labor demands for "an increasing share of profits" limited reinvestment and forced businesses to turn to government funding for expansion. "This is socialism," Keller decried, and the greed of the laboring classes was the root cause. When profits were limited, so, too, were the entrepreneurial spirit and the incentive to take risks. Fewer new products and less competition threatened American freedom.

Echoing figures like John Dinneen, Keller saw the capitalist system as a reflection of democracy in which the consumer casts a vote with her "dollar ballot." The risks involved with giving consumers a choice could only be overcome when the entrepreneur was given the chance at a healthy profit. The alternative was to "destroy the freedom of choice of the consumer by dictating what he shall eat and wear; how he shall live; what recreation he shall enjoy, etc." In other words, the alternative looked a lot like communism. Profits and wealth were merely "the cost which a free economic system must pay for the freedom of the customer."[50]

Inflation—a topic of special concern in the early 1950s—was also traced to the growth of labor unions and failed government fiscal policy. High inflation had given consumers the false impression that profits were rising, when the opposite was true, Keller argued. Nor was the expansion of "big business" to blame, for larger businesses were able to operate more efficiently and actually keep prices down. Contrary to distributists, small-scale production would increase costs so significantly that it would wipe out "the very uncertain 'social' gains" that some claimed it would reap. No, it was deficit spending, agricultural subsidies, and the overproduction of money that fueled inflation, not capitalist greed. Greed was a term only applicable to labor unions that had "been able to force increases in their incomes greater than the increasing cost of living." He bemoaned the fact that while union workers made up only a minority of the total labor force, they could drive up inflation for the rest of the nation with their demands. It was "economic fiction"

---

50. Keller, "Who Gets Our National Income?" 44–47; Edward Keller, "Are Profits Too High?" *Social Justice Review* 43 (July–August 1950): 113–14.

that management set prices, he contended. Instead, "management must base prices upon costs which are largely determined by union policy."[51]

Keller's most comprehensive attempt to illustrate that the American capitalist system was consonant with Catholic social teaching came in *Christianity and American Capitalism*. The book was divided into nine chapters, each dealing with an economic topic ranging from "Big Business" to "Big Government" to "Big Labor." Chapters were framed by a collection of relevant quotations, primarily from *Rerum Novarum*, *Quadragesimo Anno*, and speeches from Pius XII (whom conservatives believed to have been sympathetic to capitalism—just as liberals had believed he was suspicious of it). The quotations served the purpose of authorizing Keller's own commentary.

Keller began by stressing that the Church had rejected all forms of socialism, "even when Socialism yields to truth and justice by rejecting false doctrines." Key to Keller's rhetorical strategy, and reflective of his own ideology, were papal statements about economic nationalization and the commonly used phrase "welfare state" as synonyms for the term "socialism." In contrast to the Church's condemnation of socialism stood "American capitalism" that had been "founded on the basic institutions of Private Property, Freedom of Competition, Freedom of Enterprise, and Freedom of Contract. The Social Encyclicals," he emphasized, "do not condemn these institutions." Only the "unrestricted laissez-faire Capitalism" that absolutized property rights and operated according to "blind forces of a completely free and unlimited competition" had been condemned. Because no such system had ever truly existed in America (or anywhere, for that matter), the American system escaped the Church's censure. He even cited McKeon's article in *Social Order* that pitted "New Capitalism vs. Old" to document America's progress, along with a report of the Council of Economic Advisors that narrated a long history of government regulation of capital for the public good in America. Doing this placed Keller in the awkward position of holding up government regulation as evidence for an improving economic system while at the same time calling for decreased regulation and government interference in business affairs.[52]

---

51. Edward A. Keller, "The Morality of Profits: Conclusion," *Social Justice Review* 43 (October 1950): 187–89; Edward A. Keller, "The Morality of Profits: I," *Social Justice Review* 43 (September 1950): 147–49.

52. Edward A. Keller, *Christianity and American Capitalism* (Chicago: The Heritage Foundation, 1953), 13–26, 46–48.

In keeping with the encyclicals, Keller never denied the right to unionize. He was concerned, however, by what he saw as an attempt to blur the lines between labor and management—a risk that involved subverting a natural social hierarchy that had been defended by both Leo XIII and Pius XI. Too many Catholics, under the guise of "freedom of contract," had misunderstood the encyclicals as demanding "a partnership-contract whereby workers would share with owners the right to manage business." These Catholics distorted the "rather mild advice of Pius XI" in *Quadragesimo Anno* that "the work-contract be *somewhat modified* by a partnership-contract" between labor and management, and they painted it as a call for full equality. They were guilty not only of misreading but also of making "what was an observation of secondary importance, a statement of major and mandatory social policy."[53] Moreover, the American system had fulfilled Pius XI's call through widespread ownership of stocks. Though the distribution of stock ownership fell short of Keller's ideal, he saw it as the key to protecting the nation from "being seduced by the siren voice of Socialism." It was not business that stood in the way of this progress but rather the refusal of labor unions to invest more of their coffers in stocks and the "excessively heavy burden of Federal taxation" that undermined the motivation for investment and came "dangerously close to the limit against which Pope Leo XIII warned" in *Rerum Novarum*.[54]

The greatest threats to the freedom of the American people came from "Big Government" and "Big Labor." The growth in government was the most ominous feature of the economy, in Keller's view. Since the New Deal, the government had been part of a modern trend toward collectivism, he warned. He cited a speech of Pius XII's cautioning that "in many countries the modern State is becoming a gigantic administrative machine."[55] Though government posed the greatest threat to freedom, "Big Labor" was a close second. Reflecting the concern of many conservatives in Keller's day, he maintained that "union leaders wield an economic power greater than that of big business." Business owners and

---

53. Ibid., 26–30, emphasis in original.
54. Ibid., 34–37.
55. Ibid., 63; one critic of Keller's, Joseph P. Fitzpatrick, pointed out that Keller had conspicuously left out the passage that preceded Pius XII's quotation. This passage had focused on the dangers of gigantic industrial corporations. To have included it may have threatened Keller's own argument that large businesses are actually better for society as a result of their efficiency. See Joseph P. Fitzpatrick, "The Encyclicals in the United States: What of the Human Person?" *Thought* 29 (Autumn 1954): 396.

managers were the victims in Keller's narrative, bullied by unions that controlled their fate with unreasonable demands. By the 1950s, as described in Chapter 3, the success of labor unions had certainly made it more difficult to portray them as a David facing the Goliath of the captains of industry. For Keller, their growth was "dangerous . . . because it is uncontrolled monopoly power so concentrated and so effective that entire industries can be shut down at the word of a single union leader and the entire economy seriously threatened by crippling strikes in basic industries." Depicting labor as a monopoly echoed the rhetoric of the NAM and a concerted effort to associate unions with monopolies that dated back to the late 1800s.[56] With some irony, Keller described the union leaders as "the laissez-faire individualists of today," skillfully aligning them with the ideology that had been condemned in the encyclicals. "Paraphrasing the 19th century argument used by businessmen," Keller continued, union leaders "say what is 'Good for Labor is good for the country.'"[57]

American unions were tantamount to monopolies, Keller cried. "To minimize the danger inherent in such labor monopoly power is to close one's eyes to reality," he argued. The solution was to hold unions to the same standards as businesses and apply antitrust legislation to them. While "some will argue that subjecting labor monopolies to the antitrust laws would destroy free unionism," because it was precisely a union's ability to unite that gave it leverage, Keller held that "such an argument is just as illogical as the argument that the anti-trust laws have destroyed free business; actually, they have strengthened free business." Furthermore, by preventing "union monopolies," including the AFL and the CIO, another Catholic social principle would be upheld: the principle of subsidiarity. In doing so, "the members of a local union could regain and exercise their personal rights, liberties, and consciences," which Keller felt had been stifled by national union organizations.[58]

All informed Catholics on every side of the economic debate took for granted the need for moral renewal. For conservatives like Keller, however, morality was the precondition for any positive social change and

---

56. Keller, *Christianity and American Capitalism*, 67–68; on the depiction of labor as a monopoly, see Fones-Wolf, *Selling Free Enterprise*, 259–60; she cites Sarah Lyons Watts, *Order Against Chaos: Business Culture and Labor Ideology in America, 1880–1915* (New York: Greenwood Press, 1991).

57. Keller, *Christianity and American Capitalism*, 67–68.

58. Ibid., 72–73.

would transform the social order more effectively than any grand schemes for economic restructuring could. Liberals were continually accused of ignoring this dictum at their peril. "The renewal of morals must, as Pius XI points out, precede the reconstruction of social institutions because the mere changing or improvement of social institutions will not change human nature," Keller wrote. Liberals were guilty of falling victim to the "modern tendency of 'salvation by organization.'" The beauty of this conservative argument that substantive change should only follow moral renewal rested in moral renewal's resistance to measurability. At what point could such renewal prove adequate to precipitate structural change?

Christianity and American Capitalism caused quite a stir, and Keller's critics were not shy.[59] The review that created the most waves was, not surprising, published in George Higgins's Yardstick column. Higgins accused Keller of adding to the confusion regarding Catholic social teachings by utilizing "the familiar device of pinning the Socialist label on those with whom he happens to disagree." Though Keller did not give names, Higgins assumed that the accusation had been pointed at men like Msgr. John Ryan and the late Bishop Francis Haas (a prominent mediator of labor disputes and the first director of the government's Fair Employment Practices Commission in 1943). Presumably, Higgins felt personally attacked as well. Keller's socialist adversary, Higgins argued, was "a straw man of his own creation," given that "there is not a single practicing Catholic in the United States who holds that the wage contract is essentially unjust and therefore must be replaced, in the name of commutative justice, by compulsory co-management or co-determination." On this point, Higgins was willing to wager "a ticket to a Notre Dame football game." Playfully, Higgins noted that Keller himself could be accused of being a socialist in his advocacy of a compulsory strike vote enforced by the government (a tactic Keller believed would take power out of the hands of labor leaders and place it into the hands of rank-and-file members).[60]

---

59. For more examples of these criticisms, see Fitzpatrick, "The Encyclicals in the United States," 391–402; Philip S. Land, "Uncritical Defender?" *America*, March 6, 1954, 603–4; Franz H. Mueller, "Christianity and American Capitalism: A Book Review," *Social Justice Review* 47 (May 1954): 43–45.

60. George G. Higgins, The Yardstick for release the week of February 8, 1954, in Rockhurst University Archives (hereafter RUA), Kansas City, Missouri, "Institute for Social Order" Collection, Box 1. On Bishop Haas, see Msgr. George G. Higgins and William Bole, *Organized Labor and the Church: Reflections of a "Labor Priest"* (New York: Paulist Press, 1993), 30–31.

The review stirred the ire of a young organization based in Chicago, the Council of Business and Professional Men of the Catholic Faith (CBPM). The group cited *Quadragesimo Anno*'s call that "employers and managers of industry" would also organize into associations to promote a Christian social order (sec. 38) as their inspiration. Charged with studying and incorporating "in business practice the social teachings of the Roman Catholic church and thereby to increase love of God and country," as well as with the need "to defend by the vocal and written word, church and country, based on the Constitution of the United States and the Bill of Rights," the CBPM joined the social justice debate.[61] They launched a letter-writing blitz to bishops, Catholic universities, and Catholic periodicals defending Keller's book and taking Higgins's review to task. At the heart of their attack, authored by the chairman of their Social Action Committee, Frank Flick, was the claim that John Ryan and Bishop Haas did in fact deviate from the teachings of the encyclicals. Ryan and Haas, the CBPM believed, advocated the very "compulsory co-management" that Higgins himself had rejected.

The CBPM letter made its way into a handful of diocesan papers, despite the organization's claims that they wished to keep the debate out of the public eye. Higgins responded in both a letter and in a Yardstick column by illustrating what he took to be the CBPM's misunderstanding of the Church's position on "co-management." Marxism, wrote Higgins, taught that the wage contract was unjust by nature, thereby arguing that "compulsory co-determination or co-management is a requirement of natural law or commutative justice." In contrast, *Quadragesimo Anno* defended the justice of the wage contract, rendering codetermination or comanagement "not a requirement of natural law." Citing a recent letter from Monsignor Montini, the Vatican pro-secretary of state, workers did not have a natural right to comanagement. They were entitled, however, "through legitimate means—among which, presumably, collective bargaining is one—[to] seek it as an ideal. In the past, such voluntary agreement granting workers a share in management have been productive, as Pius XI noted. . . . Finally, where the common good indicates the need, the state may legitimately provide that in certain enterprises the workers be given a voice in policy-making." The distinction, then, turned on the question of whether comanagement came voluntarily through

---

61. "By-Laws of the Council of Business and Professional Men (of the Catholic Faith)," in RUA, "Institute for Social Order" Collection, Box 1.

collective bargaining, or whether it was, as the Marxists held, a natural right and compulsory. "If co-determination or co-management is not required by the natural law or commutative justice, it may, however, be required under certain circumstances by virtue of *social justice,*" Higgins replied, citing a list of Catholic luminaries who agreed with his position.[62]

The CBPM responded, essentially, by changing the subject. In an apparent reversal, they stated that they "believe . . . that all American Catholics past and present including yourself [Higgins], Bishop Haas and Monsignor John A. Ryan are in full agreement with the orthodoxy of Father Keller's ideas on co-determination and co-management as expressed in his book." If Higgins rejected Keller's claims that some Catholics taught compulsory comanagement, then "no one is hurt by this statement" because such individuals do not exist. At the very least, Keller's claim might have clarified the point for some Catholics who were confused, and therefore merited praise rather than condemnation.[63]

The debate between Higgins and the CBPM serves to illustrate how much the arguments between conservatives and liberals hinged on their distinctive use of terms—usage often shaped by their sympathies. In the same manner, the encyclicals themselves provided a common language to all Catholics while still depending on individuals to invest that language with distinctive meanings. Conservatives were no more likely than liberals to believe that the United States had achieved the fullness of economic justice, and all pointed to factors in the American system that posed a risk to freedom and human dignity, or seriously inhibited that freedom already. The devil was in the details. Conservatives, urban labor activists, and agrarian distributists were divided on where the risk was coming from. For conservatives, the risk was identified with encroaching government regulations and a growing labor movement. America's capitalist system, they believed, was structurally capable of delivering the sort of just social order that the encyclicals had envisioned. The bedrock of this system, private property and the freedom to use that property—with some limitations—as one saw fit, through a system of competition within a marketplace that guaranteed freedom of contract, would provide the best way to assure just wages, adequate

---

62. Msgr. George G. Higgins, The Yardstick for release the week of May 10, 1954, in RUA, "Institute for Social Order" Collection, Box 1.

63. Letter to Monsignor George Higgins from Frank Flick, Social Action Committee Chairman, CBPM, June 28, 1954, in RUA, "Institute for Social Order" Collection, Box 1.

leisure time, and the ability to develop fully in relation to God. Original sin would prevent the social order from ever achieving perfection, a perfection promised by Marxism. But the communists, as Keller noted in 1947, failed to heed the words of Leo XIII when he said that "to suffer and to endure is the lot of humanity."[64] There would always be differences between the rights of capital and the rights of labor, though the American system freed the workers to join the ranks of ownership through the purchase of stock as well as the right to step forward and compete on their own as entrepreneurs. The failings of capitalism were nothing more than the failings of the human person tainted by sin, and no amount of social planning would change that. By the end of the 1950s, many Catholics continued to embrace the "New Capitalism"—the "People's Capitalism"—that they believed had evolved in the United States, and they resisted calls to change it.

64. Keller, "The Church and Our Economic System," 265.

(5)

Catholics and Right-to-Work Laws

So far, our study has looked at manifestations of the Catholic ideology as they developed within particular organizations or among individuals dedicated to distinctive economic positions, like the promotion of the capitalist system. The remaining two chapters will instead focus on two topics that serve as case studies for making sense of the fissures within Catholic economic thought: debates over right-to-work laws, and the range of attitudes toward the Catholic Industry Council Plan. In doing so, we will see how the umbrella myth of natural law and the mythic texts, *Rerum Novarum* and *Quadragesimo Anno,* informed diverse and at times antithetical conceptions of justice among those attempting to bring the authority of the Church to bear on economic perspectives.

Debates over right-to-work (RTW) laws became the center of national attention during the 1950s and revealed much about the multivalence of natural-law theology as well as the encyclicals themselves. They also help to highlight the way that Catholic discourse was distinguishable from the discursive strategies of non-Catholic parties to the debate, because Catholics of all stripes approached the topic with a vocabulary born of the Church's theology. Issues regarding the obligations of a Christian to join a union, the character of the unions themselves, the preconditions for the establishment of unions, and the role that unions played in the promotion of the Catholic conception of the common good all remained points of contention in the 1940s and 1950s among Catholics in the United States. The compatibility of RTW laws with competing ideals of justice was tested in arguments involving familiar themes such as the dignity of the individual, the principle of subsidiarity, the understanding of the common good, and the rights and duties of both the worker and the employer as demanded by natural law. Notably, however, the right to unionize—in some form or another—was not a viable question among Catholic commentators as it remained with a significant minority of the population at large.[1] Even the staunchest of Catholic conservatives had bowed to the clear language of the encyclicals on this topic. Yet the right to unionize was distinguishable from questions relating to the form, strength, and efficacy of those unions. It was in this gray area that the battle lines were drawn in the RTW debates.

Nonsectarian sources on both sides of the issue used rhetorical appeals to the Constitution, the Bill of Rights, the "Founding Fathers," and the "American way." Catholic sources were cited in nonsectarian books and tracts with surprising frequency. The work of Edward Keller and the Jesuit John E. Coogan appeared often in the literature of the National Association of Manufacturers and other pro-RTW groups, though, except on rare occasions, their theological appeals to concepts like natural law, subsidiarity, the common good, and social justice were glossed over.[2]

The most common discursive strategies in non-Catholic sources aligned arguments with symbolic references that elicited broad emotional appeal. For instance, in a union-published pamphlet, AFL-CIO President George Meany characterized RTW laws as deceptive for failing to "guarantee any right to work to any citizen of our land." Highlighting the "un-American" character of the laws, Meany maintained that the "only country which has a real right-to-work law is Soviet Russia," leaving no doubt in the minds of Cold War Americans that RTW laws were undesirable.[3] William T. Harrison, executive secretary of the National Right to Work Committee and a former union member who had been expelled for taking "violent exception" to the sanctioning of the union shop, published *The Truth About Right-to-Work Laws: The Union Arguments, the People's Case* in 1959. Harrison couched his rhetoric in the Founding Fathers, John Paul Jones, the Constitution, and the Magna Carta. Like some others engaged in the argument, he was not above eliciting God's sanction—though by the common route of identifying the liberty invoked in the Declaration of Independence as deriving by the

---

1. See Derek C. Bok and John T. Dunlop, *Labor and the American Community* (New York: Simon and Schuster, 1970), 19.

2. An example of an exception to this can be found in William Taylor Harrison, *The Truth About Right-to-Work Laws: The Union Argument, the People's Case* (Washington, D.C.: National Right to Work Committee, 1959), 131–33.

3. George Meany, "Labor's View—'Right-to-Work' Laws," pamphlet published by the AFL-CIO and written by George Meany; cited by Harrison, *The Truth About Right-to-Work Laws*, 66.

Grace of the Creator.[4] Catholic debates in the public realm were no less likely to appeal to these sources of authority but were interested especially in aligning their beliefs with the teaching authority of the Church itself.

The Terms of Debate

Before exploring the intra-Catholic debate in detail, it is important to define terms and describe the context of these debates. RTW laws were enacted by individual states, not the federal government. They were crafted to prevent workers from being required to join unions as a condition for employment. Proponents of RTW laws claimed that they were enacted to protect individuals from having to submit to corrupt and dictatorial unions or, in some cases (though with much less frequency by the late 1950s), Marxist-dominated unions. Opponents characterized RTW laws as having no other purpose than to weaken unions and stifle organizing attempts.

The public was often confused by the terms of the debate. It was common parlance to refer to the "closed shop" as the target of RTW laws, yet the closed shop was only one method of ensuring union security and was not the only method outlawed by the RTW laws. The four basic means by which unions sought security were the closed shop, the union shop, maintenance of membership, and the checkoff. Though the specifics of the terms fluctuated over time and were subject to differing nuances from source to source, closed shops required that employers only hire workers supplied by the union under contract. This method, reflecting the practices of the guild system that predated modern labor unions, had actually been outlawed by the Taft-Hartley Act of 1947, but its application as a federal law to only interstate commerce left open the possibility of the closed shop within the states. The union shop allowed employers to hire anyone, but new employees were then given thirty days to join the union contracted by an employer. Because it did not restrict employers' ability to hire the people of their choice, it was perfectly legal under the Taft-Hartley restrictions. The maintenance of membership did not require employees to join the union but did require those

---

4. For instance, see Harrison, *The Truth About Right-to-Work Laws*, 162–63. See also Elizabeth Fones-Wolf, *Selling Free Enterprise: The Business Assault on Labor and Liberalism, 1945–1960* (Urbana: University of Illinois Press, 1994), especially chaps. 8 and 9.

who chose to join to remain members until any union contracts with the employer had expired. In doing so, workers could not cease paying their dues as soon as their union successfully negotiated better contract terms with employers. Finally, the checkoff method of union security simply required that the employer would deduct union dues from the paychecks of those union members who authorized this deduction. The authorization would be valid for one year or until the end of the union's contract, whichever was shorter. According to John C. Cort, "all 'right-to-work' laws forbid the closed shop, the union shop, and maintenance of membership," while only "some also made check-offs illegal."[5]

For decades before the issue came to the public eye, labor unions maintained the necessity of one of these forms of security, favoring the closed or union shops. And for decades—formally since 1903—the National Association of Manufacturers (NAM) rejected the idea of a closed shop in favor of an "open shop." The former appealed to the need for unity and the legitimacy of collective bargaining as a means by which union security could be assured, while the latter appealed to the "American way" and the primacy of the individual over the collective. Even during the Second World War, when leaders of government, business, and labor met and agreed to a three-point program ensuring a coordinated wartime production, including a "no strikes or lockouts" pledge, a promise to handle disputes peacefully, and an agreement that the president could appoint a War Labor Board to handle disputes, the issue of a closed shop could not be resolved. Management was as bitterly opposed to the closed shop as labor was wholeheartedly in support of it.[6] So even in the spirit of compromise inspired by a mutual sense of patriotic duty during wartime, accord could not be reached on this issue. Despite the Wagner Act's protection of the primary forms of union security, the first RTW laws were passed by states in 1944, and with the Taft-Hartley Act of 1947, Section 14(b), states were ceded the right to pass their own laws regarding union security restrictions.[7]

By the end of the 1950s, RTW laws designed to prohibit closed and union shops had been approved in eighteen states, mostly in the South.

5. John C. Cort, "The Battle over 'Right-to-Work,'" *The Commonweal* 62 (April 22, 1955): 75–76; on the nuances in the definitions of these terms, see Jerome L. Toner, *The Closed Shop* (Washington, D.C.: American Council on Public Affairs, 1942), 26–50.

6. Toner, *The Closed Shop*, 23–24; Benjamin L. Masse, "Does the Closed Shop Destroy the Right to Work?" *America*, January 24, 1942, 425.

7. Bok and Dunlop, *Labor and the American Community*, 98–99; Fones-Wolf, *Selling Free Enterprise*, 261.

And virtually all of the RTW states were agricultural as opposed to industrial. Union lobbying had been successful at repealing RTW laws in Louisiana in 1955, though success in Kansas during the same year depended on a gubernatorial veto. Highly publicized attempts by the United Auto Workers to close the factories of the Perfect Circle company through methods that sometimes resulted in violence prompted Indiana, in 1957, to become the eighteenth state to enact RTW laws (they repealed the laws in 1965),[8] though more states had placed some restrictions on "compulsory" union membership contracts.[9]

Increasing demands for RTW laws must be seen in the context of a change in the public perception of unions. Gallup polls from the mid-1930s through the years of Vatican II never showed public approval of labor unions dipping beneath 60 percent; support was on the rise into the first half of the 1950s. Yet the sense that unions were the "underdogs" in a brutal fight with the powerful forces of capital had begun to diminish after World War II. Some polling data showed a very clear downward trend of those who believed "unions should grow larger" beginning at the war's end and continuing for the next two decades. The turning point was 1957, with the beginning of U.S. Senate hearings chaired by John L. McClellan of Arkansas. Between 1957 and 1959, the McClellan hearings (with the help of the young chief counsel, Robert F. Kennedy) exposed substantial corruption in unions, including ties to organized crime and illegal activities by the Teamsters union led by Jimmy Hoffa. Not only did union approval ratings dip from nearly 80 percent to barely above 60 percent within the year, but the number of Americans believing "unions have grown enough or are too large now" rose from 51 percent to 68 percent between 1957 and 1960, peaking at 73 percent in 1963.[10]

   8. Keith Lumsden and Craig Petersen, "The Effect of Right-to-Work Laws on Unionization in the United States," *The Journal of Political Economy* 83 (December 1975): 1237–48, esp. 1237.
   9. Harold G. Vatter, *The U.S. Economy in the 1950s: An Economic History* (1963; Chicago: University of Chicago Press, 1985), 238; Gerard D. Reilly, "State Rights and the Law of Labor Relations," in *Labor Unions and Public Policy*, ed. Edward H. Chamberlin et al. (Washington, D.C.: American Enterprise Association, 1958), 93–121, esp. 110; see also Fones-Wolf, *Selling Free Enterprise*, 261.
   10. Vatter, *The U.S. Economy in the 1950s*, 239; John E. Coogan, S.J., "Pastoral Care of the Labor Unionist," *Pastoral Life* 7 (January–February 1959): 10; on Gallup poll labor approval ratings, see Bok and Dunlop, *Labor and the American Community*, 12–15; on polling data regarding labor's growth being too low or too large, see Opinion Research Corporation, *The Public Looks at 14 (b) and the Right to Work Issue: A Comprehensive, Nationwide Survey of General Public Attitudes* (Princeton, N.J.: ORC, 1966), iv. The particular

Religion played a role in RTW debates across the spectrum. Some labor unions distributed a "booklet containing moral studies of right-to-work laws by Father William J. Kelley, Rabbi Israel Goldstein, and the Reverend Dr. Walter G. Muelder." Protestants participated in the fray over RTW laws as liberals and conservatives staged debates at the meetings of the National Council of Churches (NCC). Unlike Catholics who appealed almost entirely to encyclical references and quotations from representatives of the Church's magisterium, biblical references authorized the positions of Protestant commentators on the debate. The NCC's Department of Church and Economic Life (roughly the equivalent to the NCWC's Social Action Department) drafted a biblically informed statement of "Union Membership as a Condition of Employment" that prompted an "impassioned five-hour debate," remembered as the "longest ever conducted on any single subject" at the council. Conservatives successfully persuaded the general board to table the statement that had been sympathetic to labor interests. *Christian Century,* the progressive Protestant weekly, berated the NCC for not taking a firm stand on behalf of unions.[11]

Catholics on Both Sides of the Fence

This was the context of Catholic debates over RTW laws in the 1950s. As one historian put it, "of the three major faiths, Catholic clergymen were loudest and most persistent in their opposition to laws banning union security."[12] But significant clerical support did not translate into Catholic unanimity on the subject. In keeping with the attitudes of the public at large and despite disproportionate ties to the "working classes" that exceeded those of Protestants and Jews, the Roman Catholic laity were far more likely to support RTW laws than the Roman Catholic clergy.[13] In fact, the RTW debates led to cases of open opposition to members of the hierarchy at times, particularly among Catholic business

---

study was commissioned by the partisan National Right to Work Committee, but the data had been collected by ORC long before the study was commissioned and is a reliable indicator of public attitudes on this question.

11. Fones-Wolf, *Selling Free Enterprise,* 263–65.
12. Ibid., 263.
13. Masse, "Does the Closed Shop Destroy the Right to Work?" 425; "Semantics of Right-to-Work," *America,* March 29, 1958, 744–45.

owners. In New Orleans, for example, a group of sixty-six Catholic businessmen took out a large ad in the city paper to counter their own archbishop, who had gone on record opposing RTW laws as a violation of Catholic principles.[14] By the mid-1950s, despite opposition to RTW laws on the part of the large majority of Catholic clergy, the sporadic voices among the clergy supporting the laws grew louder. After all, the Church never had anything approaching an "official" stance on the topic, and while at times bishops took very public positions on the issue—such as when the six bishops of Ohio released a statement claiming RTW laws "would not solve our problems," or when the bishops of Hartford, Connecticut; Santa Fe, New Mexico; and Spokane, Washington, condemned the new laws—the bishops were not unanimous in their opposition and refused to correlate a stance on the issue with theological orthodoxy.[15] Neither side could claim victory by decade's end.

The ideological battlefields for Catholics engaged in these debates related to questions of maintaining human dignity—especially by preserving human freedom—and fulfilling the common good. Though one might intuitively suspect that individual freedom was pitted against the common good, the truth was that both sides of the RTW issue insisted that its stance best fulfilled both prerequisites for a just social order. The debate played out in the pages of Catholic periodicals, especially in 1957 and 1958. Two of the most lively exchanges took place in magazines aimed especially at the clergy themselves. In October 1957 Edward Keller squared off with Jerome Toner in the pages of *The Homiletic and Pastoral Review*. Toner was a Benedictine priest and the dean of industrial relations at St. Martin's College in Washington. He had authored a monograph on the closed shop in a series on labor published by the American Council on Public Affairs in 1942 and was a protégé of Msgr. John Ryan. Keller had authored a book on RTW laws, a book that Barry Goldwater himself credited with "putting in words" the senator's position on the topic. In a letter to Keller, Goldwater lightheartedly begged Keller's forgiveness for having "plagiarized [Keller's] book considerably" in his own speeches.[16] The following year, John Coogan, a Jesuit with a Ph.D.

14. Cort, "The Battle Over 'Right-to-Work,'" 76.
15. Fones-Wolf, *Selling Free Enterprise*, 273; Bob Senser, "Your 'Right to Work,'" *The Catholic Mind* 56 (May–June 1958), 245.
16. Letter from Senator Barry Goldwater to Edward A. Keller, February 5, 1958, University of Notre Dame Archives (hereafter UNDA), Notre Dame, Indiana, Rev. Edward Keller Files, A 837, Box 1: "'Edward Keller, CSC' Personal Papers," Folder: CKEL Barry Goldwater [1958–70].

in sociology from Fordham University, defended RTW laws in *The Priest*, eliciting a response from John F. Cronin, an editor of the magazine and a prominent voice of the Social Action Department of the NCWC. The intra-clerical dialogue among these figures and others illustrates vividly the difficulties arising from applying natural-law theology and the encyclicals to the nuts and bolts of economic policy.

Freedom and Subsidiarity

Opponents of RTW laws framed their arguments around the rhetoric of freedom, the common good, and the rights and duties of the worker. Contracts between unions and employers were entered into freely. A closed or union shop would not and could not exist unless an employer, weighing the available options, willingly entered into an agreement to create such a shop. The imposition of either federal or state law to impede the parties' entering into such a contract violated the principle of subsidiarity as articulated by Pius XI. As such, it would limit the freedom of the individual worker who benefited from collective bargaining but was always "free, if he values his own bargaining position more than that of the group, to vote against [union] representation." RTW laws also limited the union's freedom to negotiate and the employer's freedom to offer the union a contract that had been freely negotiated.[17] Jerome Toner—no doubt with some irony, given that his debating partner was Keller—held that RTW laws, by inserting the state into contract negotiations, were "a classic case of 'creeping Socialism' clothed in the sheepish appearance of the rights of freedom of contract." Contrary to popular belief, many employers supported union security agreements for the stabilizing effect they had on the work environment and the steady mediator it provided them to work with. Toner listed Radio Corp. of America, Seagram's, and General Motors as evidence. In obstructing an employer's "freedom-of-choice," RTW laws failed to conform to the "basic justice of natural law and the moral order" brought about "naturally and necessarily" by both their objects and their effects.[18]

17. For examples of this argument, see Benjamin L. Masse, "What's Happening to Right-to-Work Laws?" *America*, May 7, 1955, 150; Francis W. Carney, "State of the Question: The Morality of Right to Work Laws," *America*, September 6, 1958, 589; Jerome L. Toner, "Right-to-Work Laws: Unjust and Harmful," *Homiletic and Pastoral Review* 58 (October 1957): 47–48; quotation found in Toner, 55–56.
18. Toner, "Right-to-Work Laws," 47–48, 53–55.

The language of freedom was just as evident among supporters of RTW laws. Keller reflected the majority of RTW advocates when he characterized the debate as one of "voluntary unionism" versus forced unionism and asserted that "Right-to-Work laws are intrinsically moral because they fully protect the wage earner in his natural right to self-organization; they are extrinsically necessary to protect the consciences of the worker and his political freedom." By his reckoning, "the basic moral issue is ... reduced to 'voluntarism,' that is, whether a worker should be permitted the freedom of choice to exercise his right of private association by being permitted legally to join or not to join." RTW laws, therefore, did not interfere with the worker's right to join a union; they merely provided the option of not joining.[19] According to Coogan, the real limitations placed on the worker's freedom stemmed from the unions themselves, which often required oaths of loyalty from their members as well as the payment of dues. He cast the image of an "average workman ... of limited education and ... short of funds," facing "a huge union upon whose favor he *practically* depends." Such a worker was "as outmatched by a huge union as by a huge corporation."[20]

The principle of subsidiarity rested at the heart of the RTW supporters' positions regarding freedom as well. Where opponents of the laws had argued that subsidiarity was violated by the state's interfering with the right of employers and unions to negotiate freely, supporters of the laws one-upped them by holding that the closed shop or union shop violated subsidiarity at its most elemental level: the level of individual choice. Individuals were being denied the right to make contracts freely with their employers. If one was compelled to contribute a portion of his or her salary to union dues and fees, the right to make a basic decision regarding unions was being undercut. True freedom and the principle of subsidiarity went hand in hand, they argued.[21] But even at the level of government, Keller cited Leo XIII's acceptance of state regulation "if

---

19. Keller, "Right-to-Work Laws: Just and Beneficial," *Homiletic and Pastoral Review* 58 (October 1957): 34, 58–59.

20. John E. Coogan, S.J., "An End to Forced Unionism," *The Priest* 14 (January 1958): 26.

21. For examples of this argument, see Goetz A. Briefs, "An Attack on 'Compulsory Unionism,'" in *American Catholic Thought on Social Questions*, ed. Aaron I. Abell (Indianapolis: Bobbs-Merrill, 1968), 515, taken from Goetz A. Briefs, "Compulsory Unionism," *Review of Social Economy* 18 (March 1960); Keller, "Right-to-Work Laws," 34; Coogan, "An End to Forced Unionism," 31–33; Ferdinand C. Falque, "Right-to-Work Laws? Yes!" *Homiletic and Pastoral Review* 58 (January 1958): 344–46.

[unions] professedly seek after any objective which is clearly at variance with good morals, with justice or with the welfare of the State" (*RN* sec. 72).[22]

Dignity and the Common Good

The line between the concepts of individual human dignity (in this case applicable to the question of freedom) and the preservation of common good is a fluid one. Catholic theology defines the common good as that social order that best enables the individual to develop the fullness of the human personality and grow toward his or her ultimate end, union with God. As such, arguments relating to individual freedom on both sides of the RTW debate bled into arguments framed specifically as relating to the common good. For supporters of RTW laws, extending the freedom to avoid unions through legislation served the common good by enabling the worker to steer clear of engaging with sin. The work of the McClellan committee in the U.S. Senate helped bolster the claim that joining a union, in practice, often meant contributing to organizations that were infested by corruption, illegal activity, and in some cases Marxism. Citing a former dean of Harvard Law School, Keller claimed that the McClellan reports verified that "labor unions and their members enjoy privileges and immunities to commit wrongs which no one else can do with impunity." Invoking *Rerum Novarum*, Keller reminded his opponents that "Pope Leo XIII states categorically" that "occasionally there are times when it is proper for the laws to oppose associations of this kind (unions), that is, if they professedly seek after any objective which is clearly at variance with good morals, with justice or with the welfare of the State. Indeed, in these cases the public power shall justly prevent such associations from forming and shall also justly dissolve those already formed" (sec. 38). The constructive engagement attempted by organizations like the ACTU was useless in light of the modern union structure, Keller believed. Echoing Pius XII, Keller feared that personal liberty was being subordinated to "a collectivist order in which morality and rights are determined by the majority vote." RTW laws, therefore, were not only acceptable in the United States, they were

---

22. Edward Keller, *The Case for Right-to-Work Laws: A Defense of Voluntary Unionism* (Chicago: The Heritage Foundation), 78.

"necessary" as a result of "the spiritual dangers to Catholics forced by compulsory unionism to belong to immoral unions, such as communist, socialist, racketeer or mobster-controlled unions; or forced to engage in immoral activities such as illegal strikes, violence and feather-bedding."[23]

Keller was not alone. Ferdinand Falque, whose own pamphlet titled "The True Purpose of Right-to-work Laws" claimed the origins of opposition to RTW laws were to be found in a communist-planned conspiracy, also saw the common good negated by the sinful activities found within unions. Opponents of RTW laws were guilty of following a "school of social thought in the Church which assumes that organization compensates for personal moral defection. . . . Freedom and brotherhood become meaningless proportionately as organization can be substituted for personal choice and personal decision."[24] Coogan and Keller both argued that RTW laws would correct the "gross evils" taking place in unions. Bringing the principles of the free market to bear on the problem, Keller argued that the "best control over a union and its leaders is the power of the members to withdraw from the union." RTW laws provided that power.[25]

Opponents of RTW laws were not blind to the problems within labor unions. The McClellan hearings had assured that any attempts to deny union corruption would be futile. Jerome Toner pointed out, however, that while unions had their share of corrupt individuals, the same could be said for the ranks of management and government. These institutions were not being condemned on the basis of their worst examples. On the contrary, business and government were conspiring through RTW laws to impose an unjust solution on unions. The fact was, according to John Cronin, American unions were "no better or no worse than any other neutral economic organizations." Immorality could be found in all facets of life. The Christian was faced with either abstaining from the world, or engaging in it and functioning as "a leaven, working with the world to raise its standards and win converts to the truth."[26]

Unions were not simply tolerable, opponents to RTW laws pointed out, but had actually been encouraged by Church teaching as a means of

23. Keller, "Right-to-Work Laws," 35, 40.
24. Ferdinand C. Falque, "The True Purpose of Right-to-Work Laws," found in Box 32 (Ferdinand C. Falque Folder), George Gilmary Higgins Papers, The American Catholic History Research Center and University Archives (hereafter ACUA), Catholic University of America, Washington, D.C.; Ferdinand C. Falque, "Right-to-Work Laws? Yes!" 347.
25. Coogan, "An End to Forced Unionism," 27; Keller, "Right-to-Work Laws," 41–43.
26. Toner, "Right-to-Work Laws," 48.

promoting the common good. Both Leo XIII and Pius XI grounded the freedom to associate in natural law as a way of developing the human personality for its union with God. Given that a person had a moral obligation to sustain himself or herself, and that sustenance could not be achieved without laboring, workers were entitled to a just wage, reasonable hours, and healthy working conditions. Without labor unions, in many cases, these prerequisites for sustenance and personality development were impossible. Anything, therefore, that seriously damaged the security of unions necessarily hindered the common good by restricting the worker's ability to address issues of sustenance effectively.[27]

Toner believed that the underlying agenda behind RTW laws was the destruction of the labor movement as a whole. He traced RTW laws to the turn of the twentieth century, when the legislative agenda of the NAM was aimed at opposing unions at every juncture. Unions threatened profits, and the NAM made no secret of its belief that labor unions not only had no right to exist and threatened the American way of life but also threatened Christianity itself. Any law originating with the NAM could never be considered anything less than a direct assault on unionism, regardless of the milder rhetoric with which the NAM couched its agenda, argued Toner.[28]

Maintaining Viable Unions

If sustenance was required to develop spiritually, and unions were a prerequisite to sustenance for some, then the common good was fulfilled by those measures that assured union security, like the closed shop and the union shop. A study defending the need for union security measures by the Jesuit Leo C. Brown, appearing in *The Catholic Mind* in 1955, was frequently cited in the literature of RTW opponents. Under the Taft-Hartley Act, Brown noted, the only grounds on which employees could be dismissed from a union job was for failure to pay union dues. While RTW supporters pointed to such measures as evidence that workers ran

---

27. For examples of these arguments, see Masse, "What's Happening to Right-to-Work Laws?" 150; Toner, "Right-to-Work Laws," 52–54; Carney, "State of the Question," 589; The Bishops of Ohio, "'Right-to-Work' Laws," *The Catholic Mind* 56 (September–October 1958): 477–79, a reprint of a statement issued by the Ohio Catholic Welfare Conference and signed by the bishops of the six dioceses within the state, March 20, 1958.

28. Toner, "Right-to-Work Laws," 48–50.

the roost rather than management, Brown contended that the measure was meant precisely to protect employees who had criticized union leadership from losing their jobs for political reasons. Now RTW supporters were seeking to end the practice of making union dues and initiation fees a condition of employment—a step that would ultimately come back to haunt the workers themselves. The problem, Brown argued, was that "effective and stable unionism is impossible without security," and paying dues and initiation fees were necessary for maintaining that security.[29]

Demographic changes brought his argument into clearer focus. The "unparalleled horizontal and vertical mobility" of the American workforce itself threatened union security. Between April 1940 and April 1947, nearly 60 percent of the "civilian male population over fourteen changed residence," motivated primarily by change in employment. From these statistics, Brown concluded that in order to keep one hundred jobs filled during a ten-year span, more than four hundred people may have needed to be hired. Without a union security contract, union organizers would be engaged in a constant game of catch up, continuously having to make up for losses stemming from worker mobility. A majority of workers originally agreeing to a union may have left the shop within a few years, forcing the continuous enlistment of a whole new crop of workers. Backed by a healthy supply of statistics, Brown concluded that "beyond question . . . in large areas in American industry effective and stable union organization is practically impossible without some form of union security or without a sustained organizing campaign at prohibitive costs and . . . continuing turmoil." The costs associated with such a campaign alone would render the papal injunctions to unionize meaningless on a practical level. Union workers forced to share their shop with an ever-growing number of nonunion workers would find their workplace divided, placing disproportional power in the hands of the employers and enabling employers to drive down wages and limit benefits.[30] This was the principal threat that the so-called scab worker posed to unions, for as long as there were individuals willing to work for lower wages (and depending on the economic climate, there usually were), then the ability of the union to bargain effectively was severely undercut.

29. Leo C. Brown, S.J., "Right-to-Work Legislation," *The Catholic Mind* 53 (October 1955): 606–12.
30. Ibid.

John F. Cronin reiterated Brown's sentiments. Even with the dramatic changes in union empowerment since the 1930s, Cronin felt that "compulsory unionism is often necessary to protect the very right of labor to organize, in spite of assurances that these [RTW laws] do not hinder such organization." Overcoming workers' fear that forming a union would threaten their jobs was only part of the battle:

> Once a majority is convinced, and signatures obtained, the union may petition for an election. At this point the employer could discharge the workers who are most actively pro-union and intimidate the rest. The union has no alternative but to press unfair-labor-practices charges. This can mean a delay of several years through the NLRB and possibly the courts. In the meantime expenses mount, workers leave for other jobs and the union is forced to continue organizing under most unfavorable circumstances. If the union finally succeeds, it must still continue organizing in order to make up for members lost through formal turnover, as well as those who backslide through fear of the employer. The only way this process can be stopped is by the union shop. Then the workers know that their union is secure and that the union itself can be spared the suicidal drain of continuous organizing campaigns. If there is a right-to-work law in the state, then the union might as well give up.[31]

Cronin noted that an adversarial relationship between employers and unions was inherent in the act of organizing, given that organizing stemmed from an emphasis on worker grievances. The paradox that Cronin posed was that the best way to fight class antagonism—an antagonism rendered a distortion of nature by the Church—was to allow unions to establish themselves with less difficulty and support them with security agreements: "Only when the status of the union is finally settled can it devote its energies to constructive relationships with the employer."[32]

Conservative supporters of RTW laws had their own statistics to indicate that RTW laws did not harm unions, individual workers, or the

---

31. John F. Cronin, S.S., "'Forced Unionism': A Reply," *The Priest* 14 (February 1958): 116.
32. Ibid., 121.

general public. Keller had done an analysis of those states where RTW laws had been enacted. Opponents of RTW laws believed that even if the laws had been written with the best of intentions for labor unions, as supporters had claimed, the laws still produced "evil" effects, thus undermining the common good, and rendered "evil" in and of themselves. Keller, however, cited evidence from the National Bureau of Economic Research showing that "the twelve states which had enacted Right-to-Work laws in 1947 or prior showed an increase in union membership of nonagricultural workers during the period 1939–53 of 186% compared to 155.5% for the states which did not have Right-to-Work laws and to 158.1% for the total United States." Making no reference to the possibility that these numbers reflected the fact that non-RTW states had already been disproportionately unionized compared to the RTW states, especially in the South, Keller went on to cite other studies making the same point. One study showed that "of the lowest 29 states in degree of unionization, 12 were RTW states and 17 were non-RTW states. These statistics," argued Keller, "indicate that Right-to-Work laws had little to do with the organization or lack of organization of nonagricultural workers in the various states."[33]

Where Keller's argument was aimed at reassuring opponents of RTW laws that the natural right to unions was fully preserved with their passage, Goetz A. Briefs, a German refugee and professor at Georgetown University, approached the issue of the common good from a different angle. Briefs asked whether unions, secure or not, were a necessity for the common good. Though never questioning the right to unionize, he sought to undermine the assumption that workers and the general public benefited from unions in the big picture. He asserted that unions did not improve the standard of living for the working class, as such, but only the standards of their own members. This resulted in unions competing against one another with one union's success potentially damaging the quality of life for workers everywhere else. Improving wages for the union worker through collective bargaining could result only in three possibilities: "firstly, shifting increased costs to consumers, secondly, from unions cutting the profit margin, and thirdly, from an increase in the rate of productivity." Either way, improved wages demanded consumer sacrifice, a reduction in fringe benefits, or longer hours. Unions were playing in a zero-sum game and unwittingly putting the squeeze

33. Keller, "Right-to-Work Laws," 39.

on the working class.³⁴ If working-class people struggled to make ends meet, they could blame their neighbors or themselves for successfully bargaining for a higher wage. As another RTW supporter reasoned, "if the prime goal of unions is to produce greater wages and shorter hours at an inverse ratio and on a quarter-to-quarter or year-to-year basis, there is serious reason to ask if they are serving the nation well." The end result would be that "when the union man gets his four-day week, the man in the middle will have to increase his own work load or cut down his standard of living."³⁵ If RTW laws did have the effect of weakening unions, the common good would be well served.

Finally, disagreements involving the natural rights and duties of workers were plentiful. Was there really a right to work? Was not the avoidance of sin both a right and a duty? Did the worker have a duty to join a labor union? Did the refusal to join a union where a union existed make that worker a "free rider," benefiting disproportionately from the work of peers? These were "hot-button" questions that drove much of the dispute.

Opponents of RTW laws were placed in the somewhat awkward position of arguing that no absolute right to work existed. The awkwardness stemmed from their concurrent insistence that labor was necessary for sustenance, unions were necessary to ensure adequate sustenance, and joining unions itself was the worker's duty, as they understood the encyclicals. As Jerome Toner put it, while everyone had the right to seek work with whomever he or she chose, workers were ultimately bound to restrictions imposed by the employer, including qualifications for employment and other stipulations. With this in mind, "a union-security contract, that is mutually agreeable to stockholders and management, the majority of the employees and their legal representative—the union," needs to be seen as a legitimate condition of employment and one of the many inherent restrictions on the so-called right to work. Furthermore, the Supreme Court had decided that the "loss of a particular job or position (the 'right to work') is not a loss of life or liberty" and therefore not a violation of the Constitution. Therefore, supporters of RTW laws had no grounds to claim that failure to keep a job or contract for a job as a result of a closed or union shop contract was tantamount to a

---

34. Briefs, "An Attack on 'Compulsory Unionism,'" 511.
35. Frank Morriss, "Right-to-Work Laws? Yes!" *Homiletic and Pastoral Review* 58 (March 1958): 548.

violation of rights. The Supreme Court, Toner held, viewed unions as "voluntary associations," and as such "no one has a legal right to join any voluntary association." Their voluntary nature allows them to restrict individuals from joining. Because there was "*no legal right to join a union,* the corollary legal *right not to join a union,*" which Keller and others had claimed "necessarily rests on the *right to join a union,* is baseless and void."[36]

The director of the Institute of Social Education at St. John's College in Cleveland, Ohio, Francis W. Carney, S.T.D., added to the argument against a right to work. Because all had a duty to perfect themselves through work, there must also be a right to work in order to fulfill that duty. Yet this right was not "absolute and unconditioned." Carney detailed the exceptions to the right: "He has no right to work that physically is beyond his endurance or that will lead to physical injury. He has no right to work that will dull his mental faculties and cause deterioration of his personality. He has no right to work that will place him in danger of wrongdoing or unethical conduct. Finally, a man has no right to work in situations that impede his development as a social being or bring harm upon the society of which he was a part." It was with the last stipulation that Carney rejected RTW laws. Failing to join one's coworkers in a union was tantamount to bringing harm on their society of workers. One "may not in pursuing his own perfection place obstacles to" the perfection of coworkers. The fallacy of the "right" to work laws rested in their failure to acknowledge the conditions associated with the "right" itself.[37]

Neutral Unions

Carney's list of conditions could have been co-opted by supporters of RTW laws on the subject of placing the worker "in danger of wrongdoing or unethical conduct." The right and the duty to avoid sin were tantamount in the eyes of conservatives. As noted, the McClellan hearings validated the fear that in many cases, union membership was tantamount to condoning and supporting sin. The issue of union sinfulness provided an entryway for conservatives to raise an issue that pro-labor

36. Toner, "Right-to-Work Laws," 51–52.
37. Carney, "State of the Question," 588.

Catholic activists had hoped was put to rest with *Quadragesimo Anno*: the morality of neutral unions—as opposed to Catholic unions.[38] Keller's book-length treatment of RTW laws devoted several pages to the concerns expressed by popes, beginning with Leo XIII, of Catholic involvement in associations that were not committed to the social principles of the Church. *Quadragesimo Anno* placed the power of judging the morality of Catholic participation in particular unions with the bishops of the Church. "It is clearly the office of bishops," wrote Pius XI, "when they know that these associations are on account of circumstances necessary and are not dangerous to religion, to approve of Catholic workers joining them keeping before their eyes, however, the principles and precautions laid down by Our Predecessor, Pius X of holy memory" (sec. 35). Pope Pius X, who had been canonized by the time Keller wrote his book, had cautioned that Catholic union members "should never permit the unions, whether for the sake of material interests or their members of the union cause as such, to proclaim or support teachings or to engage in activities which would conflict in any way with the directives proclaimed by the supreme teaching authority of the Church."[39] The issue was not merely abstract. The bishop of El Paso, Texas, Sidney Metzger, had already directed the workers of his diocese to flee from a union the bishop believed to be dominated by communists. Without a Texas RTW law protecting the jobs of these workers when they withdrew from their union, the responsibility extended to the bishops by the popes would have proven unmanageable, Keller asserted.[40]

Despite his admission that non-neutral unions were impossible in the American context, RTW supporter John Coogan found the neutral unions in existence in the United States to be "seriously defective." He pointed to a 1950 statement made by the Catholic hierarchy in the civil province of Quebec. The statement had been prefaced with a declaration by the cardinal secretary of the Sacred Consistorial Congregation in Rome verifying that the conclusions of the Quebec hierarchy were harmonious with the papal encyclicals. The pastoral statement argued that unions are formative institutions for Christian laborers and, therefore,

---

38. See Michael J. Schuck, *That They Be One: The Social Teaching of the Papal Encyclicals, 1740–1989* (Washington, D.C.: Georgetown University Press, 1991), 84.

39. Pius X quoted in Keller, *The Case for Right-to-Work Laws*, 70; Keller cites *All Things in Christ: Selected Encyclicals and Documents of Saint Pius X*, comp. and ed. Rev. Vincent A. Yzermans (Westminster, Md.: Newman Press, 1954), 193.

40. Keller, *The Case for Right-to-Work Laws*, 70–71.

when this formation occurred "in a Christian way," adhering "in its very constitution, to the social principles of Christianity, and if the leaders who shape its actions are capable, through their living faith in the authority of Christ and the Church," such a union was acceptable: "*Otherwise the association will lead the worker astray to materialism; it will imbue him with a false concept of life made known by harsh claims, unjust methods, and the omission of the collaboration, necessary to the common good.*"[41] American unions, Coogan believed, did not come close to meeting these standards. He cited the prominent sociologist Will Herberg, along with Catholic luminaries such as archbishop of North Dakota and leader of the NCRLC Aloysius J. Muench, and an array of pro-union Catholics (whom he knew well to be opposed to RTW laws) like Msgr. John Ryan, Ed Marciniak, and John F. Cronin, as giving testimony to the immorality present in the American labor movement. He expressed his amazement that "almost any John Doe who has given a pat on the back to labor unions can get a headline from Catholic union apologists. But the entire hierarchy of the greatest Catholic region in North America can in our day solemnly proclaim with Roman approval a warning against the dangers of neutral unionism . . . and not rate a line!"[42]

It appears that seeing his name being used in an argument to support RTW laws and condemn neutral unions prompted John Cronin's reply to Coogan. He accused Coogan of misleading readers by using quotations from RTW opponents to support those laws. With direct reference to the hierarchy of Quebec, Cronin pointed out that if Coogan's argument of their opposition to neutral unions was correct, then the bishops of Quebec had placed themselves in an inconsistent position. As Cronin wrote, the Quebec hierarchy was permitting "Catholic unions of that province to engage in merger negotiations with the 'secularist' unions of the A. F. of L. –C.I.O." When this fact was coupled with the claim in the same pastoral letter that Christian workers had an "obligation" to join unions, the weakness of Coogan's argument became clear. If the merger were to take place, Cronin wrote sarcastically, "one shudders at the fate of workers" who read the injunction to join unions.[43]

Coogan had been guilty of decontextualizing his quotations, said Cronin (an accusation that both sides of the RTW debate leveled against

---

41. Coogan, "An End to Forced Unionism," 28, emphasis in original; Coogan makes a similar argument in "Pastoral Care of the Labor Unionist," 10–14.
42. Ibid., 28–33.
43. Cronin, "'Forced Unionism': A Reply," 116.

one another with some frequency). "If a Lenten pastoral, for example, were to dwell upon the dangers of worldliness among Catholics," Cronin explained, "it could be quoted in such a way as to leave the impression that the Church also is a hotbed of secularism." As to the right to belong to neutral unions in America, "doctors, lawyers, businessmen, and farmers also belong to groups that are neutral in regard to religion," and immorality could be found in these groups as well. Compared to European neutral unions, American unions were remarkably well inclined toward religion, he argued. The long history of Marxism and anticlericalism in European unions only served to highlight the quality of American unions in this regard. By Cronin's reckoning, American unions since the early 1950s were more anticommunist than the U.S. government itself, refusing to participate in exchanges or meetings with delegations from any Iron Curtain countries. Also, great strides had been made by unions in ridding themselves of corruption, exemplified most vividly by the AFL-CIO's expulsion of the Teamsters union. In the end, Cronin concluded, RTW laws were designed only to make unionism more difficult. The end result would be their bringing "about more evils than those they purport to cure."[44]

Duty and the Free Rider

The most omnipresent dichotomy invoked by opponents of RTW laws was the belief in one's duty to unionize pitted against the image of the "free rider." The view that the encyclicals prescribed the duty to join a union was common, as discussed in Chapter 3. Jerome Toner explained his "personal *opinion* that there is a *per se* general duty and obligation (although *per accidens* in particular circumstances there may be no duty or obligation), for all employees covered by a legal collective-bargaining contract under federal law in the United States today (1) support and (2) join the union making and executing that contract." Though this was distinct from a "general duty and obligation binding all workers to" form or join a union, he contended that this broader conception of duty had been endorsed by bishops, theologians, and Rome itself. He cited a recent speech by Pius XII teaching "the *duty* and right to organize labor belongs above all to the people immediately interested; employers and

44. Ibid., 117–19, 122.

their workers." The authority of those in support of a general duty to join unions only strengthened his narrower argument that RTW laws were immoral. The free rider was in violation of that solemn duty but was legitimized by RTW laws. "An employee may be opposed to having the union represent him," Toner wrote. "He may consider the union to be controlled by communists, racketeers, radicals, socialists, Protestants, Catholics, Jews, Democrats or Republicans. However, if the prospective employee wishes to exercise his right to work for that collective-bargaining employer, then he must freely, voluntarily, mutually and consensually hire and employ the union to represent and protect him. Those are the legal terms of every federal collective bargaining contract." The failure of the free rider to comply with the terms of a collective-bargaining agreement and withhold support for a union was a failure to comply with the common good. Pius XI's encyclical *On Atheistic Communism* insisted that social justice "demands from each individual all that is necessary for the common good." Toner concluded that "social justice, therefore, demands and commands that each employee working under a legal collective-bargaining contract must join the union that he has hired and employed to represent and protect him."[45]

Keller, like nearly all conservatives, rejected the idea that the encyclicals taught the duty to unionize. He noted that Pius XI had even quoted Leo XIII in saying of private associations that one "is quite free *to join or not*" (QA sec. 87). Keller used extended quotations from Francis J. Connell, C.S.S.R., dean of the School of Sacred Theology at Catholic University; Ferdinand Falque; and Dennis J. Comey, S.J., to support his claim that there is not a "universal moral obligation to belong to a union." Comey, the former president of St. Peter's College in Jersey City, New Jersey, and founder of one of the earliest industrial relations schools at Saint Joseph's College, carried particular weight for his status as a staunch supporter of labor rights; he had negotiated peace between management and the Philadelphia longshoremen's union while simultaneously striving to rid the union of corruption. Keller compared the issue to procreation and the "natural right to marry." It is only in the context of a marriage that procreation (another "natural right") can be exercised morally, he said. "Moreover, marriage must be completely free; if either party to the marriage contract is compelled . . . the marriage is null and void." Keller knew of "no theologian who argues that God has

---

45. Toner, "'Right-to-Work Laws,'" 57–59.

placed an equally strong moral condition on the right to work, namely, that it can be exercised morally only in the association of a union."[46]

As for the free rider argument, conservative economists like Goetz Briefs chose to question whether the nonunionized employee working in a shop with a union that has exclusive rights to bargaining actually benefited from the union. Briefs wrote that in many cases, some of the "highly skilled crafts" within manufacturing industries have actually paid a price for giving up their bargaining rights to larger industrial unions. Like Keller and others, Briefs believed that the improved wages that had been garnered by unions over the years were the result of factors that had nothing to do with the power of collective bargaining.[47]

By far the most creative argument against those Catholics who condemned the free rider came from Francis J. Connell, who was enthusiastically cited by Coogan, comparing the status of the free rider to that of the Roman Catholic Church in America. The free rider argument could be used as easily to force religious organizations to pay taxes on property and income, for they "too receive the benefits of government." Catholics on all points of the ideological spectrum were united in their opposition to taxing the Church. From Coogan's perspective, it would be preferable to recognize how the free rider could contribute to his or her shop by "setting a high example of a conscientious, diligent worker, or by visiting his fellow workers in their sickness," or other means that did not require membership and payment of dues to immoral unions.[48]

By the early 1960s, the RTW debates died down as Americans became consumed by civil rights issues and Vietnam. Catholics also turned their attention to the winds of change that blew from Vatican II. The claims made by Catholics on both sides of the RTW issue did not deviate in substance from those being made in nonsectarian circles. But Catholic debates were set apart by their language and their appeals to distinctively Catholic authorities. The controversy over RTW laws reveals the difficulties that arise when multiple ideological threads intersect to address one issue. What it meant to be "free," to be "just," and to be "fair" were entangled with competing conceptions of "duty," of "rights," and of the morality of social organizations. There was no definitive Catholic answer. While the weight of Catholic clerical voices opposed RTW laws, Catholic

46. Keller, *The Case for Right-to-Work Laws*, 59, 48–53.
47. Briefs, "An Attack on Compulsory Unionism," 510–11; Keller, *The Case for Right-to-Work Laws*, 37–41.
48. Coogan, "An End to Forced Unionism," 34.

supporters of those laws effectively undermined the impression some had hoped to give of a Church that spoke with one voice. They did so by appealing to the myth that they all shared and bringing competing ideological impulses to bear on that myth, always with the conviction that their approach best fulfilled the encyclical call to an authentically Christian social order.

(6)

Industry Councils

Rerum Novarum spoke wistfully of the days when the guild system served as a buffer between the family and the state (secs. 36–38). *Quadragesimo Anno* expanded on this vision with a call for structuring economies according to vocational orders. Rather than be divided by class, Pius XI promoted a socioeconomic system organized according to the economic functions people performed. In the generation before Vatican II, Pius XI's vision evolved into a concept known as an Industry Council Plan among American Catholics and served as their most comprehensive outline for a Christian reconstruction of the social order. *Quadragesimo Anno* was short on specifics, and variations of the Industry Council Plan (ICP) were plentiful—though common threads could be found in all of them. In the same way that an American Catholic's position on right-to-work laws revealed much about the manner in which he or she interpreted the social encyclicals, how Catholics felt about the ICP shed light on the malleability of the mythic texts to suit the needs and preferences of competing economic perspectives. All points of view in this debate were bound by their commitment to seeing the Church point the way toward a just social order, yet divided in their conceptions of precisely where the Church was pointing.

Abolishing the unnatural state of class conflict was at the heart of Pius XI's proposed vocational-group system. The elimination of class division was the duty of both the state and "all good citizens," taught Pius XI, and the "reestablishment of functional groups" was the key to eliminating the tension between labor and management that strained the social fabric. *Quadragesimo Anno*'s analysis held that

> the demand and supply of labor divides men on the labor market into two classes [management and labor], as into two camps,

and the bargaining between these parties transforms this market into an arena where the two armies are engaged in combat. To this grave disorder which is leading society to ruin a remedy must evidently be applied as speedily as possible. But there cannot be question of any perfect cure, except this opposition be done away with, and well-ordered members of the social body come into being: functional "groups"; namely, binding men together not according to the position they occupy in the labor market but according to the diverse functions which they exercise in society. For as nature induces those who dwell in close proximity to unite into municipalities, so those who practice the same trade or profession, economic or otherwise, constitute as it were fellowships or bodies. These groupings, autonomous in character, are considered by many to be, if not essential to civil society, at least a natural accompaniment thereof. (*QA* sec. 83)

Aquinas himself was cited as identifying these functional groups, commonly known as orders, as existing naturally in society. For example, everyone involved in the production of lumber, from the tree farmers to the lumberjacks to those who treated the wood to those who managed the operations and owned lumber companies were all bound by a common task: the production of lumber for the marketplace. Just as each level in this social hierarchy worked toward the same social function, each was vested with the obligation to provide for the common good. With a shared vision, Pius XI argued, harmonious cooperation between all levels conformed to nature. Disharmony was the fruit of human sinfulness. Only the greed of capitalists coupled with the envy stirred up by Marxist rhetoric created an artificial state of class opposition.

The seeds of the vocational-group order *Quadragesimo Anno* described could be found in the work of the German Jesuit economist Heinrich Pesch. In fact, Pesch's protégé, Oswald von Nell-Breuning, S.J., was the primary figure in drafting *Quadragesimo Anno*, and the fingerprints of his mentor could be seen throughout the text.[1] Pesch's five-volume work *Lehrbuch der Nationalokonomie*, written in the early 1920s, was

---

1. John T. McGreevy, *Catholicism and American Freedom: A History* (New York: W. W. Norton, 2003), 150; cites Oswald von Nell-Breuning, S.J., "The Drafting of *Quadragesimo Anno*," in *Official Catholic Social Teaching*, ed. Charles Curran and Richard A. McCormick (New York: Paulist Press, 1986), 60–68; Francis X. Murphy, "Oswald von Nell-Breuning: Papal Surrogate," *America*, October 26, 1991, 293–95; Paul Droulers, *Le Père Desbuquois et l'Action populaire* (Paris: Éditions ouvriers, 1980), 152–56.

called by one Jesuit commentator the "source book" for Pius XI's encyclical. In these volumes, Pesch left his mark with a paradoxical theory of value. Essentially, the "optimum" price of a good was understood to be the "competitive price." At the same time, however, it was competition that led "to a divergence from this optimum." From Pesch's perspective, vocational groups that preserved some competition while loosely regulating prices with the help of consumer groups would best serve to maintain prices at their optimum level. The freewheeling competition of laissez-faire, as much as the state price controls of a communist economy, pulled prices—the market value of goods—away from their ideal levels. The consequences would be felt throughout the economy as either competition would disproportionately pull down the wages of labor in an effort to undercut competitors' prices, or in the communist scenario, true capital expenditures and incentives would be ignored in an effort to maintain labor costs. The cooperation fostered by vocational groups would prevent these undesired outcomes.[2]

While the influence of Pesch on Pius XI's thinking was undeniable, the social environment in which *Quadragesimo Anno* was released was also reflected in the plan for vocational groups. The Catholic conception of society as an organic unity existing to do God's will led to an affinity for the corporative elements of Mussolini's fascistic ideology. In fact, the encyclical addressed Italian fascism directly. It described how syndicates (or unions) were granted official recognition by the state. Corporate bodies "composed of representatives of the unions of workingmen and employers of the same trade or profession" were designed by the state as instruments for coordinating economic activity. In the fascist corporative model, strikes were prohibited and disputes were decided through the intervention of a public authority. Pius XI concluded his overview of the fascist corporate system by judging that "little reflection is required to perceive the advantages in the institution thus summarily described." In its maintenance of "peaceful collaboration of the classes, repression of socialist organizations and efforts," as well as in its application of "the moderating authority of a special ministry," Italian fascism fulfilled many requirements for a just social order (*QA* secs. 88–95).

The problem with fascist corporatism, from Pius XI's perspective, lay not in its structure so much as its aims. The fascist vocational-group

---

2. See Richard E. Mulcahy, S.J., "The Peschian Value Paradox: A Key to the Function of Vocational Groups," *Review of Social Economy* 10 (March 1952): 32.

system had as its ultimate aim the promotion of the Fascist Party and the fascist state. As such, it risked "substituting itself in the place of private initiative" and degenerating into "an excessively bureaucratic and political character." Most important, as a result of the primacy given to the party, the fascist order had the potential of "serving particular political aims rather than contributing to the restoration of social order and the improvement of the same" (*QA* sec. 95). Transforming fascist corporatism into an acceptable system required that its ultimate end be the promotion of Catholic principles (sec. 96). In essence, for corporatism to work, it must develop in the context of the Roman Catholic ideology—an ideology that stood in competition with that of the Italian fascists in its totalism.[3]

In light of Peter D'Agostino's work on "the Roman question," it would be foolish to read *Quadragesimo Anno* in a manner that separated it from its context as an encyclical authored in the midst of the Vatican's attempt to consolidate its renewed status as a territorial authority—an authority granted to the Church by Mussolini with the Lateran Pact of 1929. In this environment, ruling over Vatican City while surrounded by the fascist regime, it is clear that Pius XI aimed at peaceful coexistence and a measure of ideological reconciliation while consistently maintaining the Church's primacy in judging all matters of individual and social morality. Still, for all Pius XI's praise of the structural elements of corporatism—comparing it with the often romanticized medieval guild system (sec. 97)—*Quadragesimo Anno* did offer a "critique of a single state-controlled labor system," as opposed to the Catholic conception of corporative bodies that were meant to be *voluntary* associations. This prompted the retaliation of Mussolini, who shut down the offices of Catholic Action youth groups. Only weeks later, Pius XI retorted with an attack on Italian fascism, *Non Abbiamo Bisogno*, and a climate of crisis ensued that threatened the Lateran Pact. But by the end of the year the crisis had cooled and relative harmony prevailed between the two ideological forces until the late 1930s.[4]

The undeniable parallels between Pius XI's vocational-group idea and central elements of the fascist corporatist system appear to have grown

---

3. On totalism, see Martin E. Marty, *The One and the Many: America's Struggle for the Common Good* (Cambridge, Mass.: Harvard University Press, 1997), 10–11.

4. Peter D'Agostino, *Rome in America: Transnational Catholic Ideology from the Risorgimento to Fascism* (Chapel Hill: University of North Carolina Press, 2004), 224–29, esp. 224 and 228.

from the common romantic visions of societies as organisms working in unison toward the promotion of a particular ideal: the fascist state or the Roman Catholic social order. It is important to recognize that for all the enmity that periodically arose between the Italian fascists and the Church—enmity that Mussolini sought to opportunistically downplay through most of the period between 1923 and 1938—fascism was not yet associated with gas chambers and attempts at global domination. Moreover, while Catholic and non-Catholic historians tend to speak of fascism as a phenomenon of the 1930s and early 1940s, fascism began to dominate in Italy by the early 1920s. Most Catholics in the United States and abroad approached fascism with less enmity than communist and socialist economic orders.[5]

While Catholic attacks on fascism became common by the 1930s, D'Agostino's research revealed only two American Catholic antifascists whose critiques of the system date back to the early 1920s: fathers Giuseppe Ciarrocchi and James Gillis. Notably, the Vatican attempted to silence both of them under pressure from the Italian fascist government. This willingness to engage the Italian fascists resulted largely from the Vatican's efforts and ultimate success at securing territorial autonomy in 1929, and the overriding importance of this issue assured that most Catholics in Italy and the United States maintained an open posture toward the fascist regime. This posture was solidified by the Vatican's acquiescence to Mussolini's reining in the leftist-Catholic Partito Popolare Italiano. The American Catholic press unanimously praised Mussolini for his agreement to the 1929 Concordat, and with the exception of a 1931 standoff between Pius XI and Mussolini over the Catholic Action movement in Italy—which resulted in the publication of the antifascist encyclical *Non Abbiamo Bisogno*—the Vatican's relationship to Mussolini (and the attitude of Catholic intellectuals toward fascism) ranged from neutral to warm until the mid-1930s. Pius XI even awarded Mussolini the Papal Order of the Golden Spur in 1932, just a year after *Non Abbiamo Bisogno* was published! Only with the threat of German fascism and the advent of World War II did attitudes change significantly,

---

5. Many historians have put forward this assessment, including Patrick Allitt, *Catholic Intellectuals and Conservative Politics in America, 1950–1985* (Ithaca, N.Y.: Cornell University Press, 1993), 25; David J. O'Brien, *American Catholics and Social Reform* (New York: Oxford University Press, 1968), 82–86; John P. Diggins, *Mussolini and Fascism: The View From America* (Princeton, N.J.: Princeton University Press, 1972), 182–203; George Sirgiovanni, *An Undercurrent of Suspicion: Anti-Communism in America During World War II* (New Brunswick, N.J.: Transaction Publishers, 1990), 150.

as did attempts to revise the historical record "to insist that the Church had always been anti-Fascist."[6] For our purposes, we must recognize that associations made between Pius XI's corporatism and that of Italian fascists played a role in the failure of the Industry Council Plan—inspired as it was by *Quadragesimo Anno*—to gain long term popularity in the United States.

Americans and the Vocational-Group Order

Beyond the context of the encyclical's composition, the principles of a just Christian social order outlined by Pius XI found a receptive audience among Roman Catholics in the United States. Vocational groups, as opposed to the class-based divisions that marked the capitalist economy, were seen as a viable means of attaining the "natural" organic character of the socioeconomic order that Catholic social activists were prone to believe existed. One of those primarily responsible for translating Pius XI's call to action into a plan for the American economy was John A. Ryan of the Social Action Department.[7] Ryan's 1935 work *A Better Economic Order* built substantially on *Quadragesimo Anno*'s ideas. Because individualism had been "the root cause of all our economic evils," Ryan proposed self-governing "occupational groups" as the primary means of countering the individualistic impulse without lapsing into state-run collectivism. These groups maintained private property rather than ceding industrial ownership to the public. Ryan lamented the demise of a medieval guild system that united masters, journeymen, and apprentices. It had instead given way to the "employing capitalist" and the "propertyless employee." Through the establishment of occupational groups according to "a graded hierarchical order, a system of subsidiary organizations between the individual and the State," class antagonism could be abolished and a sense of common purpose could be restored within the social organism.[8]

---

6. For a thorough treatment of the interplay between the Vatican and Mussolini, see D'Agostino, *Rome in America*, chaps. 6 and 7; on D'Agostino's conclusions regarding the state of American antifascism, see 159–60, 309.

7. George G. Higgins, "American Contributions to the Implementation of the Industry Council Plan," *American Sociological Review* 13 (March 1952): 15. Higgins writes that Ryan increasingly stressed the "industry council plan" after 1931.

8. John A. Ryan, *A Better Economic Order* (New York: Harper and Brothers, 1935), 177–79.

This idea that something was needed to stand between the powerful state and the individual, something that also protected individuals from capitalist exploitation—provided that that "something" looked to Roman Catholic principles as its guide—was key to Pius XI's encyclical and to the work of many American Catholics after *Quadragesimo Anno*. Nearly a decade after Ryan's book, the Jesuit Wilfrid Parsons, a professor of political science at the Catholic University of America, expressed this sentiment vividly when he wrote that "there is now nothing that stands between the individual and Leviathan. Once the individual had the protection of the guild to which he belonged. In fact, in a pluralistic world he belonged first to his guild and then to the State." In the world of medieval Europeans, Parsons elaborated, "the guild, not the individual, was the real member of the State, in the sense in which Pius XI uses the word *member*, we had an organic society composed of cells of which the individual was a member."[9] Guilds, like vocational groups suggested by *Quadragesimo Anno*, served as a buffer between the individual and the state.

Harold Francis Trehey's book-length treatment of vocational groups was one of the most influential in the development of the Industry Council Plan. *Foundations of a Modern Guild System*, published in 1940, was a revision of Trehey's dissertation under the direction of John Ryan at the Catholic University of America. His book outlined practical steps toward the implementation of a guild system in America. The system would be based on seven principles—principles that continued to be rearticulated in variations of the Industry Council Plan that circulated over the next twenty years. Beginning with the principle of organic structure as a counter to the "atomistic-mechanistic conception" of society that recognized only individuals and the state as constituting society as a whole, the social order was defined as a "collection of classes, 'orders,' or occupational groups which form living organs in the social body" and whose cooperation was needed "for its health and prosperity." The principle of subsidiarity would keep higher orders, especially the state, from assuming too much authority. Classical liberalism, Trehey taught, prevented individuals "from forming associations to govern their own lives free from governmental interference since it created conditions which could only be remedied by the State." A measure of autonomy

---

9. Wilfrid Parsons, S.J., "The Function of Government in Industry," *The Catholic Mind* 31 (March 1943): 8, emphasis in original.

would be achieved with subsidiarity, coupled with the principle of self-government to enable workers and employers to organize free from state interference.[10]

Autonomy, both for the individual and the free association, had limitations, and individual rights were not all equal in value (the right to life, for instance, superseded the right to property). Trehey explained that groups and societies possessed a "hierarchy of rights" that was evident in his fourth principle, graded structure. Through this principle, the social order was arranged according to a hierarchical ranking. This was reflected in the ranking of social groups in the modern guild system, in which local organizations of labor and management would, when necessary, cede authority to regional groups, who in turn would cede authority to national groups. For this authority system to function effectively, the vocational order would require the principle of public-legal status to be maintained. Subsidiary occupational groups were to be public bodies in that the rules and regulations that they agreed to would have the force of law within the state. Failure to include an enforcement mechanism, Trehey argued, would render these groups impotent.

Like the medieval guild, membership in the modern guild would not be optional for those seeking to participate in a profession or industry, in the same way attorneys could not practice law without being a member of a bar association (private institutions with a publicly recognized status). "In the society of Catholic social teaching," Trehey wrote, "each Guild would be a self-governing quasi-State, with a right to existence just as valid as that of the State itself, yet subordinate to it in those matters included within the State's proper jurisdiction." Finally, these guilds would be bound to the principle of the common good, working to promote an environment that allowed for the "harmonious development of a person's natural perfection." As such, guilds, and especially the state, had to abide by Trehey's last principle, that of intervention. Deviating from the anarchist leanings of some in the Catholic Worker movement, Trehey argued that "adequate social order demands that some authority, whose sole reason for existence is to protect and promote the good not merely of individuals but of all, should have the power to supervise [i.e., intervene in] the activities of all." Ultimately, it was up to the state to

---

10. Harold Francis Trehey, *Foundations of a Modern Guild System* (Washington, D.C.: Catholic University of America Press, 1940), 1–2, 44–53.

fulfill its "God-given" role as the protector and promoter of the common good, for the member groups within the social order "could not or would not concern themselves effectively with the good of all."[11]

The reestablishment of the organic social order that Trehey described depended on spiritual renewal, and logically, Trehey pointed to the Roman Catholic Church as the guide to such a renewal. Acutely aware that parallels between the Catholic and fascist visions of a corporative order had become a substantial liability by 1940, Trehey vigorously denied the connections, claiming instead that the "Catholic Church is, and always has been a defender of liberty, and of the innate and inalienable rights which are the basis of American democracy." Two decades before John Courtney Murray's famous attempt to do so in *We Hold These Truths*—and in the same year Luigi Ligutti and John Rawe applied a similar tactic in *Rural Roads to Security*—Trehey grounded democracy and democratic principles in the work of the Angelic Doctor himself, Thomas Aquinas. It was a move that would likely have confused his priestly counterparts in Rome and throughout Europe. The modern guild system described by Pius XI and elaborated on by Trehey was merely carrying on the Catholic tradition of protecting the very liberty and democracy so dear to his American audience.[12]

By broadening our scope, we may begin to see the call for a modern guild system or a vocational-group order as an element of the Roman Catholic ideology that was especially appropriate to the situation of the Church in that era. Having been conceived as a territorial Church for centuries, it had functioned as both a state and a spiritual institution mediating the grace of God in the world. The tumultuous consequences of the rise of the nation-state, paired with Enlightenment liberalism, directly challenged the Church's self-conception. Even with the restoration of territorial authority through the Lateran Pact in 1929, the Church remained at the mercy of an erratic fascist regime for its territorial integrity. In a sense, just as the individual in the modern world was at the mercy of the state—a state that either let capitalists have free reign or that substituted itself for the capitalist—the Church was at the mercy of the state as well. Without the support of the state, either through the active promotion of the Church's agenda or through a policy of toleration

11. Ibid., 55–59, 62–69.
12. Ibid., 1–2, 12.

for that agenda, the Vatican feared the Church would be powerless. With the voluntary creation of intermediary organizations like guilds, a new venue for the promotion of the Roman Catholic ideology would be established at the same time that the power of the state's hold on the individual would be weakened. Guilds created a buffer zone not only for individuals but for the Church's hold on the people as well. Of course, if those guilds were established by and answerable only to the state, as the fascist system dictated, they would be of little use to the Church and would fail to serve the protective function they had been envisioned to serve in *Quadragesimo Anno*.

American Precursors to the ICP

The Industry Council Plan evolved from Roman Catholic ideology but had American inspirations as well. Ryan and Trehey, after all, developed their ideas against the backdrop of the New Deal. The National Recovery Administration (NRA), the primary element in the National Industrial Recovery Act passed by Congress in Roosevelt's first one hundred days, was seen by both men as evidence that the vocational-group order they envisioned would eventually become a reality. Roosevelt described the NRA as a nationwide plan for "the regulation of production." The act established industry-wide codes governing working hours, minimum wages, production, and business conduct. In all, 557 separate codes for industries were established with the NRA. Congress set aside antitrust laws. Leaders in major industries worked to draw up the codes with a goal of sustainable development aimed at putting people back to work and maintaining growth over time. The NRA was nothing short of a planned economy, though the promoters of the idea were not primarily government figures; they were leaders of big businesses in America. In fact, it was the head of General Electric who introduced the proposal that became the NRA, and consequently, the fruits of the NRA were reaped primarily by large corporations at the expense of small businesses. Despite establishing the most sweeping protections of labor unions and collective bargaining the nation had seen, labor was largely excluded from the decision-making process in the NRA. Consumers also had no voice. These factors, combined with a well-organized Republican attack on the plan, diminished the NRA's popularity. By 1935, the Supreme

Court ruled the NRA to be unconstitutional due to the powers the act granted the federal government to regulate interstate commerce.[13]

Despite its having failed, both Ryan and Trehey took the NRA to be a precedent for the future ordering of vocational groups. Though faulting the NRA for failing to include the full participation of workers, consumers, and small-business groups, they believed that with adjustments that granted these groups full participation in drawing up the industrial codes and implementing them, the NRA could be made acceptable. Shortly before the NRA was found unconstitutional, Ryan had expressed fears that the program was more likely to slip into fascism than into the sort of occupational group system that he had in mind. Though he welcomed the Church's compromise with fascist Italy in the Lateran Pact and downplayed the theological challenges that accompanied the move, Ryan was one of the few American Catholics to publicly proclaim his wariness of fascism as early as 1926, and his concerns remained evident in 1935. Yet the very attempt of the NRA to employ comprehensive economic planning to sustain growth and jobs was encouraging from Ryan's perspective.

The rhetoric Ryan used in support of the act pushed the boundaries as he called on discouraged Catholics who had given up working toward implementing a vocational-group order "to reflect that it [the NRA] is the only practical alternative to Fascism or Communism, even in our beloved country: hence they ought to realize that inaction is *apostasy from Catholic social principles and treason against America*."[14] Five years after the NRA had failed, Trehey pinned the blame on both the lack of worker involvement and the "dominant lack of moral standards and adequate social education."[15] In keeping with the Church's taxonomy of the social order that sees itself as the essential legitimating feature of any social arrangement, Trehey's second critique was not unusual among Catholics who lamented the NRA's demise.

As the 1940s began, Pius XI's vocational-order plan maintained a tenuous hold on the American Catholic imagination. Ryan, Trehey, and a handful of other vocal activists promoted the idea, but much of their

13. George E. Mowry and Blaine A. Brownell, *The Urban Nation, 1920–1980* (New York: Hill and Wang, 1981), 85–101.
14. J. Ryan, *A Better Economic Order*, 187–88, 176, emphasis added; Kevin E. Schmiesing, *Within the Market Strife: American Catholic Economic Thought from "Rerum Novarum" to Vatican II* (Lanham, Md.: Lexington Books, 2004), 87; D'Agostino, *Rome in America*, 214–18, 186–89.
15. Trehey, *Foundations of a Modern Guild System*, 178.

early energy was expended deflecting charges that the plan was fascistic. Virtually every article written in support of Catholic corporatism in the 1930s alluded to this charge and felt obliged to rebut it. The Catholic ideal was democratic, these authors claimed. "Fascist corporations do not blend the two factors of production, capital and labor, but only prevent them from indulging in disputes," wrote Charles Bruehl, a Catholic sociologist. In contrast, he continued, "the Pope's vocational groups are autonomous bodies, built on the combined interests of capital and labor and free to adopt their own regulations." Yet even as he tried to distinguish the Catholic plan from that of the fascists, Bruehl nodded to the "well-deserved praise which the Holy Father bestows on the achievements of Fascism with regard to social and moral improvements."[16]

By 1941, however, the movement for a vocational-group order was significantly recharged thanks to the work of Philip Murray, the head of the CIO. Murray—who, as we noted in Chapter 3, was a Catholic educated in the social teachings of the Church—proposed a plan to coordinate U.S. production in the face of impending warfare, and he actively promoted his plan in the pages of Catholic periodicals. The failure of American industry to respond adequately to the needs of World War I resulted from a lack of coordination and planning, Murray argued. He offered a proposal calling for the coordination "of several groups in the vital defense industries, labor, management, consumers and government." Murray wanted to meet the needs of defense and presented his ideas to President Roosevelt in a two-hour meeting. The plan would be called the Industry Council Plan, named after its primary feature, national industry councils in each of the important sectors of the defense industry. Labor and management would be equally represented from each industry and would coordinate all elements of production. He hoped that his plan would "reduce to a minimum the possibility of industrial disturbances, strikes, or stoppages occurring in any of these industries," because the councils would facilitate "the process of joint reasoning" and "intelligent collective bargaining to settle disputes." Government would coordinate production, and the chair of each committee would be a government representative as a way to maintain, Murray argued,

---

16. Charles Bruehl, D.D., "Structure of Vocational Groups," *Homiletic and Pastoral Review* 38 (February 1938): 450; other examples of attempts to defend the plan from an association with fascism include George T. Andrews, "Order in Industrial Economy," *The Modern Schoolman* 14 (March 1937): 56–57, and Edward Mooney, D.D., "The American Tradition," *The Catholic Mind* 36 (June 8, 1938): 217.

impartial leadership. Government, using competent economists and statisticians, would also provide "facts" to the councils to guide them in setting policy.[17]

Murray's Industry Council Plan was never implemented, and the governing board established by the Roosevelt administration during wartime to handle production was not modeled along industry council lines. Murray's plan lacked the comprehensive quality of a vocational group encompassing an entire industry beginning at the plant level and rising through a graded hierarchical structure extending to regional and national councils. Instead he favored a system composed of elites from each industry. Still, many Catholics saw Murray's plan as an encouraging sign, reflecting some of the rudimentary elements of *Quadragesimo Anno*. John C. Cort of the ACTU wrote that Murray's idea was "at least representative of [a vocational group], forming an initial connecting link between the two halves, employers' association and union." This link, Cort believed, "could easily serve as the beginning of a common organization."[18]

Others, like Leo Brown, S.J., a prominent sociologist and director of the Institute for Social Order at Saint Louis University, argued that Murray's plan as it stood did not conform adequately to Catholic principles as articulated in the encyclicals. In lieu of natural, organic vocational orders, Murray's plan offered an artificial construction for the benefit of existing elites and was nothing more than a glorified labor-management committee. The only thing separating the plan from the NRA, which favored big business over small companies, was the addition of the highest ranks of labor in the decision-making process. "I find it hard to see," Brown wrote,

> where these principles (the principle of subsidiarity and the principles of social justice and social charity) compel us to throw the weight of Catholic thought behind a socio-economic structure, basically composed of organized labor and organized capital, fused together in some way at a second or higher stage of

---

17. Philip Murray, "CIO Looks Forward," *Christian Social Action* 6 (January 1941): 10–12; Murray, "Looking Forward," *Christian Social Action* 6 (June 1941): 187.

18. Aaron I. Abell, *American Catholicism and Social Action: A Search for Social Justice, 1865–1950* (Garden City, N.Y.: Hanover House, 1960), 267–69; John C. Cort, "Are We Missing a Bus? Why Not Support the Murray Industry Council Plan," *The Commonweal* 36 (August 14, 1942): 394.

the economic hierarchy.... Merely joining a large labor union to a large trade association does not, by the fact of juxtaposition, knit them together. It is entirely conceivable that such a structure would point up class warfare in a much more violent fashion.[19]

Catholic supporters of Murray's plan favored it not so much for its detail as for the direction in which it pointed. It inspired similar plans by other labor leaders, including Walter Reuther, then vice president of the United Automobile Workers, whose plan included consumer representatives on industry councils to ensure their working for the general welfare of the public. It was not long before programs like Murray's and Reuther's were being considered as a means of achieving social justice in peacetime as well as in war, and all the talk about economic planning became the subject of intense scrutiny among Catholic intellectuals in the pages of the American Catholic press.[20]

Developing an American Catholic Plan

With several plans competing for attention, each with its own name and distinctive terminology, cultivating momentum for a "Catholic plan" was difficult. In response, the American Catholic Sociological Society (ACSS) created a committee in 1946 aimed at not only examining the feasibility of vocational groups in the American economy but also more clearly defining and labeling precisely what sort of economic system they were proposing. So many different titles had been given to the proposals originally outlined by Pius XI in *Quadragesimo Anno*, and each title conjured up different images. The ACSS committee rejected the titles of "Papal Plan for Reconstructing the Social Order" and "Pius XI's 'Industries and Professions,'" because they were both too long and too closely associated with sectarian Roman Catholic origins to have broad public appeal. Harold Trehey's phrase "Modern Guild System" was rejected for being too closely tied to a system that had already failed. "Vocational Group System" was rejected for sounding too vague and being too easily

---

19. Brown quoted in Abell, *American Catholicism and Social Action*, 269.
20. Murray, "Looking Forward," 192; see also Robert L. Shannon, F.S.C., "The Industry Council Plan as an Instrument of Reconstruction," *Review of Social Economy* 1 (December 1942): 87–99; and John Brophy, "The Industry Council Plan," *The Commonweal* 49 (November 12, 1948): 110.

confused with religious vocations. Another widely used title, "Occupational Group System," was favored by many in the committee for its emphasis on the "natural group," deemed essential to its philosophical defense, and because it embraced all professions rather than being restricted to those in industries. Several also favored the title "Industrial Democracy," though it sounded more like a slogan to some than a plan for economic restructuring. In the end, and somewhat peculiarly, the committee settled on the title "Industry Council Plan." That the title had already been used by the CIO chief, Philip Murray, prompted some reservations among those who feared that the plans would be confused. Yet Industry Council Plan was ultimately deemed to indicate "the essential element of the idea (the council) as well as the focal point of the problem (industry)," and from that point forward, Catholics co-opted Murray's title for their own program to implement the changes called for in *Quadragesimo Anno*. The ACSS committee quickly became known as the Industry Council Committee and continued to meet for over a decade.[21]

Now that the plan had a name, it needed to be defined. The Industry Council Committee sociologists revised the definition seven times between 1948 and 1953. The original definition reflected Murray's own focus on unions working with associations of employers to plan production. At the same time, the committee wanted to emphasize an expansive scope of economic planning not limited to a national governing board for each industry. Their 1948 definition identified their plan as being "based on democratically selected councils of employers' associations and labor unions which would meet to discuss and solve problems on the local, regional, and national levels." The definition was judged simple and straightforward, while preserving the multivalence of the encyclicals themselves in allowing for a wide array of possible implementation strategies. By 1953, complaints that earlier definitions left no room for consumer and agricultural representation had influenced the committee's attitudes, as had the increasing public cynicism regarding the role of government control in economic planning. These concerns were reflected in the seventh definition of the Industry Council Plan, identifying their conception as "a proposed system of social and

---

21. Gerald J. Schnepp, "Ten Years of the Industry Council Committee," *American Catholic Sociological Review* 17 (March 1956): 30; Schnepp, "Let's Call It the Industry Council Plan," *America*, February 21, 1948, 572–73.

economic organizations which would be functional, democratic, legally recognized but not government controlled, and balanced to achieve the recognition of both individual rights and the general welfare."[22] The transformation illustrated a notable increase in specificity regarding the principles of the ICP, while at the same time being considerably more vague than the 1948 definition with respect to the ICP's structure.

A Top-Down Versus Bottom-Up Approach

While the ACSS was active in promoting the Industry Council Plan, few promoters were as prolific and prominent as the NCWC's Social Action Department and the ACTU. Both organizations tried to garner support for the ICP among both Catholics and the general public through articles, pamphlets, and the curriculum of labor schools. Even before Philip Murray's plan, *The Michigan Labor Leader*—an early incarnation of the Detroit ACTU's *Wage Earner*—had begun an almost weekly barrage of articles calling for "Corporatism Now!" The papal plan for vocational groups, the paper claimed, aimed at avoiding "economic dictatorship," promoting healthy competition and a "revolutionary form of social change" directed toward a true "economic democracy."[23]

The barrage continued in ACTU newspapers for over a decade. Yet, as discussed in Chapter 3, the SAD and the ACTU differed considerably in structure and strategy, and while their common interest in promoting labor unions and infusing them with Catholic values made them frequent allies, fissures would sometimes develop. While both organizations supported the ICP, they emphasized different means of implementing it. Under the leadership of Raymond McGowan and George Higgins, the SAD tended to envision the ICP's coming to fruition primarily through legislative initiative. As early as the Bishops' Program of 1919, which

---

22. Schnepp, "Ten Years of the Industry Council Committee," 31–32; Schnepp, "Let's Call It the Industry Council Plan," 573; Joseph B. Schuyler, S.J., "The Industry Council Idea: Is It Adaptable to the United States?" *American Catholic Sociological Review* 18 (December 1957): 293; 1953 definition quoted from Schuyler in Mary Eberdt, C.H.M., and Gerald Schnepp, S.M., *Industrialism and the Popes* (New York: P. J. Kennedy and Sons, 1953), 1–3. The book was the product of two committee members and emerged from the work of the Industry Council Committee.

23. "Corporatism Now!" *The Michigan Labor Leader*, July 19, 1940, 4; "Corporatism ... and Competition," *The Michigan Labor Leader*, July 5, 1940, 2; "Industry Councils Will Speed Victory," *The Michigan Labor Leader*, January 9, 1942, 4.

was replete with calls for legislative change, the SAD concentrated on lobbying efforts—efforts made even more visible through John Ryan's close personal ties to Roosevelt and the New Deal administration. McGowan carried on Ryan's emphasis on government's important role in economic planning. In a 1938 address to the National Catholic Social Action Conference, McGowan stressed that "a government must . . . so regulate property, income and work, and competition and the new domination by wealth, corporations and finance, that the people will all have work and all have a good livelihood." Furthermore, government must "as far as possible, protect, foster, rely on and guide the people's own organizations in industry, farming, trade and the professions so they themselves will be establishing justice and promoting the general good."[24]

Needless to say, ensuring that all Americans had "a good livelihood" as well as viable mediating organizations on which to depend presented government with an enormous responsibility. But the set of principles guiding government behavior, McGowan argued, "justifies a far-reaching program of laws and government action." While the aim of legislation was to "devolve as much power as possible on organized industry and the professions so they themselves, the growing Christian Social Order itself, can do the job of ending the unemployment, the poverty and the waste," the first step was drawing up and passing good legislation. In McGowan's view—one that appears to have prevailed within the SAD—there was, "in Catholic social teaching . . . no trace of anti-government."[25]

The SAD, under McGowan's leadership, put out a statement in 1949 calling for a new labor law that would "go beyond governmental guarantee of collective bargaining and government intervention to settle disputes." With an eye toward industry councils, the preamble of this law should declare government's support of labor-management cooperation, while adding teeth to the plea with the creation of "a federal committee made up of all departments and agencies dealing with business and labor to search out ways of encouraging" this cooperation. These committees, the SAD implored, should then be extended to "regions, states and to cities" as well.[26]

24. Neil Betten, *Catholic Activism and the Industrial Worker* (Gainesville: University Presses of Florida, 1976), 41–44; Raymond A. McGowan, "Government and Social Justice," *The Catholic Mind*, June 8, 1938, 223–25, from a speech delivered May 1, 1938.
25. McGowan, "Government and Social Justice," 223–25.
26. "Labor Legislation: Statement of the Social Action Department, National Catholic Welfare Conference, Signed by Reverend Raymond A. McGowan, the Director," *Catholic Action* 31 (February 1949): 3.

In the same year, McGowan's eventual successor, Msgr. George Higgins, complained that the Wagner Act, while an important step, did not go far enough in fulfilling the Christian economic ideal. Higgins proposed a new labor law that would substitute for Taft-Hartley and "lift the sights of the Federal Government" toward a more expansive plan of labor and management cooperation. Though it went "without saying that government cannot—and dare not even attempt to—force cooperation upon industry and labor," because cooperation was voluntary by definition, it could still legislate to "encourage labor-management cooperation by writing into the preamble of the new labor law a forceful declaration favoring the cooperative approach and by writing into the text of law itself a number of provisions designed to implement the philosophy of the preamble," as the SAD's official statement had suggested. All of this was meant to "point the way towards" industry councils. Later in 1949, Higgins articulated the SAD's agenda by holding that while the long-term goal was the establishment of the Industry Council Plan, the promotion of "piece-meal legislation" was an essential and practical way to enact social change. Assorted laws were not enough, but a vital step along the path toward "the organic reconstruction of the social order."[27]

Higgins and the SAD were quite conscious of the risk that overreliance on legislation could "innocently lead us into statism." But their means for implementing the Industry Council Plan relied heavily on government assistance. Certainly their experiences with the Depression and the New Deal had reinforced their conviction that legislation was the most effective and efficient way to enact sweeping social change. Of course, the SAD was also a branch of the organized structure of the American Catholic hierarchy, clergy working on behalf of the bishops. The fact that they tended to argue for the implementation of the ICP from "the top down" was in keeping with the worldview of the NCWC's own membership, especially prior to Vatican II.[28]

In contrast, the ACTU—particularly its most prominent spokesperson, John Cort—tended to advocate a "bottom up" approach to enacting the ICP. Unions, while often supporting legislation to benefit workers, had

---

27. George G. Higgins, "Cooperation Rather than Conflict," *Catholic Action* 31 (February 1949): 4–5; Higgins, "Social Action Program of the National Catholic Welfare Conference," *Review of Social Economy* 7 (September 1949): 37–38.

28. George Higgins, "Toward a New Society," *The Catholic Mind* 54 (November 1956): 631.

traditionally viewed government intervention in labor-management relations as potentially damaging to their long-term interests. Government interference often undermined the power that came with the threat of strikes and was rarely as effective in promoting workers' interests, they believed, as collective bargaining. Like all ACTU members, Cort was a unionist, and this attitude was reflected in a late 1948 article for *The Commonweal*. Following a string of statements made by the American Catholic Bishops and the SAD supporting the ICP, Cort had grown weary of the rhetoric and feared that the ICP would "remain just another eloquent appeal." Admitting that he had been guilty of promoting the ICP "as seen from above" in his own column, he asked his readers to consider "the approach from below." After all, because Catholics were supposed to support the principle of subsidiarity, they should "try a little harder to apply the Industry Council Plan on the plant level while we're waiting around for a sympathetic government to show up." Since World War II, nearly three thousand labor-management committees had been formed, commonly called Joint Production Committees. But only a fraction of these committees remained intact after the war had ended. Still, despite the low numbers of those that remained, they were "more than the number of industry councils we have operating at the present time." Though businesses resisted cooperation, "what evidence there is indicates that reconciliation [between management and labor] can be made by men who have the mind, the heart and the will to do it." The Joint Production Committees were the first steps toward the goals of the ICP, and Cort reasoned that "we should concentrate on walking before we run."[29] Cort's approach reflected the ideology of the ACTU that took its task as serving as "leaven" to the union movement and promoting Catholic values to one small group of unionists at a time. The fact that it was an organization made up exclusively of lay members, as opposed to the SAD's clerical makeup, may have also influenced the affinity for an approach "from below."

Christian Industrialism?

In one of the articles in which John Cort advocated adopting the ICP from the bottom up, he instigated a debate that revealed another deep

---

29. John C. Cort, "The Labor Movement: Reform Begins at the Plant Level," *The Commonweal* 48 (October 1, 1948): 597.

division within the Roman Catholic camp. The Catholic Worker movement had long involved itself in addressing the plight of the industrial worker. It assisted in the organization of strikes and promoted legislation benefiting the working class, though most members—led by the group's cofounder, Peter Maurin—rejected Roosevelt's NRA, believing that it did not go far enough toward controlling the ill effects of capitalism and could lead to fascism or another form of statism. Moreover, they were never satisfied with the makeup of labor unions as they existed in the United States as a vehicle for organizing a Christian social order. Industrial unions, especially, were viewed as a far cry from the guilds embraced by Pius XI. Standing in firm opposition to mass industrialism, which it saw as endemic to a flawed capitalist system, the CW was unapologetically utopian in its outlook. Only an agrarian-distributist social order could conform to the mandates of the Christian faith.[30]

Cort's October 1, 1948, article on the Industry Council Plan in *The Commonweal* provided him with an opportunity to critique the Catholic Worker perspective on industrialism. Despite the CW's being one of the primary intellectual inspirations for both Cort and the ACTU as a whole, the visions of the two movements had diverged significantly. The English distributist and ideological beacon for the CW, Eric Gill, asked the question, "Can mass production be reconciled with the demands of the human personality?" While the question was a good one, Cort wrote, the CW wrongly assumed that the answer to the question was "no." "It's really tragic," he continued, "that so many young zealots have been sold on the more romantic and intolerant editions of agrarianism without first asking either themselves or Dorothy Day the question: How do you know the answer is 'no' when you cannot point to one example of an industrial enterprise that has earnestly and intelligently tried to reconcile the two, and failed?" As Cort and most ACTU activists saw it, the dehumanization that accompanied industrial capitalism stemmed from its being directed toward unrestricted profit and conditioned by greed rather than being directed toward the common good by self-maintained controls—the sort hoped for with the ICP. Those businesses that had tried to do the right thing found themselves crushed by unscrupulous competitors. The ICP could change that. "To paraphrase Chesterton,"

---

30. Betten, *Catholic Activism and the Industrial Worker*, 70–72; Dorothy Day, "Days Without End," *The Catholic Worker* 1 (April 1934): 3–4.

Cort wrote, "Christian industrialism hasn't failed because it has never been tried."[31]

Cort's swipe at the heart of the CW anti-industrial worldview precipitated a debate in the pages of *The Commonweal* that raged on for months. The first respondent to Cort's article was Philip Burnham, a maverick Catholic intellectual and a regular contributor to *The Commonweal*. Burnham questioned Cort's use of the term "Christian industrialism" and regarded it as an oxymoron. Mass-production industrialism fostered "two possible extremes of social and personal organization," Burnham wrote. It could breed either "a suffocating unitary centralization" or "a freezing divisive separateness." Large-scale industrial production required the "central and unitary organization and control of men and resources in their economic existence. The larger the industrialism, the wider the centralization." Centralization meant that the freedom of the laborer was diminished while the importance of the laborer grew as a result of the "extreme interdependence of economic parts and functions." The result had been the explosion of population in the cities "in a particular kind of heaped-up, inhuman conurbation, for which even that isn't a bad enough word," Burnham exclaimed. The individual as a commodity had been splintered from society. "Have the Christian industrialists developed such remedies," Burnham asked, "that they are willing to junk reformers [like CW activists] who do away with the dominance of industrialism itself?" For the agrarian distributist, the problem of industrialism did not lie in the question of who controlled the factories or "whether the boss represents widows and orphans and worthy capitalists, or the hands that work the machinery, or the undifferentiated humanity which must live, one way or another, on the stuff produced." The problem with industrialism was industrialism itself.[32]

Cort responded by weeding through Burnham's words and focusing on the issue of "mass production." The word "mass," Cort argued, was being abused in Burnham's commentary. Cort "thought that 'mass production' meant that technique of producing large quantities, through the use of machinery, which has made it possible to distribute to a large number of people." The assertion that "greed and profiteering" have plagued mass production was not the same thing as arguing that they

---

31. Cort, "The Labor Movement," 597.
32. Philip Burnham, "Christian Industrialism?" *The Commonweal* 48 (October 8, 1948): 609–10.

were inherent to it. From a practical standpoint, Cort maintained that "overwhelming bigness of our giant corporations [is] not essential to efficiency." In contrast to conservative economists like Edward Keller, Cort thought that smaller, decentralized production centers were more efficient. Still, it was not the massive scale of industry that tainted it; it was human sinfulness. Moreover, Cort viewed Burnham's remarks as an opportunity to tease the Catholic Worker for its inability to balance its distaste for heavy machinery with the benefits it reaped from that machinery. Recalling that Eric Gill had devoted an entire article to justifying his use of a typewriter despite his condemnation of the method by which the typewriter had been produced, Cort asked rhetorically: "Okay, Mr. Gill. Industrialism as we know it stinks. Monopoly capitalism stinks. But how are you going to produce typewriters cheap enough so that men like yourself can buy them? Gill never answered that question." Cort maintained, "it wasn't his line. His line was sweeping condemnation, eloquent, bitter and usually wrapped in a hard core of truth and righteous indignation. But a constructive, carefully-thought-out blueprint of how typewriters could be produced cheaply and still not violate Christian values? That was much too difficult," Cort concluded.[33]

Cort reprinted sections of Robert Ludlow's response in *The Catholic Worker* to Cort's earlier statements that characterized the fundamental difference between the CW and the ACTU as resting "not only in the extent to which we [the CW membership] accept industrial methods, but also on the question of class collaboration." It was on this point that Cort and Ludlow seemed to be talking past one another. Ludlow had written that the ICP, whether at the state or plant level, "assumes class collaboration. This we reject as an impossibility under the capitalist system and as a betrayal of the workers." Ludlow's phrasing left him open to the charge of disagreeing with the social encyclicals in their call for class harmony. The specifics of the CW position were somewhat more refined. From early on, Peter Maurin had expressed his disappointment with elements of *Quadragesimo Anno* that he took to have "not [held] up the ideal of personal responsibility voiced by [Pius XI's earlier] encyclical on St. Francis of Assisi" as well as it could have. Maurin and his compatriots at the CW feared the encroachment of the state on every facet of human life above all and believed that if *Quadragesimo Anno*

---

33. John Cort, "The Labor Movement: Is Christian Industrialism Possible?" *The Commonweal* 49 (October 29, 1948): 60.

was not read comprehensively, within a broad framework of Catholic personalism, it risked being seen as calling for too great a role for the state. Organizations like the ACTU, the YCW, and others that were willing to operate within the framework of the existing capitalist order distorted what the CW took to be the authentic meaning of the Church's teachings. When Ludlow rejected class collaboration, the rejection stemmed from his belief that class itself was a by-product of a capitalism his organization rejected wholesale. The key to eliminating class antagonism was not the institution of an adequate network of grievance committees or even the greater cooperation of labor and management, but the abandonment of industrial capitalism in favor of an agrarian-distributist social order. "Under the capitalist system," he later wrote, "class war is inevitable and cannot be dissolved except by a dissolution of acquisitive class society." The vocational groups that Pius XI spoke of should be thought of as only a starting point, "minimum programs" that "should not prevent us from going beyond them to the advocacy of a society which (economically) would be distributist or communitarian." Still, Ludlow's stated rejection of class collaboration left Cort challenging the CW's commitment to the encyclical teachings and belittling their ideology as "extreme Wobbly stuff with an agrarian twist" having "nothing to do with Christianity or with Catholic Doctrine."[34]

Letters poured into *The Commonweal* to defend the Catholic Worker position. Elbert Sisson defended the philosophy of Eric Gill while castigating "the secular reformers" such as Cort, the ACTU, and the Social Action Department of the NCWC: "Father Higgins and his colleagues eschew the radical approach of distributism. Theirs is the approach of the specialist and the bureaucrat." Even the organization of the NCWC reflected the unhealthy compartmentalization of the industrial production process: "The Department of Social Action at the NCWC will refer you to specialists in the Department of Education if your question be in that field, or to Family Life should your concern apparently be there." This fragmentation illustrated the breakdown of the personalist approach to Christianity within Catholicism itself. "Mr. Cort and the NCWC officials," wrote Sisson, "like good little specialists and bureaucrats, probably see nothing objectionable in dealing with religion, the family, economics,

34. Ibid., 60–62; Dorothy Day, "Days Without End," 3–4; Day, "Catholic Worker Celebrates 3rd Birthday: A Restatement of C. W. Aims and Ideals," *The Catholic Worker* 3 (May 1936): 1, 6; Robert Ludlow, "Communications," *The Commonweal* 49 (November 19, 1948): 139–40.

Catholic Action all as separate unrelated items. The vision of the restoration of the *whole* man in the family, in work, and in the community is to Mr. Cort, perhaps, 'romantic.'"[35]

Dorothy Day's son-in-law David Hennessy wrote that looking forward to "Christian Industrialism" was tantamount to looking forward to "'the Trinitarianism of Mahomet' and the 'Military Strategy of the Quakers.'" Industrialism and the nature of the human person were irreconcilable, and "that is why Mr. Cort will look forever in vain for a Christian Plan, for only so long as man remains whole he remains Christian." The "evil essence of industrialism . . . reduces man to a subhuman condition of intellectual irresponsibility." Pius XI had said so himself in *Quadragesimo Anno* when he referred to the factory as "an instrument of strange perversion." It was Cort and the ACTU who were truly guilty of impracticality, not the CW. Their benediction of the ICP ignored the reality of industrialism in favor of their hopes for an industrialism that could never be. In keeping with personalism, Hennessy judged that no soul was worth sacrificing in the attempt to reconcile the irreconcilable: industrialism and Christianity.[36]

Nearly a month later, Father Daniel Cantwell of the Catholic Labor Alliance castigated Hennessy for using a quotation from one of Cantwell's articles to help bolster Hennessy's argument. Cantwell made clear that he was on Cort's side of the debate. Agrarianism, though worthwhile, noble, and worthy of promotion, should not be approached "as an absolute and a dogma." The CW's strategy was, for Cantwell himself, "distressing and wearying." Borrowing from the work of Father Victor Dillard, S.J., Cantwell suggested that if Christ had come to earth in modern times, Christ's love for steel would have matched his love for wood, "and that He would have become a steel worker" instead of a carpenter.[37]

Cantwell's letter prompted Philip Burnham to rejoin the fray. He chided thinkers like Cantwell and Cort for speaking as though the archetypal worker being discussed

> were the great, brawny, bare-chested man at the forge, glistening with honest and highly esthetic sweat. It is something the

---

35. Elbert R. Sisson, "Communications," *The Commonweal* 49 (October 29, 1948): 66.
36. David Hennessy, "Communications," *The Commonweal* 49 (October 29, 1948): 63.
37. Daniel M. Cantwell, "Communications," *The Commonweal* 49 (November 19, 1948): 139.

way leisure-class women like their men to be "civil engineers" who build steel suspension bridges before breakfast. These romantics make "know how" what it is in current advertising. Industrialism appears as the fascinating night glow over the colorful valleys of Allegheny County, and as the beautifully marshaled loading platforms of Detroit with those abstract masses whose poetry Sheeler paints capably for modern museums. "Trade Union" becomes the contemporary equivalent of "the Church," and Industry Council Plan substitutes for Augustine's prognostications on the City of God. Father Cantwell lets us suppose that Christ "would have become" a steel worker. The historic fact is, Christ was a carpenter and a wanderer, Who lived as a man in Palestine about nineteen hundred years before the assembly line was invented in America.[38]

Burnham went on to suggest that the romanticism of the industrialists was also misguided for celebrating an economy that was ceasing to exist. "The current economy," he wrote, "and evidently the emerging dominant system—is not properly 'industrial' at all. This is not an age of primary, basic industry, but an age of red tape, bureaucracy, and waste, and war. Kafka, and not Henry Ford, is its prophet."[39]

By the end of the year, both Cort and Day did their best to tone down the venom that had crept into the debate. If, as some had suggested, Cort was "guilty of snide remarks in the attempt to gain an empty advantage," Cort apologized and hoped that his "victims" would forgive him. For Day's part, she wrote in *The Catholic Worker* that the American bishops' suggestion to work toward the Industry Council Plan still held out the chance that the councils of labor and management might turn their attention to "the problem of decentralization and the control proposals of such men as Hilaire Belloc." She never wavered in maintaining that large-scale industry was not in keeping with Christian standards but tried to characterize the controversy as a good thing. "So let us keep up the controversy," Day wrote, "for the clarification of thought, and it will be with good will, because we have the basic unity of those of one faith."[40]

38. Philip Burnham, "The Romance of 'Christian Industrialism,'" *The Commonweal* 49 (December 10, 1948): 221.
39. Ibid.
40. John C. Cort, "The Labor Movement: Christian Industrialism III," *The Commonweal* 49 (November 26, 1948): 174–75; Dorothy Day, "On Distributism: Answer to John Cort," *The Catholic Worker* 15 (December 1948): 1, 3.

While the furor died down, the controversy over the compatibility of industry with Christianity continued through the 1950s, and the arguments did not change substantively.[41] By 1952 Robert Ludlow had clarified his position by noting that industrialism was not necessarily wrong in and of itself, but it was capitalism that made industrialism wrong. No social order preserving capitalism, including the ICP, could hope to cure the ills of factory life. In the same year, Michael Harrington, who in the next decade would go on to become one of America's most prominent social activists, lamented the American bishops' support for the ICP as a means of creating class harmony. Echoing the concerns of a vocal ICP supporter, Wilfred Parsons, Harrington argued that the success of the ICP as a tool for class cooperation was dependent on continued economic expansion. In times of economic decline, however, "the antagonistic interests of labor and capital are sharpened. It no longer becomes a question of 'fringe benefits' but of the dog-eat-dog right to work." Perhaps of greater concern to Harrington than Catholic support for the ICP was his contention that "the Bishops, at their most conservative, are about five leagues more radical than a great amount of American Catholics." The larger Catholic population's uncritical acceptance of capitalism left plans for industry councils or other forms of a guild system doomed to failure.[42]

In the end, CW opposition to the ICP stemmed from its belief that the institution of such a plan would be an impediment to the widespread agrarian distributism they deemed necessary for a truly Christian social order. Some, like Ed Marciniak, Chicago Catholic Labor Alliance cofounder and editor of the magazine *Work,* tried to bridge the gap between the ICP and hopes for a distributist society. Quoting directly from the literature of the Distributist Association of the United Kingdom, Marciniak

---

41. For more examples of letters, see "Communications," *The Commonweal* 49 (December 17, 1948): 254–56 and (December 24, 1948): 276–79; on the continuing controversy, see Robert Ludlow, "Industrialism—Not Evil in Itself," *The Catholic Worker* 18 (April 1952): 1, 6; Thomas Campbell, "Industrialism and Christianity," *The Catholic Worker* 18 (March 1952): 2; Michael Harrington, "The American Bishops on the Social Order," *The Catholic Worker* 18 (October 1952): 3, 6; "Catholic Worker Positions," *Catholic Worker* 21 (September 1954): 5; Dorothy Day, "Distributism Versus Capitalism," *The Catholic Worker* 21 (October 1954): 1, 6; Ed Marciniak, "Clarification on Distributism," *The Catholic Worker* 21 (November 1954): 1; John Thornton, "From the Mail: Green Revolution," *The Catholic Worker* 21 (December 1954): 4; Lawrence Moran, "From the Mail: Hennessy and Marciniak," *The Catholic Worker* 21 (December 1954): 4; Frank Petta, "Distributist," *The Catholic Worker* 21 (January 1955): 4.

42. Ludlow, "Industrialism—Not Evil in Itself," 1, 6; Harrington, "The American Bishops on the Social Order," 3, 6.

supported "a society where 'property and power are as widely and fairly distributed as possible amongst all people.'" By his account, the ICP was a way that property could be distributed more fairly because labor would finally have a say in the division of profits. The ills of factory mechanization would be confronted and dealt with by a newly empowered labor force were the ICP to be implemented. In Marciniak's mind, distributism and the industry council idea shared all of the same objectives. Where he parted company with the CW, however, was over "the need for the functional, organic reorganization of the major industries and occupations to serve the common good." For the CW, the very industries and occupations themselves were part of the problem. Because the distributism of the Catholic Worker movement "would never help any coal miner," Marciniak argued, industry councils were needed.[43]

CW activists remained unconvinced by Marciniak's attempt to bridge the gap.[44] While the ideology of the CW represented only a small minority of Catholics, promoters of the ICP took their arguments seriously enough to engage in them regularly. Their debates illustrate a fundamental gap with respect to interpreting the mythic texts of *Rerum Novarum* and *Quadragesimo Anno,* and they go far toward demonstrating the complex interweaving of ideological strands among Catholics who shared the framework of the Roman Catholic theology.

Government: Friend or Foe?

Another major division among American Catholics regarding the practical aspects of the ICP stemmed from the question of what role, if any, government was to play in their creation and function. Shortly before World War II, when Catholics began the rush to distance the corporatist vision they articulated in the ICP from any association with fascism, government authority became a hot-button topic. Unlike fascism, they insisted, the ICP limited government's role to *promoting* the general welfare rather than *providing* it.[45] The American bishops' statement of November 1948 described the role of the government in the ICP as "the

43. Marciniak, "Clarification on Distributism," 1, 8.
44. Thornton, "From the Mail: Green Revolution," 4; Moran, "From the Mail: Hennessy and Marciniak," 4; Petta, "Distributist," 4.
45. Edward Mooney, "The American Tradition," *The Catholic Mind* 36 (June 8, 1938): 215–20.

responsible custodian of the public interests." Its role "should be to stimulate, to guide, to restrain, not to dominate." These words echoed those of *Quadragesimo Anno*, which had characterized the state's function as that of "directing, watching, urging, restraining," but not overtaking the functions of subsidiary organizations (sec. 80).[46]

When Philip Murray of the CIO originally proposed his Industry Council Plan, government played a central role in it. After all, Murray was inspired to assist the government in planning for the needs of the nation's defense. Government officials were to serve as chairpersons of each council and function as "impartial" directors whose job included providing adequate information to labor and management with respect to economic data. Murray charged the government with organizing the councils rather than relying on the grassroots cooperation between workers and owners.[47]

There was substantial variation among Catholics regarding the role of government in the day-to-day mechanics of the ICP. Compared to the SAD representatives like Raymond McGowan and George Higgins, the ACTU saw government as less crucial to initiating the reforms of the ICP. Still, it played an important supervisory role in the process. John Cort and his compatriots in the Detroit ACTU, among others, were vocal supporters of Murray's original Industry Council Plan that involved government in an intimate way. In fact, the ACTU credited itself with keeping Murray's plan alive.[48] As Catholics strayed from the details of Murray's plan, Cort and other unionists continued to stress the supervisory role of government while being careful to emphasize that supervision did not equal control. Cort himself raised important questions on the subject, asking in one article how they would "prevent the government representatives [on industry councils] from casting the decisive votes." "In short," he continued, "how can we prevent the council from degenerating into a system of compulsory arbitration by government?" Ultimately, however, Cort was confident that a solution was possible and

---

46. "Bishops' Statement on 'The Christian in Action,'" *Catholic Action* 30 (December 1948): 13; Karl Alter, "The Industry Council System and the Church's Program of Social Order," *Review of Social Economy* 10 (September 1952): 104.

47. Murray, "Looking Forward," 188.

48. For example, see "Industry Councils Will Speed Victory," *The Michigan Labor Leader*, January 9, 1942, 4; Cort, "Are We Missing a Bus?" 392–95; John C. Cort, "The Labor Movement: A Plea for Economists," *The Commonweal* 47 (March 19, 1948): 567.

that the feared degeneration could be controlled, though he pleaded for professional economists to provide the details. Years later, Cort's vision of the ICP had developed to include councils in which the government would not only have one impartial representative, as Murray's original plan had called for, but would instead have equal representation with labor and management. He reasoned that even with equal representation, government would still be freed from much of the burden that it already bore in regulating economic issues.[49]

More conservative Catholics were clearly uncomfortable with the possibility that government would play a substantive role in the ICP. Wilfrid Parsons, though an avid supporter of the ICP, was cautious about government's role. In both articles and sermons, Parsons argued that the economic "orders" in industry and agriculture had all too often been misinterpreted as voluntary associations that individuals join of their own free will. Such a view ignored the "naturalness" of the social order described by Pius XI. There was a need to break up the two-class system and return to what he described as "an organic, hierarchical order." Catholics were mistaken to imagine that these vocational orders needed to be fashioned through any sort of government action. Pius XI's intention was not to create this natural hierarchical order but rather to change our conceptions of society so that we would see that the order already existed. Government interference was not required to bring the new structure about.[50]

Parsons admitted that Pius XI had referred to government as the "supreme arbiter" of the new vocational order, a phrase that had often been cited by ICP advocates. By couching the phrase in a sentence that undercut the importance of government, however, Parsons concluded that Pius XI had actually intended to downplay the state's significance. Pius XI envisaged a "society in which the State is *merely* a 'supreme arbiter,' whose sole function is the more *general* one of 'guiding, watching, urging, and curbing' the *self-governing* activities of subsidiary groups." The state's role in the ICP would be minimal because the only

49. Cort, "The Labor Movement: A Plea for Economists," 567–68; John C. Cort, "A Dream of Industrial Peace," *Catholic Digest* 18 (May 1954).
50. Wilfrid Parsons, S.J., "What Are Vocational Groups?" *Thought* 17 (September 1942): 464–69; sermon delivered by Wilfrid Parsons, S.J., at Saint Francis Xavier Church, New York, New York, May 16, 1941, Fordham University Archives (hereafter FUA), New York, "Xavier Institute of Industrial Relations Collection," Box 2, Folder 46.

reason for its participation in the economic order at all was to protect the public from "uncurbed free enterprise . . . laissez-faire liberalism." The self-governing vocational orders, Parsons believed, would render such interference superfluous.[51]

The most vocal opposition to government participation in the ICP came from Edward Keller. While putting an end to class conflict in favor of cooperation through a "system of voluntary self-regulatory bodies" appealed greatly to Keller, he shared the ACTU's desire to see the Industry Council Plan (a title he wished to abandon for its connections to the CIO concept promoted by Murray)[52] develop from the "bottom up," beginning on the local level before moving to the national scene. But his plan reflected a somewhat pared-down version of those floating around in most Catholic circles. At its heart would be Union-Management Production Committees consisting of equal numbers of management and union representatives. These committees would meet regularly at the local level to "prevent waste, save expense, cut costs [and] improve production." At the national level, there would be an "Economic Advisory Committee" aimed at informing the president and Congress regarding economic issues and problems. This committee would consist of "representatives of labor and the different industries, professions and consuming public." Keller was adamant, however, that "the government would have no official representation on these boards; the function of government would be merely to foster and promote the establishment of a Christian social order and to keep a watchful eye upon its functioning once it is established." On this score, Keller's conception of the ICP differed significantly from most plans, denying government a function as either an equal partner or an impartial observer within the committee structure. The New Deal reforms were evidence enough for Keller that "the greatest danger from giantism in the United States" was posed by government, and a Christian social order kept the role of government to an absolute minimum.[53]

51. Parsons, "What Are Vocational Groups?" 473–73, emphasis added.
52. Sentiment found in paragraph 3 of Keller's "Comments on the Interim Report" of the Industrial Council Committee of the NCWC, found in Rev. Edward Keller Files, University of Notre Dame Archives (hereafter UNDA), Notre Dame, Indiana, AC 8 3 7, CKEL Box 1, "'Edward Keller, CSC' Personal Papers," Folder: "Industrial Council Committee (National Catholic Welfare Conference) 1950–1951," Comments on the Interim Report; Edward A. Keller, *Christianity and American Capitalism* (Chicago: The Heritage Foundation, 1953), 67.
53. Keller, *Christianity and American Capitalism*, 79–89, 61.

Lines Between Labor and Management

Of almost as much concern to Keller as government intervention in the ICP was the overlapping of rights and responsibilities charged to both labor and management, an issue that proved to be the most hotly debated among Catholics.[54] Keller held that "partnership between labor and management must be at best a very broad cooperative partnership because justice would be violated if there were enforced an actual sharing of management by labor." His Union-Management Committees explicitly avoided giving labor a say in issues of wages, prices, and profits, "the determination of what products would be produced and what their quality and quantity would be; the determination of the allocation of capital facilities, etc." These committees, Keller argued, "incorporate many of the advantages of co-management without the annihilation of the rights and functions of private management." Invoking the words of *Quadragesimo Anno* and Pope Pius XII, Keller alluded to a "danger" that stemmed from granting workers authority of the means of production. Such a system "would be disguised socialism and a fundamental violation of the right of private property."[55]

Keller's concerns reflected an important sticking point as Catholics sought to harmonize their competing conceptions of the ICP. Was the ICP a proposal for "co-determination," granting labor an equal share of running businesses with management, or would labor defer to managers and owners themselves on crucial questions? In the earliest phase of discussions regarding vocational groups, characters like John Ryan envisioned organizations of employers and employees empowered "by law to fix wages, interest, dividends, and prices, to determine working conditions, to adjust industrial disputes, and to carry on whatever economic planning was thought feasible." ACTU representatives also anticipated that labor would have a say in determining policy in these areas. John Cort described the ideal factory as encouraging workers "in the making of all basic management policy. The word 'all' . . . includes price

---

54. See Karl J. Alter, "Industry Councils," *The Sign* 29 (May 1950): 52. Alter describes this question as the "chief difficulty" among ICP advocates.

55. Rev. Edward Keller Files, UNDA, AC 8 3 7, CKEL Box 1, "'Edward Keller, CSC' Personal Papers," Folder: "Industrial Council Committee (National Catholic Welfare Conference) 1950–1951," Comments on the Interim Report, paragraph 10; Keller, *Christianity and American Capitalism*, 68, 81–90.

policy, which directly affects the worker because it determines whether or not he is going to continue working."[56]

One of the most outspoken supporters of the ICP was John F. Cronin, assistant director of the SAD. On the issues of wages, prices, and profits, Cronin differed with some of his SAD colleagues by suggesting that these decisions were not the role of the ICP to manage. Cronin believed that industry councils would be opportunities for labor and management to work together on issues in which they shared a common interest, like productivity, economic expansion, and preventing economic depression. Wages, hours, prices, and profits, however, were not "within the sphere of common interests of owners and workers" because a "natural" disagreement would tend to rise over these issues. In lieu of industry councils, these issues needed to be determined through collective bargaining, Cronin believed. While industry councils at the national level could certainly suggest minimal standards for each issue, collective bargaining would rule at the level of the plant.[57]

More Obstacles to the ICP

Divided over questions of the nature of industrial labor, the role of government, and the respective rights and responsibilities of labor and management, some American Catholics viewed the obstacles to establishing the ICP to be overwhelming. For nearly twenty-five years, the institution of a vocational-group order had been seen as the crown jewel of the Catholic social imagination, advocated by a broad range of thinkers. So central was it to the conception of a just economic order among some prominent American Catholics that John Ryan had labeled Catholic opponents of the ICP as apostates and treasonous to the faith. But skeptical Catholics were not hard to find.

Philip Land, S.J., of the Institute of Social Order at Saint Louis University and his departmental colleague George P. Kluberantz, S.J., argued that a close examination of natural-law theology presented people with an "obligation . . . to embrace only what can be shown to be a reasonable program for a particular nation at a specific time." From this

---

56. J. Ryan, *A Better Economic Order*, 179; Cort, "The Labor Movement," 175.
57. John F. Cronin, *Catholic Social Principles: The Social Teaching of the Catholic Church Applied to American Economic Life* (Milwaukee: Bruce Publishing, 1950), 228–33.

assumption, the Jesuits suggested that the ICP might not meet that criterion. They scolded Catholics who assumed that "the indifference with which professional economists meet their proposals of reform stem from bias." This was simply not true in many cases. "What has happened," they continued, "is that the economist has been alienated by what he must inevitably consider sheer utopianism, since it is not accompanied by any reputable economic analysis." Chiding the Catholic reformers, Land and Kluberantz argued that economists are in agreement that "'you must have wealth before you can talk about sharing it.' We have seen reformers so concerned about the division of wealth that they failed to provide the energy and incentive needed to produce the goods to be divided." They feared the ICP fell into this category.[58]

A visiting German Jesuit of Gregorian University in Rome, Gustav Gundlach, remarked at a European conference in 1951 that the United States was not prepared for the vocational-order system proposed by Pius XI. In the United States, "the anti-capitalistic tendencies are not yet powerful either; an almost naïve trust in unlimited progress still holds sway over there." Gundlach's comments offended some Americans, like George Higgins.[59] But the analysis of Joseph P. Fitzpatrick of Fordham University suggested that Gundlach's observations may have only scratched the surface of the sociological circumstances in the United States that impeded the progress of the ICP.

Fitzpatrick insisted that the ICP "will never exist as an effective organization of social economy . . . unless it becomes integrated into the social structure of the society in which it is adopted." Yet this was precisely the plan's Achilles' heel. The energy of the Catholic community in the United States had been focused almost exclusively on questions of structure: How will the ICP be organized? What role will government have? How much say will labor have in management? Fitzpatrick pointed out, however, that the impact of the plan on social relations had scarcely been mentioned. The ICP "would presuppose changes in motivation; modification of complicated systems of status, prestige, authority;

---

58. Philip S. Land and George P. Kluberanz, "Practical Reason, Social Fact, and the Vocational Order," *The Modern Schoolman* 28 (May 1951): 261–66. They cite Pius XII's letter to M. Charles Flory, July 19, 1947, published in *The Catholic Mind* in November 1947.

59. George G. Higgins, "American Contributions to the Implementation of the Industry Council Plan," *American Catholic Sociological Review* 13 (March 1952): 10; Higgins cited Gundlach's speech, "The Social Question as Seen from Rome" (address to the Social Meeting of the Catholic People of Germany, Fall 1951). Translation was made available by the NCWC, Washington, D.C.

new concepts of the social function of work and business. In brief, the Industry Council Plan would be, more than anything else, a new social organization." Social dynamics were not susceptible to change through authoritative fiat but instead developed naturally over time. The ICP, reminded Fitzpatrick, is a social institution. Its *idea* is a concept of society in which the individual achieves the fullest expression of his personality in an orderly relationship to social groups. It is based on a concept of human dignity, of social justice and social charity. It suggests a pattern of social behavior in which this will be realized. But two things are clear about the Industry Council Plan: First, the pattern of behavior outlined in the plan had definitely been suggested by the evils of industrial capitalism that had subordinated social welfare to the needs of production. Second, the pattern of behavior was primarily aimed at subordinating the productive system to the social welfare.

The ICP, therefore, stood in tension with the social fabric of the nation: "Americans have always tended to think of our basic ideas of human dignity, freedom, ability for self-development in terms of free institutions and associations." While nearly everyone noted the potentially negative consequences stemming from expressing these ideas and values, they remained "sharply defined in the American mind." Yet the ICP countered some of these fundamental American values and assumptions by proposing "a pattern of behavior in which men will be compelled to do that which is for the common good." In doing so, it would run "the risk of being easily misunderstood and seriously misrepresented in the American mind."[60]

For many, the idea of organizing seemed to be a typical American phenomenon. But Fitzpatrick cited several studies pointing to organized activity as largely a middle-and upper-class phenomenon. Even with the apparent success of unionism, labor unions only represented one-quarter of the nation's workforce. Still, the ICP was premised on a demand for "an extraordinary degree of participation from people who have either never bothered to join an organization or have never bothered to be active in those they have joined." This posed the risk that the ICP would yield power and authority to a small group of individuals, or even the government itself, as a result of public apathy: "To say that this will not happen under the Industry Council Plan is to misread the warnings of history.

---

60. Joseph P. Fitzpatrick, "The Industry Council Plan as a Form of Social Organization," *American Catholic Sociological Review* 14 (October 1953): 146–53.

To suggest, as has been suggested, that the creation of the formal institution will evoke the spontaneous participation of the members is to deny all that Industrial Sociology has been able to tell us about the participation of men in any organization." Moreover, when one considered that it took nearly a century of struggle, trauma, and violence to bend the American economic system to the common good through government intervention and labor unions—and even after that century there remained much to do—how could a system as comprehensive as the ICP have even the potential to develop at any point in the foreseeable future? ICP advocates, Fitzpatrick concluded, should be satisfied with smaller steps toward promoting healthy social change, for the ICP was a long way from becoming a reality.[61]

Fitzpatrick's projections regarding the fate of the ICP were confirmed over time. Intra-Catholic disagreements alone assured that nothing of substance would ever become of any of the proposals modeled on *Quadragesimo Anno*, at least not on a national level. The optimism of figures like Ryan and Trehey in the wake of Pius XI's encyclical was understandable, given the circumstances of their day. Sweeping economic reconstruction plans were being enacted in places like Italy, Portugal, and Germany, while the apparent early successes of the New Deal pointed the way toward a new economic order in the United States. For all of the concerns on both the left and the right wings of the political spectrum regarding these changes across the globe, there was clearly a sense that profound change was inevitable. The economic dislocation of the postwar period continued to provide what many believed to be fertile ground for the ICP.

By the 1950s, however, criticisms and concerns such as those discussed in this chapter, coupled with increased contentment with American economic growth, crippled the ICP's momentum. Memories of fascism and the failed NRA had embedded themselves in the American consciousness, and early attempts to associate the vocational-group order with both economic experiments only backfired with time. Eventually, unions themselves became concerned that the ICP would inhibit collective bargaining rights, and conservatives like Keller wasted no time pointing the finger of blame at union leaders for standing in the way of the ICP's implementation. All the while, the ICP never gained popularity in management circles. But as Fitzpatrick's criticisms indicated, the barriers to promoting

61. Ibid., 153–55.

the ICP in the United States ran deeper than class divisions.[62] By 1953, Daniel Bell had written in *Fortune Magazine* that "the occasional demand for 'industry councils'" made by CIO representatives and Catholic theorists, amounted to nothing more than "rhetorical flourishes of convention making."[63]

By the mid-to-late 1950s, most Catholics were left maintaining their faith in the ICP by arguing that the U.S. economy as it stood near the end of the decade was much closer to the plan than previously imagined. An article in a 1954 *Catholic Business Education Review* catalogued several "approximations to the Industry Council Plan" that had been implemented and appeared successful. Most were labor-management committees, similar to the Joint Production Committees championed by John Cort and the ACTU. Other planning groups mentioned included "The Committee of Twelve of the Anthracite Coal Industry," "The Council on Industrial Relations in the Electrical Industry," "The New York City Trucking Authority," and "The Millinery Stabilization Industry." These groups succeeded in taking steps toward fulfilling the papal call toward ending class antagonism and empowering labor unions.[64] Another ICP supporter suggested that collective bargaining alone had succeeded in bringing many of the ICP ideals to fruition. Americans had only to finish what they had started rather than "begin tilling another, unknown field."[65] By the standards set by the early advocates of the ICP, however, the economy of the mid-to-late 1950s bore little resemblance to Pius XI's plan. Class antagonism had been diminished, but by no means eliminated. And the economy under Eisenhower was even less planned than it had been toward the end of the Roosevelt Administration. For better or worse, it was not the ICP.

Every advocate of the ICP, and even its American Catholic opponents, appealed to *Rerum Novarum* and, especially, *Quadragesimo Anno* to authorize their own vision of the plan. All agreed that a truly Christian order must reflect the "organic nature" of society, be governed by the principle of subsidiarity, eliminate class antagonism—seen as an artificial by-product of either the capitalist mind-set or the sin of human greed—

---

62. "NCWC Calls for Employers' Associations," *The Commonweal* 48 (September 3, 1948): 488; Alter, "Industry Councils," *The Sign*, 52; Keller, *Christianity and American Capitalism*, 83.

63. Daniel Bell, "The Next American Labor Movement," *Fortune*, April 1953, 123.

64. Isabelle Morello, "Approximations to the Industry Council Plan in American Industry," *Catholic Business Education Review* 5 (June 1954): 57–66.

65. Schuyler, "The Industry Council Idea," 290–300, esp. 300.

and work to promote the dignity of the human person by conforming to the common good. The devil was in the details, of course, and Catholics struggled to apply Pius XI's call for vocational orders to their American context. The title Industry Council Plan was misleading in the sense that Catholics shaped by varying ideological streams put forward dozens of plans; these plans were bound by a common authority and a common language, but at times separated by mutually exclusive details and assumptions about what an authentically Catholic social order involved.

Conclusion

Americans coming of age by Vatican II had experienced the devastation of the Great Depression, the rise of totalitarian regimes with sweeping plans for new forms of social organization, the brutality of modern warfare and genocide, unprecedented consolidation of federal power, rapid technological change, the dawn of the nuclear age, and the economic consequences of a burgeoning globalization that transformed the method and meaning of work in the United States. In the midst of those transformations, people did what people have always done: impart meaning to the events taking place around them. Those meanings were shaped by experiences including personal encounters with coworkers and bosses on the shop floor, family relationships, writing checks to the Internal Revenue Service, competing with the new corporate farm in town, or losing a child, a sibling, a friend, or a spouse to war in Europe or the Pacific. Exposure to political conventions, radio commentaries, campaign rhetoric, newspaper editorials, and stories unfolding on the silver screen were only some of the means by which countless explanatory narratives helped citizens to evaluate and order their world.

We negotiate our place in the world amid a vast array of ideological strands that shape our thinking. Among these strands of ideology are those we identify as "religious," serving as powerful filters through which we make sense of our lives. For Roman Catholics in the United States in the generation before Vatican II, the ideology of the Church, with its "system of representations, perceptions, and images"—as James Kavanagh's characterization of ideology describes it—encouraged "men and women to 'see' their specific place in a historically peculiar social formation as inevitable, natural," and a "necessary function of the real itself."[1] No doubt natural-law theology contributed to the sense that the truths they held were timeless.

Judging from the ritual complaints among prominent Catholic social activists, most Catholics in the pews had, at best, a passing acquaintance with *Rerum Novarum* and *Quadragesimo Anno,* and in all likelihood, a majority knew nothing about either text. But for those Catholics seeking to publicly shape opinions on issues of economy and social order, the social encyclicals achieved the status of myth. Seen as credibly articulating a divinely ordained social order, the two encyclicals were the primary authorizing agents for socioeconomic views on all ends of the Roman Catholic spectrum for three decades. Rural homesteaders, anarcho-distributists, industrial union workers, activist clergy, business executives, and champions of American capitalism could—and did—see their perspectives reflected in these texts.

But the meanings imputed to the encyclicals were elements of a complex dynamic. The encyclicals, as artifacts embedded in time and place, shaped the contours of Catholic knowledge by providing a narrative history of the social order, painting pictures through its words, and, perhaps most important, developing a common language to be shared by its readers that reflected the tradition of natural law. The lexicon of "social justice," with its principles (subsidiarity, a "just wage," vocational orders, class harmony, etc.), was reproduced in union halls, Catholic newspapers, pamphlets, prayer breakfasts, labor schools, retreats, and face-to-face dialogue. The lexicon ensured that no Catholic could successfully appeal to the Church to defend an economic system they labeled "socialism," any more than they could appeal to the Church for a defense of a system they labeled "laissez-faire." Still, the potential ambiguity of both terms enabled Catholics to depict their intellectual adversaries as falling prey to either ideology when such an association might score points for their causes.

The Roman Catholic ideology was not distinctive for its rejection of both socialism and laissez-faire economics, because many if not most in the Western world refused to identify themselves wholeheartedly with either system and positioned themselves somewhere "in between." Its distinction, instead, lay in its taxonomy of the social order that placed the authority of the Church, through the teachings of the papacy, in the

---

1. James H. Kavanagh, "Ideology," in *Critical Terms for Literary Study,* 2nd ed., ed. Frank Lentricchia and Thomas McLaughlin (Chicago: University of Chicago Press, 1995), 310.

seat of primacy. Within the natural-law framework of this taxonomy, true social justice on a global or national scale could never be achieved as long as the Church's authority to interpret nature, define social roles, and mediate the grace of God were rejected. While Catholics may have contested those interpretations and definitions among themselves, all the individuals and organizations we have discussed were bound by their common commitment to see Rome as their guide and by their faith that the encyclicals revealed a prescription for a Christian society that only the Church seemed to understand fully.

The umbrella myth of natural law remains significant to the Roman Catholic magisterium's method of discernment today. Yet several important developments, beginning with Vatican II, affected the status of natural law as the central organizing principle for intra-Catholic dialogue. Both *Rerum Novarum* and *Quadragesimo Anno* share a framework for expounding on natural law that saw the papacy and the hierarchy as bearing responsibility for dictating the appropriate interpretation of natural law while also distilling from those interpretations broad applications for addressing the problems of the day. In the realm of individual moral choices, this pattern has remained the same to this day. But in the area of social questions such as those relating to economics, the message from the magisterium changed significantly by the early 1960s.

As theologian Stephen J. Pope explained it, beginning in 1965 with *Gaudium et spes,* near the conclusion of Vatican II, Catholic social teaching exhibited a redirection of focus in four key aspects. First, the sense of openness to the modern world that pervaded the council began to be reflected in the Church's texts. The new openness was tied to the second change in focus, coming to grips with itself as a historically situated institution shaped by the world it inhabited. This was a major deviation from its earlier self-understanding. Moreover, recognizing that in a complex world of individuals from the broadest range of sociocultural conditions, *Gaudium et spes* expressed a willingness to engage competing perspectives. As Pope put it, "the natural law theory employed by Catholic social teachings up to the Council had been crafted under the influence of ahistorical continental rationalism. The kind of method employed by Leo XIII and Pius XI developed a modern 'morality of obligation' having its roots in the Council of Trent and the subsequent four centuries of moral manuals." Where Leo XIII and Pius XI were often astounded that others would draw differing conclusions from their own, confident that these deviations resulted from "ignorance, fear, faulty reasoning, and prejudice, the authors of *Gaudium et spes* were more attuned to the fact that not all human beings possess a univocal faculty called 'reason' that leads to identical moral conclusions." The third shift in focus involved a move away from abstract natural-law reasoning to a greater attention to scripture and especially the Jesus of the Gospels. Finally, as a logical extension of the previous three aspects, the document signaled a greater emphasis on the dignity of the individual person and that person's "conscience as a source of moral insight."[2]

Whether these shifts were judged favorably or unfavorably, few doubted that such shifts had indeed taken place. In his telling study of the published addresses of the four Catholic Theological Society of America presidents between 1967 and 1970, the Jesuit theologian Roger Haight observed that all four "testif[ied] to an experience of revolution within the discipline: it had changed overnight in its situation, premises, and the problems it faced." Among the common themes emerging from these addresses was the recognition of a "sudden abandonment and loss of a unified framework for theology, for scholasticism was suddenly gone," Haight maintained. Since then, efforts to resurrect a "unified framework" have continued to confront the realities of a very different theological playing field than that which existed in the years covered by this study.[3]

While later social encyclicals ranging from Pius VI's *Populorum Progressio* (1967) to John Paul II's *Centesimus Annus* (1991) could be depended on to echo the attacks on materialism, communism, and laissez-faire capitalism that their predecessors had delivered, the organicist model of the social order, with its hierarchically arranged conceptions of class and social stations put forward in the language of natural law, had ceded space to new authorizing agents in the form of scriptural citations and appeals to experience. To be sure, natural law remained vital to the Church's social teachings—only now the laity and other interested conversation partners were invited to explore issues of justice from a range

---

2. Stephen J. Pope, "Natural Law in Catholic Social Teachings," in *Modern Catholic Social Teaching: Commentaries and Interpretations*, ed. Kenneth R. Himes, O.F.M. (Washington, D.C.: Georgetown University Press, 2005), 53–55.

3. Roger Haight, S.J., "How My Mind Was Ruined, or Saved: Later Reflections of a Nice Catholic Boy Who Came to the Divinity School in 1967," *Criterion* 45, no. 2 (2006–7): 9–13; Haight cites his earlier work on the presidents of the Catholic Theological Society, "Presidential Address: Fifty Years of Theology," *The Proceedings of the Catholic Theological Society of America* 50 (1995): 1–14.

of avenues.[4] A new engagement with democratic pluralism worldwide, coupled with ecumenical engagement, the earliest hints of the postmodern movement, and a Roman Catholic population in the United States that, for the first time, felt secure in claims to their status as Americans, all assured that the Church's new openness would have significant consequences for intra-Catholic dialogue in the United States.

This study has illustrated a tremendous diversity of thought among Roman Catholics in the pre–Vatican II era as they voiced competing views as to what constituted a just and Christian social order. These Catholics differed on methods for distributing resources, methods of production, the definition of "freedom," the value of legislation, the nature of acceptable unions, the roles of the laity and the clergy, the structure of class, or even the very existence of class. What all their arguments shared were appeals to common sources of authority, the encyclicals, and the assumptions at the foundation of natural-law reasoning from which the encyclicals grew. With the Second Vatican Council, Roman Catholics in America and around the world were far less likely to be speaking from within a common mythic framework. American Catholics in 1975 were probably not significantly more diverse in their views of economic justice than they were in 1945. But the players on the public stage were no longer reading from the same script.

Myths become myths because we impart authority to them, and as such, their meanings are colored by our own concerns. In the hands of the National Catholic Rural Life Conference, *Rerum Novarum* and *Quadragesimo Anno* were a validation of the Jeffersonian ideal of the yeoman farmer as the bedrock of democracy and freedom. Private property, escaping the class structure of the industrial economy, the focus on the family with its own gendered hierarchy, and subsidiarity's preferential option for smallness were among the elements of the myth that helped to spawn the NCRLC's efforts at homesteading, farming cooperatives, and establishing a firm foothold for Catholicism in rural America. The Catholic Worker movement, inspired as much by its desire to escape urban industrialism as by stopping the exodus from the farm to the factory, saw in the encyclicals the keys to authorizing an anarchic distributism that gave rise to Catholic farming communes nationwide.

---

4. Stephen Pope's overview of this process is the clearest and most balanced I have read to date. See his "Natural Law in Catholic Social Teachings"; for a collection of papal encyclicals dealing with economic issues, see David J. O'Brien and Thomas A. Shannon, eds., *Catholic Social Thought: The Documentary Heritage* (Maryknoll, N.Y.: Orbis Books, 1992).

Farms were not a top priority for the Social Action Department of the National Catholic Welfare Conference, but addressing the challenges posed by industrial labor with its entrenched class antagonism was. For the SAD, the encyclicals laid out a plan for a just social order that could be shepherded in through strong unions, improved labor-management cooperation, and an expansive legislative agenda at the federal level. The Association of Catholic Trade Unionists, and organizations like it, took the encyclicals as their cue to infuse the labor movement with the Catholic ideology, transforming the social order from the bottom up. The Young Christian Workers did not limit themselves to unionists, but spread the Catholic message to management and labor alike. Both the ACTU and the YCW were comfortable in an industrial arena that the Catholic Worker rejected as incompatible with human dignity, and that the NCRLC approached with suspicion. The ability of organizations like the SAD, the ACTU, and the YCW to fuse pro-labor progressivism with the anticommunism and conservative moral structure of Roman Catholicism goes far toward explaining the confrontations between blue-collar workers and antiwar activists in the early 1970s that had surprised labor historian Melvyn Dubosfsky.

When the time period covered in our study began, there was widespread cynicism toward free-market economies and a fear that the concentration of capital posed a danger to liberty. Each of the groups mentioned above were born out of a sense of social dislocation, much like the encyclicals themselves. Something was very wrong with the world, they believed, and the wisdom of the Roman Catholic Church would light the path toward fixing it. Restoring a lost order—an order "remembered" for having recognized the bishop of Rome as its head—provided these groups with a sense of mission, believing that even with the monumental transformations in ideas, technologies, and human organization that had taken place in the intervening centuries, society could still be "whole" again. Society was an organism, after all, and we had merely lost sight of this truth. Catholic activists, inspired by Catholic Action, saw themselves as bearing responsibility for carrying out God's will on earth, shouldering the burden of fulfilling the teleology in which they placed their faith.

By the 1950s, the climate in which these movements were born had changed in the United States. Catholics were fleeing the "ghetto" in droves for the "greener" pastures of middle management and beyond. America was a "superpower" engaged in a Manichean struggle with an atheistic foe, shielded not only by her weaponry but by an economic engine that had come to be the world's most powerful. Americans were growing receptive to the prophets of a "New Capitalism," a "People's Capitalism," said to be filled with promise and opportunity. Catholics like Richard McKeon, John Dinneen, Francis Graham Wilson, Ferdinand Falque, and Edward Keller were among those prophets, and paved the way for later thinkers like William F. Buckley, George Weigel, and Michael Novak. Where others had found in *Rerum Novarum* and *Quadragesimo Anno* the prescription for greater economic centralization or protective legislation, they found the foundational elements of American capitalism: the sacrality of private property, subsidiarity's cautious stance toward government, a clear denunciation of socialism, and the castigation of class conflict. The American economy had not fulfilled the Christian ideal, but the key components were already there and nothing else held out as much promise for the future.

The comparative contentment with the American economy reflected in figures like Dinneen and Keller had a profound impact on the fortunes of the other groups we have explored. The grassroots-style framework on which several of the Catholic activist organizations depended for their expansion was curtailed by a diminishing sense of outrage toward the apparent social inequities that remained. Certainly the standard of living for most Americans had improved. But working conditions and life circumstances that might have been seen two decades earlier as symptomatic of a failed system had come to be characterized as an anomaly; as examples of those who had "slipped through the cracks" of an otherwise sound economic structure. Organizations like the ACTU functioned until the early 1970s, and the Catholic Worker continues today, but their impact never reclaimed the levels they had achieved in earlier decades. Though the Catholic Worker's rhetoric maintained its radical edge, assuring its growing marginalization within an ever more "mainstream" American Catholic culture, organizations like the SAD, the NCRLC, and the YCW reined in their calls for sweeping reform by the mid-1950s in favor of tactical measures aimed at fulfilling the charge of the encyclicals as they understood them.

Whether *Rerum Novarum* and *Quadragesimo Anno* genuinely invoked divine laws and eternal truths, they were certainly products of their time and place in history. American Catholic activists were energized by the vision outlined in these texts, and by what they saw of their own visions reflected in them. Through their respective organizations, and as individuals, they reconstituted the encyclical mythology to meet the needs of their own constituencies, weaving the Catholic ideology through the thicket of economic and political ideologies that prevailed in mid-twentieth-century America.

"The Catholic Social Tradition" became a shorthand phrase in some circles to describe a laundry list of policies and plans that the Church has promoted—at least since 1891—for the establishment of justice in the world. I suggest that scholars would be better served by looking at this "Tradition" not as a socioeconomic platform that can be traced in a linear fashion through the past, but instead as a site for dialogue and debate. Attempting to redescribe the history of a select range of Catholic thinkers over a limited span of time by borrowing categories common to religious studies, and refraining from the temptation to choose heroes and villains measured against reified theological categories, reveals a rich texture of activity, thought, belief, and passion. With their words and actions, they struggled to consecrate in the name of the Roman Catholic faith those features of American economic life that they held dear, while striving to transform those elements they rejected in the name of an authentically Christian social order.

Bibliography

Along with the following sources, my research for this book included archival work at the American Catholic History Research Center and University Archives at The Catholic University of America, Washington, D.C.; Fordham University Archives, Bronx, New York; Marquette University Archives, Milwaukee, Wisconsin; Rockhurst University Archives, Kansas City, Missouri; and University of Notre Dame Archives, Notre Dame, Indiana.

Abbott, Philip. *Exceptional America: Newness and National Identity.* New York: Peter Lang, 1999.
Abell, Aaron I. *American Catholicism and Social Action: A Search for Social Justice, 1865–1950.* Notre Dame, Ind.: University of Notre Dame Press, 1963.
———, ed. *American Catholic Thought on Social Questions.* Indianapolis, Ind.: Bobbs-Merrill, 1968.
Agar, Herbert. *A Time for Greatness.* Boston: Little, Brown, 1942.
Alter, Karl. "Industry Councils." *The Sign* 29 (May 1950): 50–53.
———. "The Industry Council System and the Church's Program of Social Order." *Review of Social Economy* 10 (September 1952): 97–107.
Andrews, George T. "Order in Industrial Economy." *The Modern Schoolman* 14 (March 1937): 56–57.
Appleby, Joyce. "Commercial Farming and the 'Agrarian Myth' in the Early Republic." *The Journal of American History* 68 (March 1982): 833–49.
Aristotle. *The "Art" of Rhetoric.* Edited and translated by John Henry Freese. London: William Heinemann, 1926.
Banning, Lance. "Jeffersonian Ideology Revisited: Liberal and Classical Ideas in the New American Republic." *William and Mary Quarterly* 43 (January 1986): 3–19.
Becker, Joseph M. "Who Are Opposed to Social Security?" *America*, May 15, 1948, 135–37.
Bell, Daniel. "The Next American Labor Movement." *Fortune*, April 1953, 120–23, 201–6.
Belloc, Hilaire. *The Crisis of Civilization.* New York: Fordham University Press, 1937.
———. *Essays of a Catholic.* New York: Macmillan, 1931.

———. *The Restoration of Property.* New York: Sheed and Ward, 1936.
———. *The Servile State.* New York: Henry Holt, 1946.
Betten, Neil. *Catholic Activism and the Industrial Worker.* Gainesville: University Presses of Florida, 1976.
Bishops of Ohio. "'Right-to-Work' Laws." *The Catholic Mind* 56 (September–October 1958): 477–79.
Bissett, Jim. *Agrarian Socialism in America: Marx, Jefferson, and Jesus in the Oklahoma Countryside, 1904–1920.* Norman: University of Oklahoma Press, 1999.
Bok, Derek C., and John T. Dunlop. *Labor and the American Community.* New York: Simon and Schuster, 1970.
Bokenkotter, Thomas. *A Concise History of the Catholic Church.* New York: Doubleday, 1977.
Bovée, David. "The Church and the Land: The National Catholic Rural Life Conference and American Society, 1923–1985." 2 vols. Ph.D. diss., University of Chicago, 1986.
Bredeck, Martin J., S.J. *Imperfect Apostles: The Commonweal and the American Catholic Laity, 1924–1976.* New York: Garland, 1988.
Briefs, Goetz A. "An Attack on 'Compulsory Unionism.'" In *American Catholic Thought on Social Questions,* edited by Aaron I. Abell, 506–21. Indianapolis: Bobbs-Merrill, 1968.
Brophy, John. "The Industry Council Plan." *The Commonweal* 49 (November 12, 1948): 110–12.
Brown, Alden V. *The Grail Movement and American Catholicism, 1940–1975.* Notre Dame, Ind.: University of Notre Dame Press, 1989.
Brown, Dorothy M., and Elizabeth McKeown. *The Poor Belong to Us: Catholic Charities and American Welfare.* Cambridge, Mass.: Harvard University Press, 1977.
Brown, Leo C., S.J. "Right-to-Work Legislation." *The Catholic Mind* 53 (October 1955): 606–14.
Bruehl, Charles, D. *The Pope's Plan for Social Reconstruction.* New York: Devin-Adair, 1939.
———. "Structure of Vocational Groups." *Homiletic and Pastoral Review* 38 (February 1938): 449–57.
Burnham, Philip. "Christian Industrialism?" *The Commonweal* 48 (October 8, 1948): 609–10.
———. "The Romance of 'Christian Industrialism.'" *The Commonweal* 49 (December 10, 1948): 221.
Burns, Gene. *The Frontiers of Catholicism: The Politics of Ideology in a Liberal World.* Berkeley and Los Angeles: University of California Press, 1992.
Burns, John F. "ACTU Bores from Within." *Catholic Digest* 13 (April 1949): 50–53.
Camp, Richard L. *The Papal Ideology of Social Reform: A Study in Historical Development, 1878–1967.* Leiden: E. J. Brill, 1969.
Campbell, Thomas. "Industrialism and Christianity." *The Catholic Worker* 18 (March 1952): 2.
Cantwell, Daniel M. "Communications." *The Commonweal* 49 (November 19, 1948): 139.
Carney, Francis W. "State of the Question: The Morality of Right to Work Laws." *America,* September 6, 1958, 588–90.

"Catholic Worker Positions." *The Catholic Worker* 21 (September 1954): 5.

Chadwick, Owen. *The Secularization of the European Mind in the Nineteenth Century.* Cambridge: Cambridge University Press, 1975.

Chamberlin, Edward H., et al., eds. *Labor Unions and Public Policy.* Washington, D.C.: American Enterprise Association, 1958.

Chesterton, G. K. *The Catholic Church and Conversion.* New York: Macmillan, 1950.

———. *The Outline of Sanity.* London: Methuen, 1926.

Coogan, John E., S.J. "Communications from Our Readers: Right-to-Work Debate." *Homiletic and Pastoral Review* 58 (November 1957): 126–37.

———. "An End to Forced Unionism." *The Priest* 14 (January 1958): 26–34.

———. "Pastoral Care of the Labor Unionist." *Pastoral Life* 7 (January–February 1959): 10–14.

Coren, Michael. *Gilbert: The Man Who Was G. K. Chesterton.* New York: Paragon House, 1990.

Corrin, Jay P. *G. K. Chesterton and Hilaire Belloc: The Battle Against Modernity.* Athens: Ohio University Press, 1981.

Cort, John C. "Are We Missing the Bus? Why Not Support the Murray Industry Council Plan." *The Commonweal* 36 (August 14, 1942): 392–95.

———. "The Battle over 'Right-to-Work.'" *The Commonweal* 62 (April 22, 1955): 75–77.

———. "Can We Lick the Labor Problem?" *The Sign* 29 (November 1949): 32–35.

———. "Capitalism: Debates and Definitions." *The Commonweal* 61 (November 26, 1954): 221–22.

———. "Catholics in Trade Unions." *The Commonweal* 30 (May 5, 1939): 34–36.

———. "The Charms of Anarchism." *The Commonweal* 57 (November 14, 1952): 139–40.

———. "Christian Industrialism III." *The Commonweal* 49 (November 26, 1948): 174–75.

———. "A Dream of Industrial Peace." *Catholic Digest* 18 (May 1954): 89–93.

———. "From Small Groups a Big Movement." *The Commonweal* 60 (May 7, 1954): 116.

———. "Is Christian Industrialism Possible?" *The Commonweal* 49 (October 29, 1948): 60–62.

———. "Lay Apostles in the Field." *The Commonweal* 54 (July 20, 1949): 356–57.

———. "Nine Years of ACTU." *America*, April 6, 1946, 4–5.

———. "A Plea for Economists." *The Commonweal* 47 (March 19, 1948): 567–69.

———. "The Popes and the American Worker." *The Catholic Mind* 54 (November 1956): 636–41.

———. "Reform Begins at the Plant Level." *The Commonweal* 48 (October 1, 1948): 597.

———. "Right-to-Work Laws." *The Commonweal* 64 (August 3, 1956): 438–40.

———. "A Setback to AFL-CIO Unity." *The Commonweal* 59 (March 26, 1954): 623–24.

———. "Side by Side with the Unions." *The Commonweal* 59 (March 5, 1954): 552–54.

———. "Ten Years." *The Commonweal* 46 (May 23, 1947): 143–44.

———. "What Kind of Labor?" *Catholic Digest* 11 (April 1946): 24–26.
Cronin, John F. *Catholic Social Action*. Milwaukee: Bruce Publishing, 1948.
———. *Catholic Social Principles: The Social Teaching of The Catholic Church Applied to American Economic Life*. Milwaukee: Bruce Publishing, 1959.
———. "'Forced Unionism': A Reply." *The Priest* 14 (February 1958): 116–22.
———. *Social Principles and Economic Life*. Milwaukee: Bruce Publishing, 1959.
Cross, Robert D. "The Changing Image of the City Among American Catholics." *Catholic Historical Review* 48 (April 1962): 33–52.
———. *The Emergence of Liberal Catholicism in America*. Cambridge, Mass.: Harvard University Press, 1958.
Curran, Charles E. *American Catholic Social Ethics: Twentieth-Century Approaches*. Notre Dame, Ind.: University of Notre Dame Press, 1982.
D'Agostino, Peter. *Rome in America: Transnational Catholic Ideology from the Risorgimento to Fascism*. Chapel Hill: University of North Carolina Press, 2004.
Daly, Thomas F. "Letter to the Editor: What Is Capitalism?" *The Commonweal* 28 (June 10, 1938): 185.
Danbom, David. *The Resisted Revolution: Urban America and the Industrialization of Agriculture, 1900–1930*. Ames: Iowa State University Press, 1979.
Davis, Winston. "Natural Law and Natural Right: The Role of Myth in the Discourses of Exchange and Community." In *Myth and Philosophy*, edited by Frank Reynolds and David Tracy, 349–79. Albany: State University of New York Press, 1990.
———. "Natural Law: A Study of Myth in a World Without Foundations." In *Myth and Philosophy*, edited by Frank Reynolds and David Tracy, 317–48. Albany: State University of New York Press, 1990.
Day, Dorothy. "Days Without End." *The Catholic Worker* (April 1934): 3–4.
———. "A Human Document." *Sign* 12 (November 1932): 223–24.
———. "I Remember Peter Maurin." *Jubilee* 1 (March 1954): 34–39.
———. *The Long Loneliness*. New York: Harper and Row, 1952.
———. "May Day." *The Catholic Worker* 23 (May 1957): 2.
———. "On Pilgrimage—January 1959." *The Catholic Worker* 25 (January 1959): 1–2, 7.
———. "The Pope and Peace." *The Catholic Worker* 21 (February 1954): 1, 7.
Dempsey, Bernard W., S. J. ". . . But Don't Call It Capitalism." *Social Order* 4 (May 1954): 199–208.
Denning, Michael. *The Cultural Front: The Laboring of American Culture in the Twentieth Century*. New York: Verso Books, 1996.
Derber, Milton, and Edwin Young, eds. *Labor and the New Deal*. Madison: University of Wisconsin Press, 1957.
Diggins, John P. *Mussolini and Fascism: The View from America*. Princeton, N.J.: Princeton University Press, 1972.
Dinerstein, Joel. *Swinging the Machine: Modernity, Technology, and African American Culture Between the Wars*. Amherst: University of Massachusetts Press, 2003.
Dinneen, John A., S.J. "'Capitalism' and Capitalism." *The Catholic World* 180 (January 1955): 293–97.
"Distributism: A Draft for Action." *The Catholic Worker* 13 (October 1946): 5.
Distributist League. *Do We Agree? A Debate Between G. K. Chesterton and*

Bernard Shaw with Hilaire Belloc in the Chair. Oxford, U.K.: Kemp Hall Press, 1928.

Dolan, Jay P. *The American Catholic Experience: A History from Colonial Times to the Present.* Notre Dame, Ind.: University of Notre Dame Press, 1992.

Dolan, Timothy. *"Some Seed Fell on Good Ground": The Life of Edwin V. O'Hara.* Washington, D.C.: Catholic University of America Press, 1992.

Dubofsky, Melvyn, ed. *American Labor Since the New Deal.* Chicago: Quadrangle Books, 1971.

Dugan, Kerran. "Eric Gill: A Special Kind of Artist." *The Catholic Worker* 17 (November 1950): 4, 7.

Eberdt, Mary, C.H.M., and Gerald Schnepp, S.M. *Industrialism and the Popes.* New York: P. J. Kennedy and Sons, 1953.

Ellis, John Tracy. *American Catholicism.* Chicago: University of Chicago Press, 1969.

Ellis, Mark. *Peter Maurin: Prophet in the Twentieth Century.* New York: Paulist Press, 1981.

Eustace, C. J. "Which Leviathan—Big Business or the State?" *Catholic World* 166 (February 1948): 441–46.

Falconi, Carlo. *The Popes in the Twentieth Century: From Pius XI to John XIII.* Translated by Muriel Grindrod. London: Weidenfeld and Nicolson, 1967.

Falque, Ferdinand C. "Liberalism in the Guise of Uplift." *Homiletic and Pastoral Review* 57 (January 1957): 325–30.

———. "Right-to-Work Laws? Yes!" *Homiletic and Pastoral Review* 58 (January 1958): 344–47.

———. "The Theology of Work." *Pastoral Life* (May–June 1954): 23–26.

Fantasia, Rick. "From Class Consciousness to Culture, Action, and Social Organization." *Annual Review of Sociology* 21 (1995): 269–87.

Finnigan, Joyce, O.F.M. "Starting a Credit Union." *The Priest* 15 (December 1959): 1008–10.

Fisher, James. *The Catholic Counterculture in America, 1933–1962.* Chapel Hill: University of North Carolina Press, 1989.

Fitzpatrick, Joseph P. "The Encyclicals in the United States: What of the Human Person?" *Thought* 29 (Autumn 1954): 391–402.

———. "The Industry Council Plan as a Form of Social Organization." *American Catholic Sociological Review* 14 (October 1953): 146–55.

Fogarty, Gerald P., S.J. "The United States and the Vatican, 1939–1984." In *Papal Diplomacy and the Modern Age*, edited by Peter C. Kent and John F. Pollard, 221–44. Westport, Conn.: Praeger Press, 1994.

Fones-Wolf, Elizabeth. *Selling Free Enterprise: The Business Assault on Labor and Liberalism, 1945–1960.* Urbana: University of Illinois Press, 1994.

Foote, Peter. "Evolution of YCW: Notes on the Chicago Experience." *Apostolate* 7 (Spring 1960): 35.

"Founder of Jocism." *The Catholic Mind* 47 (May 1949): 292–97.

Freeman, Joshua, et al. *Who Built America? Working People and the Nation's Economy, Politics, Culture, and Society, Volume Two: From the Gilded Age to the Present.* New York: Pantheon Books, 1992.

Freemantle, Anne, ed. *The Papal Encyclicals in Their Historical Context.* 5th ed. New York: Mentor-Omega Books, 1963.

Galenson, Walter. "The Historical Role of American Trade Unionism." In *Unions*

in Transition: Entering the Second Century, edited by Seymour Martin Lipset. San Francisco: Institute for Contemporary Studies Press, 1986.
Gall, Jeffrey L. "Presbyterians, Warren Wilson, and the Country Life Movement." *The Journal of Presbyterian History* 76 (Fall 1998): 215–31.
Gargan, Edward T., ed. *Leo XIII and the Modern World*. New York: Sheed and Ward, 1961.
Genovese, Eugene. *The Slaveholder's Dilemma: Freedom and Progress in Southern Conservative Thought, 1820–1860*. Columbia: University of South Carolina Press, 1994.
Gettleman, Marvin. "The Lost World of U.S. Labor Education: Curricula at East and West Coast Community Schools, 144–1957." Paper delivered at Gotham History Festival, New York, October 5–14, 2001. Available at http://www.gothamcenter.org/festival/2001/confpapers/gettleman.pdf; accessed June 27, 2004.
Gillis, Chester. *Roman Catholicism in America*. New York: Columbia University Press, 1999.
Gleason, Philip. *The Conservative Reformers: German-American Catholics and the Social Order*. Notre Dame, Ind.: University of Notre Dame Press, 1968.
Gorman, Ralph, C.P. "Capitalism Canonized?" *The Sign* 29 (December 1949): 6.
———. "A New Capitalism in the Making?" *The Sign* 36 (October 1956): 12.
Great Encyclical Letters of Leo XIII. Edited by John J. Wynne, S.J. New York: Benziger Brothers, 1903.
Greeley, Andrew. "The Problem Approach to Social Inquiry." *Apostolate* 6 (Spring 1959): 2–5.
Gremillion, Joseph. *The Gospel of Peace and Justice: Catholic Social Teaching Since Pope John*. Maryknoll, N.Y.: Orbis Books, 1976.
Haight, Roger, S.J. "How My Mind Was Ruined, or Saved: Later Reflections of a Nice Catholic Boy Who Came to the Divinity School in 1967." *Criterion* 45, no. 2 (2006–7): 9–13, 28.
Halsey, William M. *The Survival of American Innocence in an Era of Disillusionment, 1920–1940*. Notre Dame, Ind.: University of Notre Dame Press, 1980.
Hanson, Eric O. *The Catholic Church and World Politics*. Princeton, N.J.: Princeton University Press, 1987.
Harrington, Michael. "The American Bishops on the Social Order." *The Catholic Worker* 18 (October 1952): 3, 6.
Harris, Paul T. "Communications: 'Obituary for Distributism.'" *The Commonweal* 61 (February 11, 1955): 505.
Harrison, William. *The Truth About Right-To-Work Laws: The Union Argument, the People's Case*. Washington, D.C.: National Right to Work Committee, 1959.
Hayes, Carleton J. H. *A Generation of Materialism, 1871–1900*. 2nd ed. New York: Harper and Row, 1947.
Hayes, John. "Cardijn in the World." *Apostolate* 4 (Spring 1957): 23–24.
Heaney, Larry. "Toehold on the Land." *The Catholic Worker* 14 (January 1948): 5.
———. "Toehold on the Land." *The Catholic Worker* 14 (June 1947): 4.
Heineman, Kenneth J. *A Catholic New Deal: Religion and Reform in Depression Pittsburgh*. University Park: Penn State University Press, 1999.
Heinz, John J. "Harvest Among the Harvesters." *The Priest* 5 (January 1949): 42–45.

Hellman, John. "The Opening to the Left in French Catholicism: The Role of the Personalists." *Journal of the History of Ideas* 34 (July–September, 1973): 381–90.
Hennacy, Ammon. *The Book of Ammon*. Salt Lake City, 1965.
———. "Christian Anarchism Defined." *The Catholic Worker* 22 (July–August, 1955): 3, 7.
Hennesey, James, S.J. *American Catholics: A History of the Roman Catholic Community in the United States*. New York: Oxford University Press, 1981.
———. "Leo XIII's Thomistic Revival: A Political and Philosophical Event." In *Celebrating the Medieval Heritage: A Colloquy on the Thought of Aquinas and Bonaventure*, edited by David Tracy. Chicago: University of Chicago Press, 1978.
Hennessy, David. "Communications." *The Commonweal* 49 (October 29, 1948): 63.
Hillenbrand, Reynold. "5 Point Social Program." *Apostolate* 3 (Winter 1955): 11–24.
———. "The Priesthood and the World." *Worship* 26 (January 1952): 49–57.
Higgins, George G. "American Contributions to the Implementation of the Industry Council Plan." *American Sociological Review* 13 (March 1952): 10–24.
———. "Cooperation Rather than Conflict." *Catholic Action* 31 (February 1949): 4–5.
———. "Letter: Response to the ACTU and Its Critics." *The Commonweal* 49 (January 21, 1949): 374–76.
———. "Social Action Program of the National Catholic Welfare Conference." *Review of Social Economy* 7 (September 1949): 37–38.
———. "Toward a New Society." *The Catholic Mind* 54 (November 1956): 629–35.
Higgins, George G., and William Bole. *Organized Labor and the Church: Reflections of a "Labor Priest."* New York: Paulist Press, 1993.
Himes, Kenneth R., O.F.M., ed. *Modern Catholic Social Teaching: Commentaries and Interpretations*. Washington, D.C.: Georgetown University Press, 2005.
Hodges, Harold M., Jr. *Social Stratification: Class in America*. Cambridge, Mass.: Schenkman, 1964.
Hofstadter, Richard. *The Age of Reform: From Bryan to F.D.R.* New York: Knopf, 1955.
Hogan, Edward. "The First Ten Years." *Apostolate* 5 (Summer 1958): 3.
"Holy See and Distributism." *The Catholic Worker* (April 1955): 1.
Hough, Billy. "Chat with YCW Chaplains." *Apostolate* 2 (Spring 1955): 7.
Ireland, John. "Leo XIII, His Work and Influence." *North American Review* 177 (September 1903): 321–64.
Jedin, Hubert, Konrad Repgen, and Jay Dolan, eds. *History of the Church*. Vols. 9 and 10. Translated by Margrit Resch. New York: Crossroad, 1981.
Jentunen, Arthur. "Leaven in the Unions." *Catholic Digest* 11 (November 1946): 56–60.
"JOC Survives in France." *America*, October 14, 1944, 22.
Kalven, Janet. *The Task of the Woman in the Modern World*. Des Moines, Iowa: NCRLC, 1946.
Kauffman, Christopher J. *Mission to Rural America: The Story of W. Howard Bishop, Founder of Glenmary*. New York: Paulist Press, 1991.

———. "W. Howard Bishop, President of the National Catholic Rural Life Conference, 1928–1934." *U.S. Catholic Historian* 8 (Fall 1989): 29–35.

Kavanagh, James H. "Ideology." In *Critical Terms for Literary Study*, 2nd ed., edited by Frank Lentricchia and Thomas McLaughlin, 306–20. Chicago: University of Chicago Press, 1995.

Keller, Edward A. *The Case for Right-to-Work Laws—A Defense of Voluntary Unionism*. Chicago: The Heritage Foundation, 1956.

———. *Christianity and American Capitalism*. Chicago: The Heritage Foundation, 1953.

———. "The Church and Our Economic System: 1." *Ave Maria* 65 (March 1, 1947): 263–66.

———. "The Morality of Profits: Conclusion." *Social Justice Review* 43 (October 1950): 187–89.

———. "The Morality of Profits: 1." *Social Justice Review* 43 (September 1950): 147–49.

———. "Previous Depressions." *Ave Maria* 42 (August 24, 1935): 225–30.

———. "Who Gets Our National Income?" *Catholic Digest* 12 (May 1948): 44–47.

———. "Right to Work Laws: Just and Beneficial." *Homiletic and Pastoral Review* 58 (October 1957): 34–46.

Kelly, George. "The ACTU and Its Critics." *The Commonweal* 49 (December 31, 1948): 298–302.

Kelly, John E. "The Influence of Aquinas' Natural Law Theory on the Principle of 'Corporatism' in the Thought of Leo XIII and Pius XI." In *Things Old and New: Catholic Social Teaching Revisited*, edited by Francis P. McHugh and Samuel M. Natale, 104–43. Lanham, Md.: University Press of America, 1993.

Kennedy, Keith. "YCW: A Worker's Apostolate?" *Apostolate* 5 (Spring 1958): 15–18.

Kent, Peter C., and John F. Pollard. "A Diplomacy Unlike Any Other: Papal Diplomacy in the Nineteenth and Twentieth Centuries." In *Papal Diplomacy in the Modern Age*, edited by Peter C. Kent and John F. Pollard, 11–21. Westport, Conn.: Praeger Press, 1994.

———, eds. *Papal Diplomacy in the Modern Age*. Westport, Conn.: Praeger Press, 1994.

"Labor Legislation: Statement of the Social Action Department, National Catholic Welfare Conference, Signed by Reverend Raymond A. McGowan, the Director." *Catholic Action* 31 (February 1949): 3.

LaFarge, John, S.J. "Catholic Agrarians Swing into Action." *America*, November 14, 1936, 129–30.

Land, Philip S. "Capitalism: Toward a Humane Economic Order." *Social Order* 1 (November 1951): 412–21.

———. "Uncritical Defender?" *America*, March 6, 1954, 603–4.

Land, Philip S., and George P. Kluberantz. "Practical Reason, Social Fact, and the Vocational Order." *The Modern Schoolman* 28 (May 1951): 239–66.

Leach, William. *Land of Desire: Merchants, Power, and the Rise of American Culture*. New York: Pantheon Books, 1993.

Le Berthon, Ted. "The Church and the Bracero." *The Catholic Worker* 24 (September 1957): 1, 7–8.

---. "Detroit and the Nation." *Catholic Digest* 9 (September 1945): 37–42.
Le Goff, Jacques. *Medieval Civilization: 400–1500*. Translated by Julia Barrow. Cambridge, Mass.: Basil Blackwell, 1991.
Ligutti, Luigi. "Agrarianism, Cooperatives, and the Bishops' Statement." *The Catholic Rural Life Bulletin* 3 (May 1940): 5.
---. "From Rome . . ." *Land and Home* 9 (December 1946): 95.
---. "Keep Youth on the Land." *Land and Home* 6 (September 1943): 71.
---. "Land and Home: An Introduction." *Land and Home* 5 (March 1942): 1.
---. "The Monsignor Says." *The Christian Farmer* 1 (February 1948): 1.
---. "No Room for Others." *Land and Home* 8 (June 1945): 32.
Ligutti, Luigi, and John C. Rawe. *Rural Roads to Security: America's Third Struggle for Freedom*. Milwaukee: Bruce Publishing, 1940.
Lincoln, Bruce. *Discourse and the Construction of Society: Comparative Studies of Myth, Ritual, and Classification*. New York: Oxford University Press, 1989.
---. *Theorizing Myth: Narrative, Ideology, and Scholarship*. Chicago: University of Chicago Press, 1999.
Lipset, Seymour Martin, ed. *Unions in Transition: Entering the Second Century*. San Francisco: Institute for Contemporary Studies Press, 1986.
Liu, William T., and Nathaniel Pallone, eds. *Catholics/U.S.A.: Perspectives on Social Change*. Lanham, Md.: Rowman and Littlefield, 1995.
Ludlow, Robert. "Anarchism and Leo XIII." *The Catholic Worker* 22 (September 1955): 3, 8.
---. "Communications." *The Commonweal* 49 (November 19, 1948): 139–40.
---. "Industrialism—Not an Evil in Itself." *The Catholic Worker* 18 (1948): 1, 6.
---. "A Re-evaluation." *The Catholic Worker* 21 (June 1955): 2, 8.
Lumsden, Keith, and Craig Petersen. "The Effect of Right-to-Work Laws on Unionization in the United States." *The Journal of Political Economy* 83 (December 1975): 1237–48.
Lynch, Miriam. "The Organized Social Apostolate of Albert de Mun." Ph.D. diss., Catholic University of America Press, 1952.
Lyttleton, Adrian. *The Seizure of Power: Fascism in Italy, 1919–1929*. 2nd ed. Princeton, N.J.: Princeton University Press, 1987.
Mangan, Mary Lou. "YCW Program." *Apostolate* 3 (Fall 1956): 15–17.
"Manifesto of the Young Christian Worker." *The Catholic Mind* 49 (July 1951): 462–64.
Mapel, David. *Social Justice Reconsidered: The Problem of Appropriate Precision in a Theory of Justice*. Urbana: University of Illinois Press, 1989.
Marciniak, Ed. "Clarification on Distributism." *The Catholic Worker* (November 1954): 1.
Marino, Dolores. "Y.C.W. in Our Factory." *Apostolate* 2 (Winter 1954): 20–26.
Marlett, Jeffrey. *Saving the Heartland: Catholic Missionaries in Rural America*. DeKalb: Northern Illinois University Press, 2002.
Marshall, D. "The Church and Capitalism." *Catholic World* 146 (November 1937): 177–80.
Marty, Martin E. *Modern American Religion, Volume 3: Under God, Indivisible, 1941–1960*. Chicago: University of Chicago Press, 1996.
---. *The One and the Many: America's Struggle for the Common Good*. Cambridge, Mass.: Harvard University Press, 1997.

Masse, Benjamin L. "The Church and Labor." *The Catholic Mind* 47 (October 1949): 603–8.

———, ed. *The Church and Social Progress: Background Readings for Pope John's "Mater et Magistra."* Milwaukee: Bruce Publishing, 1966.

———. "Does the Closed Shop Destroy the Right to Work?" *America*, January 24, 1942, 425–27.

———. "Right-to-Work Laws." *America*, September 1, 1956, 503–4.

———. "What Is the Taft-Hartley Act?" *America*, July 12, 1947, 406–8.

———. "What's Happening to Right-to-Work Laws?" *America*, May 7, 1955, 149–50.

Maurin, Peter. "Easy Essays." *The Catholic Worker* 2 (June 1933): 3.

McBrien, Richard P. *Catholicism*. Rev. ed. San Francisco: Harper and Row, 1994.

McCloskey, J. Michael. "The Catholic Worker Movement." *The Catholic Worker* 23 (May 1957): 4–5.

McCutcheon, Russell T. "Myth." In *Guide to the Study of Religion*, edited by Willi Braun and Russell T. McCutcheon, 190–208. London: Cassell, 2000.

McGowan, Raymond A. "Footnotes to a Document." *The Commonweal* 24 (May 8, 1936): 38–39.

———. "Further Footnotes." *The Commonweal* 24 (July 31, 1936): 339–40.

———. "Government and Social Justice." *The Catholic Mind* 36 (June 8, 1938): 223–25.

McGreevy, John T. *Catholicism and American Freedom: A History*. New York: W. W. Norton, 2003.

McHugh, Francis P., and Samuel M. Natale, eds. *Things Old and New: Catholic Social Teaching Revisited*. Lanham, Md.: University Press of America, 1993.

McKee, Arnold F. "Selling American Capitalism: A Conspicuous Failure." *Social Order* 6 (November 1956): 411–16.

McKenna, Norman. "ACTU." *The Catholic Mind* 45 (February 1947): 117–20.

———. "The Story of the ACTU." *Catholic World* 168 (March 1949): 453–59.

McKeon, Richard M., S.J. "New Capitalism vs. Old." *Social Order* 3 (March 1953): 99–102.

McLaughlin, Vincent J. "A Labor School Takes Inventory." *The Commonweal* 31 (January 12, 1940): 261–62.

McNabb, Vincent, O.P. "An Economic Creed: From 'The Church and the Land.'" *The Catholic Worker* 12 (December 1945): 6.

McShane, Joseph M. *Sufficiently Radical: Catholicism, Progressivism, and the Bishops' Program of 1919*. Washington, D.C.: Catholic University of America Press, 1986.

Meany, George. "On Labor's Future." In *American Labor Since the New Deal*, edited by Melvyn Dubofsky, 164–71. Chicago: Quadrangle Books, 1971.

Mich, Marvin L. Krier. *Catholic Social Teaching and Movements*. Mystic, Conn.: Twenty-third Publications, 1998.

Michel, Virgil. "What Is Capitalism?" *The Commonweal* 28 (April 29, 1938): 6.

Miller, Douglas T., and Marion Nowak. *The Fifties: The Way We Really Were*. Garden City, N.Y.: Doubleday, 1977.

Miller, Raymond W. *Monsignor Ligutti: The Pope's Country Agent*. Washington, D.C.: University Press of America, 1981.

Mink, Gwendolyn. *Old Labor and New Immigrants in American Political Development: Union, Party, and the State, 1875–1920*. Ithaca, N.Y.: Cornell University Press, 1986.
Misner, Paul. "The Predecessors of *Rerum Novarum* Within Catholicism." *Review of Social Economy* 49 (Winter 1991): 444–64.
Mooney, Edward D. "The American Tradition." *The Catholic Mind* 36 (June 8, 1938): 215–20.
Moran, Lawrence. "From the Mail: Hennessy and Marciniak." *The Catholic Worker* 21 (December 1954): 4.
Morello, Isabelle. "Approximations to the Industry Council Plan in American Industry." *Catholic Business Education Review* 5 (June 1954): 57–66.
Morris, Charles R. *American Catholic: The Saints and Sinners Who Built America's Most Powerful Church*. New York: Vintage Books, 1997.
Morris, George. "Using the Cloth to Hide Anti-Union Dagger." *The Daily Worker*, June 16, 1948, 1.
Morris, Rudolph Edward. "Christianity and Collectivist Trends." *Thought* 23 (September 1948): 463–74.
Morriss, Frank. "Right-to-Work Laws? Yes!" *Homiletic and Pastoral Review* 58 (March 1958): 546–51.
Mowry, George E., and Blaine A. Brownell. *The Urban Nation, 1920–1980*. New York: Hill and Wang, 1981.
Mueller, Franz H. "Christianity and American Capitalism: A Book Review." *Social Justice Review* 47 (May 1954): 43–45.
Muench, Aloisius J. "Justice for the Farmer." *Land and Home* 5 (June 1942): 1.
Mulcahy, Richard E., S.J. "The Peschian Value Paradox: A Key to the Function of Vocational Groups." *Review of Social Economy* 10 (March 1952): 32–41.
Murphy, Paul V. *The Rebuke of History: The Southern Agrarians and American Conservative Thought*. Chapel Hill: University of North Carolina Press, 2001.
Murray, Philip. "American Labor and the Threat of Communism." *Annals of the American Academy of Political and Social Sciences* 247 (March 1951): 125–30.
———. "CIO Looks Forward." *Christian Social Action* 6 (January 1941): 9–13.
———. "CIO Victory Plan." *Christian Social Action* 6 (December 1941): 288–94.
———. "Looking Forward." *Christian Social Action* 6 (June 1941): 186–92.
National Catholic Rural Life Conference. *Manifesto on Rural Life*. Milwaukee: Bruce Publishing, 1939.
———. *Rural Life in a Peaceful World*. Des Moines, Iowa: NCRLC, 1944.
"'Nation' Looks at ACTU: Misses Some Things: Fails to Understand Motives." *The Michigan Labor Leader*, January 17, 1941, 3.
"NCWC Calls for Employers' Associations." *The Commonweal* 48 (September 3, 1948): 488.
Neville, Ray. "Apostle in the Executive Suite." *The Sign* 35 (July 1956): 20–21.
Novak, Michael. *The American Vision: An Essay on the Future of Democratic Capitalism*. Washington, D.C.: The American Enterprise Institute for Public Policy Research, 1978.
———. *The Catholic Ethic and the Spirit of Capitalism*. New York: The Free Press, 1993.

———. *Freedom with Justice: Catholic Social Thought and Liberal Institutions.* San Francisco: Harper and Row, 1984.
Novitsky, Anthony. "The Ideological Development of Peter Maurin's Green Revolution." Ph.D. diss., State University of New York, Buffalo, 1977.
O'Brien, David J. *American Catholics and Social Reform: The New Deal Years.* New York: Oxford University Press, 1968.
———. *The Renewal of American Catholicism.* New York: Oxford University Press, 1972.
O'Brien, David J., and Thomas A. Shannon, eds. *Catholic Social Thought: The Documentary Heritage.* Maryknoll, N.Y.: Orbis Books, 1992.
O'Brien, W. V. "War." *The New Catholic Encyclopedia,* 14:795–801. Washington, D.C.: Catholic University of America, 1967.
Opinion Research Corporation. *The Public Looks at 14 (b) and the Right to Work Issue: A Comprehensive, Nationwide Survey of General Public Attitudes.* Princeton, N.J.: Opinion Research Corporation, 1966.
O'Rourke, Edward W. "Soil Saving—A Plan." *Land and Home* 10 (March 1947): 22–23.
Parsons, Wilfrid, S.J. "The Function of Government in Industry." *The Catholic Mind* 31 (March 1943): 7–15.
———. "The Papal Plan for Social Reconstruction." *The Catholic Mind* 40 (March 22, 1942): 1–15.
———. "What Are Vocational Groups?" *Thought* 17 (September 1942): 464–69.
Paulhus, Normand J. "Uses and Misuses of the Term 'Social Justice' in the Roman Catholic Tradition." *The Journal of Religious Ethics* 15 (Fall 1987): 261–82.
Petta, Frank. "Distributist." *The Catholic Worker* 21 (January 1955): 4.
Piehl, Mel. *Breaking Bread: The Catholic Worker and the Origin of Catholic Radicalism in America.* Philadelphia: Temple University Press, 1982.
Pollard, John F. *The Vatican and Italian Fascism, 1929–32.* Cambridge: Cambridge University Press, 1985.
Pope, Stephen J. "Natural Law in Catholic Social Teachings." In *Modern Catholic Social Teaching: Commentaries and Interpretations,* edited by Kenneth R. Himes, O.F.M., 41–71. Washington, D.C.: Georgetown University Press, 2005.
Prentiss, Craig. "Taming Leviathan: The American Catholic Church and Economics, 1940–1960." 2 vols. Ph.D. diss., University of Chicago, 1997.
"Record of Capitalism." *Ave Maria* 73 (June 23, 1951): 772–73.
Reese, Thomas J., S.J. *A Flock of Shepherds: The National Conference of Catholic Bishops.* Kansas City, Mo.: Sheed and Ward, 1992.
Reilly, Gerard D. "State Rights and the Law of Labor Relations." In *Labor Unions and Public Policy,* edited by Edward H. Chamberlin et al., 93–121. Washington, D.C.: American Enterprise Association, 1958.
Repgen, Konrad. "Foreign Policy of the Popes in the Epoch of the World Wars." In *History of the Church,* vol. 10, edited by Hubert Jedin, Konrad Repgen, and John Dolan, translated by Anselm Biggs, 35–96. New York: Crossroad, 1981.
Rice, Charles Owen. "Confessions of an Anti-Communist." *Labor History* 31 (Summer 1989): 449–62.
Roberts, Nancy L. *Dorothy Day and the Catholic Worker.* Albany: State University of New York Press, 1984.

Rogers, Elizabeth. "Report on Migrant Labor." *The Catholic Worker* 25 (April–May 1959): 1, 8.

Rosswurm, Steve. "The Catholic Church and the Left-Led Unions: Labor Priests, Labor Schools, and the ACTU." In *The CIO's Left-Led Unions*, edited by Steve Rosswurm, 119–38. New Brunswick, N.J.: Rutgers University Press, 1992.

———, ed. *The CIO's Left-Led Unions*. New Brunswick, N.J.: Rutgers University Press, 1992.

———. "Introduction: An Overview and Preliminary Assessment of the CIO's Expelled Unions." In *The CIO's Left-Led Unions*, edited by Steve Rosswurm, 1–18. New Brunswick, N.J.: Rutgers University Press, 1992.

Rubin, Louis D. *I'll Take My Stand: The South and the Agrarian Tradition*. New York: Harper, 1962.

Ryan, John A. *A Better Economic Order*. New York: Harper, 1935.

———. *A Living Wage: Its Ethical and Economic Aspects*. New York: Macmillan, 1906.

Ryan, William A. "Detroit ACTU Explains Its Decision." *The Wage Earner*, October 1956, 1.

Schackmann, J. H. "Are Catholics Committed to Capitalism?" *Catholic World* 148 (January 1939): 423–30.

Schmiedeler, Edgar, O.S.B. "Credit for the Farmer." *The Catholic Rural Life Bulletin* 3 (August 1940): 12–13, 25–27.

Schmiesing, Kevin E. *Within the Market Strife: American Catholic Economic Thought from "Rerum Novarum" to Vatican II*. Lanham, Md.: Lexington Books, 2004.

Schneider, Mary L. "Visions of Land and Farmer: American Civil Religion and the National Catholic Rural Life Conference." In *An American Church: Essays on the Americanization of the Catholic Church*, edited by David J. Alvarez, 99–122. Morgana, Calif.: St. Mary's College of California, 1979.

Schnepp, Gerald J. "Let's Call It the Industry Council Plan." *America*, February 21, 1948, 572–73.

———. "Ten Years of the Industry Council Committee." *American Catholic Sociological Review* 17 (March 1956).

Schuck, Michael J. *That They Be One: The Social Teaching of the Papal Encyclicals, 1740–1989*. Washington, D.C.: Georgetown University Press, 1991.

Schuyler, Joseph B. "The Industry Council Idea: Is It Adaptable to the United States?" *American Catholic Sociological Review* 18 (December 1957): 290–300.

Seaton, Douglas P. *Catholics and Radicals*. Lewisburg, Pa.: Bucknell University Press, 1981.

Segrè, Claudio G. *Italo Balbo: A Fascist Life*. Berkeley and Los Angeles: University of California Press, 1987.

"Semantics of Right-to-Work." *America*, March 29, 1958, 744–45.

Senser, Bob. "Your 'Right to Work.'" *The Catholic Mind* 56 (May–June 1958): 240–48.

Shannon, Robert L., F.S.C. "The Industry Council Plan as an Instrument of Reconstruction." *Review of Social Economy* 1 (December 1942): 87–99.

Shapiro, Edward. "Decentralist Intellectuals and the New Deal." *The Journal of American History* 58 (March 1972): 938–57.

Sharper, Philip. "The Catholic Layman and the Theology of Work." *Apostolate* 6 (Summer 1959): 18–22.
Sheehan, Arthur. *Peter Maurin: Gay Believer*. Garden City, N.J.: Hanover Press, 1959.
Sirgiovanni, George. *An Undercurrent of Suspicion: Anti-Communism in America During World War II*. New Brunswick, N.J.: Transaction Publishers, 1990.
Sisson, Elbert R. "Communications." *The Commonweal* 49 (October 29, 1948): 66.
Smith, Jonathan Z. *Imagining Religion: From Jonestown to Babylon*. Chicago: University of Chicago Press, 1982.
Smith, M. J., O.M.I. "The Young Christian Workers Movement: I." *Social Justice Review* 40 (January 1948): 295–98.
———. "The Young Christian Workers Movement: II." *Social Justice Review* 40 (February 1948): 333–36.
Soderini, Count Edward. *The Pontificate of Leo XIII, Vols. 1 & 2*. Translated by Barbara B. Carter. London: Burns, Oates, and Washbourne, 1934.
———. *Socialism and Catholicism*. New York: Longmans Green, 1896.
Stone, Albert E., Jr. "Seward Collins and the *American Review*: Experiment in Pro-Fascism, 1933–37." *American Quarterly* 12 (Spring 1960): 3–19.
"Summary of Resolutions Adopted at the 23rd Annual NCRLC Convention, Des Moines, Iowa, October 23–25, 1945." *Land and Home* 8 (December 1945): 92–93.
Thornton, Jack and Mary. "Five Years on the Land." *The Catholic Worker* 18 (February 1953): 1, 5.
Thornton, John. "From the Mail: Green Revolution." *The Catholic Worker* 21 (December 1954): 4.
Tocqueville, Alexis de. *Democracy in America*. Edited by J. P. Mayer. Translated by George Lawrence. New York: Harper and Row, 1966.
Toner, Jerome L. *The Closed Shop*. Washington, D.C.: American Council on Public Affairs, 1942.
———. "Right-to-Work Laws: Unjust and Harmful." *Homiletic and Pastoral Review* 58 (October 1957): 47–59.
Trehey, Harold Francis. *Foundations of a Modern Guild System*. Washington, D.C.: Catholic University of America Press, 1940.
U.S. Congress. Joint Subcommittee on Low-Income Families of the Joint Committee on the Economic Report. *Low-Income Families*. 81st Cong., 2nd sess., December 21, 1949.
U.S. Congress. Joint Subcommittees of the Judiciary. *Revision of Immigration, Naturalization, and Nationality Laws*. 82nd Cong., 1st sess., March 12, 1951.
U.S. House of Representatives. Committee on the Judiciary. *Hearings Before the President's Commission on Immigration and Naturalization*. 82nd Cong., 2nd sess., October 1, 1952.
U.S. House of Representatives. Select Committee of the House Committee on Agriculture. *Farm Security Administration*. 78th Cong., 1st sess., March 18, 1948.
U.S. Senate. Committee on Agriculture and Forestry. *Agricultural Act of 1948*. 80th Cong., 2nd sess., April 21, 1948.

U.S. Senate. Subcommittee on Labor and Labor-Management Relations of the Committee on Labor and Public Welfare. *Migratory Labor.* 82nd Cong., 2nd sess, part 1, February 11, 1952.

Vajda, Mihaly. *Fascism: A Mass Movement.* New York: St. Martin's Press, 1976.

Van Allen, Rodger. *The Commonweal and American Catholicism: The Magazine, the Movement, the Meaning.* Philadelphia: Fortress Press, 1974.

Vatter, Harold G. *The U.S. Economy in the 1950s: An Economic History.* Chicago: University of Chicago Press, 1985.

Wallace, Lillian Parker. *Leo XIII and the Rise of Socialism.* Durham, N.C.: Duke University Press, 1966.

Ward, Leo, C.S.C., ed. *The American Apostolate: American Catholics in the Twentieth Century.* Westminster, Md.: The Newman Press, 1952.

Ward, Richard J. "The Role of the Association of Catholic Trade Unionists in the Labor Movement." *Review of Social Economy* 14 (September 1956): 79–100.

Warner, Michael. *Changing Witness: Catholic Bishops and Public Policy, 1917–1994.* Washington, D.C.: Ethics and Public Policy Center; Grand Rapids, Mich.: William B. Eerdmans, 1995.

Weaver, Mary Jo, and R. Scott Appleby, eds. *Being Right: Conservative Catholics in America.* Bloomington: Indiana University Press, 1995.

Weber, Wilhelm. "Society and the State as a Problem for the Church." In *History of the Church*, vol. 10, edited by Hubert Jedin, Konrad Repgen, and John Dolan, translated by Anselm Biggs, 229–59. New York: Crossroad, 1981.

Weigel, George. *Building the Free Society: Democracy, Capitalism, and Catholic Social Teaching*, edited by George Weigel and Robert Royal. Grand Rapids, Mich.: William B. Eerdmans, 1993.

———. "The Neoconservative Difference: A Proposal for the Renewal of Church and Society." In *Being Right: Conservative Catholics in America*, edited by Mary Jo Weaver and R. Scott Appleby, 138–62. Bloomington: Indiana University Press, 1995.

Wills, Gary. *Bare Ruined Choirs: Doubt, Prophecy, and Radical Religion.* Garden City, N.Y.: Doubleday, 1972.

Wilson, Francis Graham. *The Case for Conservatism.* Seattle: University of Washington Press, 1951.

———. "Catholics and the 'New Conservatism.'" *Social Order* 6 (June 1956): 247–52.

Witte, Raymond Philip. *Twenty-five Years of Crusading: A History of the National Catholic Rural Life Conference.* Des Moines, Iowa: NCRLC, 1948.

"YCW Training Course." *Apostolate* 4 (Spring 1957): 18–19.

Yzermans, Vincent A. *The People I Love: A Biography of Luigi G. Ligutti.* Collegeville, Minn.: The Liturgical Press, 1976.

Zotti, Mary Irene. *A Time of Awakening: The Young Christian Worker Story in the United States, 1938 to 1970.* Chicago: Loyola University Press, 1991.

Index

Abell, Aaron I., 4
Abraham Lincoln Brigade, 97
Aeterni Patris, 18, 20
AFL-CIO, 88–89, 124, 170, 176, 193–94
Agar, Herbert, 42–43, 51 n. 41
agrarian myth, 15, 40–41, 43, 46, 69
Agricultural Act of 1948, 67
agricultural economy, 39–43, 49–50, 65, 69, 81
agronomic universities, 72–73
Allen, Frederick Lewis, 149
Amalgamated Clothing Workers, 86
America, 71
American Catholic Sociological Society (ACSS), 212–14
    and Industry Council Committee, 213–14, 214 n. 22
American Council on Public Affairs, 181
American Country Life Association, 41–42
American Federation of Labor (AFL), 85–88, 107
American Legion, 98
American Review, 42
anarchism, 73–77, 74 n. 127, 75 n. 128, 80, 206
Ancient Order of Hibernians, 99
Apostolate, 133, 140
Aquinas, Thomas, 18, 23 n. 16, 26, 26 n. 27, 53, 200, 207
Association of Catholic Trade Unionists (ACTU), 15, 83, 90, 102–25, 130, 140–41, 159, 184, 211, 214, 216–18, 221–22, 226, 228–29, 234, 242–43
Au Milieu des Solicitudes, 19 n. 8
Augustine of Hippo, 148, 223

"authenticity," 14, 244
    as rhetorical tool, 14
Ave Maria, 145, 148, 166

Bakunin, Mikhail, 74
Bell, Daniel, 234
Belloc, Hilaire, 43–45, 44 n. 17, 45 n. 24, 49, 77, 147, 223
Better Economic Order, A, 204
Big Change, 149
birth control, 60–61
Bishop, W. Howard, 51 n. 41
Bishops' Program of Social Reconstruction, The (1919), 91, 95, 214
Boland, John, 108
Bovée, David, 62, 69
bracero program, 67–69, 139
Briefs, Goetz A., 147, 189–90, 196
Brookings Institution, 92–93
Brophy, John, 99–100
Brown, Leo C., 186–88, 211–12
Bruehl, Charles, 210
Buckley, William F., 243
Bureau of Economic Research (Notre Dame University), 164–65, 167
Burnham, Philip, 219–20, 222–23

Cantwell, Daniel, 222–23
capitalism, 6–7, 13, 15, 34, 44, 44 n. 17, 83, 85, 89, 92–93, 143–74, 218–24, 231–32
    debates over definition of, 146–51
    and links to Protestantism, 45, 147, 147–48 n. 11
    and industrialism, 218–24
Cardijn, Joseph, 126–29, 132–33, 140
Carey, Philip A., 113–14, 122–23

Index

Carney, Francis W., 191
Catholic Action, 13, 126–28, 202, 222, 242
Catholic Business Education Review, 234
Catholic Council on Working Life, 114
Catholic Hour, The, 98
Catholic Labor Alliance (Chicago), 102–3, 114, 136, 159, 222, 224
Catholic Labor Alliance (Detroit), 136, 159
Catholic Labor Defense League (CDLD), 110
Catholic Labor Guild of Boston, 114
Catholic Mind, The, 186
Catholic Social Principles, 104
Catholic social thought, 2, 8–12, 14, 16, 244
  defined, 2
  redescription of, 8–12, 14, 16, 244
Catholic Theological Society of America, 240
Catholic University of America, The, 195, 205
Catholic Worker movement, 15, 40, 43, 48, 70–81, 83, 102, 124, 143, 206, 218–22, 225, 241, 243
  and farming communes, 78–80
  and government authority, 74–77, 81
  and industrialism, 216–22
Catholic Worker, The (newspaper), 71–72, 74, 76–79, 220, 223
Catholic World, The, 146, 152
Catholics and Radicals, 122
Centesimus Annus, 240
Central-Verein, 47–48, 147
Chávez, César, 56
Chesterton, G. K., 43–44, 49, 77, 81, 218–19
"Christ the Worker" Prayer, 119–20
Christian anarchism. *See* anarchism
Christian Century, The, 67, 180
Christian Economics, 162
Christian Family Movement, 60, 128
Christian Policy for Agriculture, A, 59
Christianity and American Capitalism, 166, 168–71
Ciarrocchi, Giuseppe, 203
City of God, 148
Civil Rights movement, 137, 196
Clancy, Raymond S., 111
class consciousness, 84–85, 88–89, 127, 136, 136–39
Clayton Antitrust Act of 1914, 166
Cogley, John, 161

Collins, Seward, 42
Columbia Magazine, 112
Comey, Dennis J., 195
Committee on Industrial Organization (CIO), 86–88, 99–100, 105, 116–17, 122, 210, 213, 234
common good, 26–27, 34, 36, 153, 172, 175–76, 181–86, 189–90, 207
Commonweal, The, 71–72, 92, 118, 130, 161, 217–19, 221
communism, 23, 34, 44, 53, 73, 78, 85–89, 95–102, 96 n. 29, 107, 109–12, 114–23, 135, 151, 154, 164, 167, 174, 185, 192, 201, 203, 209, 240, 242
Communist Worker Schools, 101, 108
Connell, Francis J., 195–96
Conrad, Arthur L., 157
Coogan, John E., 176, 181–83, 185, 192–93, 196
cooperatives, 55–56, 59, 64, 66, 74, 78–79, 80, 158, 241
corporatism, 35–36, 36 n. 53, 47, 92, 105, 201–2, 204, 207, 210, 214, 225
Cort, John C., 107, 109, 111, 117, 121–23, 130, 178, 211, 216–23, 226–27, 229, 234
Coughlin, Charles, 5, 111
Council of Business and Professional Men of the Catholic Faith (CBPM), 172–73
Council on Working Life. *See* Catholic Labor Alliance (Chicago)
Country Life Association, 41
Country Life movement, 41–42, 81
credit unions, 56, 57, 59, 66, 74
  parish affiliated, 57
Cronin, John F., 101, 104, 114, 182, 185, 188, 193–94, 230
Crosby, Donald, 98

Dachauer, Alban J., 62
D'Agostino, Peter, 19, 202
Daily Worker, The, 116–17
Davis, Winston, 18
Day, Dorothy, 70, 72–75, 117, 143, 218, 222–23
decentralist movement, 42–43
DeMille, Cecil B., 164
Democracy in America, 83
Dempsey, Bernard W., 148
Department of Church and Economic Life (National Council of Churches), 180

Dillard, Victor, 222
Dinneen, John A., 15, 152-55, 157, 167, 243
distributism, 43-46, 49-50, 73, 77-78, 80, 83, 124, 140, 167, 218-19, 221, 224-25, 241
Distributist League, 44-45
Divini Redemptoris, 58
Dolan, Jay, 13-14, 138
Dolan, Timothy, 90
Donahue, George R., 102
Drucker, Peter, 149-50
Dubofsky, Melvyn, 87, 242

Eisenhower, Dwight D., 234
Eliot, T. S., 155
Esprit, 73

Fair Employment Practices Commission (U.S.), 171
Falque, Ferdinand, 15, 157-64, 185, 195, 243
Fantasia, Rick, 84
Farm Credit Administration, 56-57
farm schools, 60
fascism, 31-33, 36, 36 n. 53, 53, 85-86, 104, 120, 201-4, 207, 209-10, 218, 225, 233
Fatima, Our Lady of, 97
Fitzgerald, Albert E., 105
Fitzpatrick, Joseph P., 231-33
Flick, Frank, 172
Fones-Wolf, Elizabeth, 145
Ford, Henry, 223
Fordham University, 108, 182, 231
Fortune Magazine, 109, 149, 234
Foundations of a Modern Guild System, 205-7
Franco, Francisco, 97-98
Free America, 42

Gaudium et spes, 239-40
Genesis, 11-12, 17, 23-24
G. I. Bill of Rights, 13, 138
Giese, Vincent, 161
Gill, Eric, 77, 218, 220-21
Gillis, James, 203
Gilson, Etienne, 74
Gleason, Philip, 47, 144
Goldstein, Israel, 180
Goldwater, Barry, 181
Gompers, Samuel, 109
Gorman, Ralph, 151
Gravediggers Union Strike (1949), 111-12

Greeley, Andrew, 137
Gregorian University (Rome), 231
Gremillion, Joseph, 7
Gundlach, Gustav, 231

Haas, Francis, 161, 171-73
Haight, Roger, 240
Harrington, Michael, 224
Harrison, William T., 176
Hart, Luke E., 112
Hayes, Carleton J. H., 1
Hayes, John M., 101
Heaney, Larry, 78-79
Heinz, John J., 61
Hennacy, Ammon, 75-76
Hennessy, David, 222
Herberg, Will, 193
hierarchy, 21-25, 32, 45-46, 51, 169
  as element of Roman Catholic ideology, 21, 21 n. 12, 24-25, 25 n. 23, 32, 45-46, 45 n. 24, 51, 169
Higgins, George, 91, 95, 102, 114, 127, 158-62, 172-73, 214, 216, 221, 226, 231
Hillenbrand, Reynold, 127-29, 133-36
historiography of Catholic social thought, 3-8, 244
Hoffa, Jimmy, 179
Hofstadter, Richard, 14, 40
homesteading, 53-55
Homiletic and Pastoral Review, The, 181
Hoover, Herbert, 164
Houses of Hospitality, 72-73, 80
Hutchinson, B. E., 164
Hutton, Barbara, 111

ideology, 8-11, 9 n. 15, 24, 37, 40, 207, 237-38, 244
  defined, 9
I'll Take My Stand, 42-43
Industry Council Committee. *See* American Catholic Sociological Society
Industry Council Plan (ICP), 15-16, 92, 105, 165, 175, 199-235
  Philip Murray's version of, 210-12, 226
  and role of government, 225-28
Institute for Social Order (St. Louis University), 211, 230
Institute of Social Education (St. John's College), 191
International Ladies' Garment Workers, 86
International Longshoremen's Association, 102
Irish Colonization Association, 47

Isidore, Saint, 63
Italian Fascism. *See* Fascism

Jeffersonian ideal, 40–41, 46–47, 50, 77, 241
Jeunesse Ouvriere Catholique, 126–27, 137, 140
Jewish Labor Committee, 103
Jocism. *See* Jeunesse Ouvriere Catholique
John Paul II, Pope, 6 n. 8, 7, 240
Joint Production Committees. *See* labor-management committees
Jones, John Paul, 176
Jostock, Paul, 147

Kafka, Franz, 223
Kavanagh, James, 9, 237
Keller, Edward A., 15, 164–74, 165 nn. 45, 46, 176, 181–85, 189, 191–92, 195, 220, 228–29, 233, 243
Kelley, William J., 180
Kelly, George, 118
Kelly, John E., 23
Kennedy, Joseph, 164
Kennedy, Keith, 138–39
Kennedy, Robert F., 179
Kent, Peter, 19
Ketteler, Wilhelm von, 47
Kenkel, Frederick P., 47–48, 147
Kluberantz, George P., 230–31
Knights of Columbus, 99, 112
Knights of Labor, 122
Kulturkampf, 19

Labor Guild (of Boston), 103
Labor Leader, 109
labor-management committees, 217, 223, 228–30, 234
labor unions, 28, 56, 67, 85–125, 131, 133, 135, 157, 167–70, 175–97, 201, 208, 214, 216–17, 232–33
    and right-to-work laws, 175–97
    and the National Recovery Administration, 208
    forms of security, 177–78
labor schools, 101, 107–9, 136, 145
laic laws, 19
laissez-faire, 34, 34 n. 46, 143, 153, 156, 166, 168, 201, 228, 238, 240
Land, Philip, 330–31
Lateran Treaties of 1929, 32, 202–3, 207, 209
Lehrbuch der Nationalokonomie, 200–201

Leach, William, 153
Le Goff, Jacques, 20
Lenin, V. I., 97
Leo XIII, Pope, 1, 18, 19 n. 8, 20–44, 48–50, 69, 76, 104, 120, 126, 134–35, 144, 163–64, 169, 174, 183–84, 186, 192, 195, 239
Lewis, John L., 88
liberalism
    Catholic opposition to, 2, 20, 22, 31–32, 53, 96, 152, 155, 207
    and individualism, 2, 53, 205
Life is Worth Living, 98
Ligutti, Luigi, 49, 53–54, 57–58, 60, 63–64, 66–67, 70, 207
Lincoln, Bruce, 8 n. 13, 9–11, 29, 29–30 n. 36
liturgical renewal movement, 62
Living Wage, A, 91
Ludlow, Robert, 76, 220–21, 224
Luther, Martin, 147

Magna Carta, 176
"Manifesto of the Young Christian Worker," 131–32
Manifesto on Rural Life, 50
Marciniak, Ed, 193, 224–25
Marino, Dolores, 133, 135
Maritain, Jacques, 74
Marlett, Jeffrey, 60, 80
Marx, Paul, 161
Marxism, 8–9, 24, 28, 41, 44, 68, 73, 81, 85–86, 89, 96–102, 115, 131, 136, 148, 161–63, 172–74, 177, 184, 194, 200
Mathews, J. B., 164
Maurin, Peter, 71–74, 74 n. 127, 218, 220
McCarthy, Joseph, 98
McClellan, John L., 179
McClellan Senate Hearings, 179, 184–85, 191
McCutcheon, Russell, 11, 14 n. 30
McDonnell, Francis J., 114
McGowan, Raymond, 92–94, 101–2, 214–15, 226
McGuire, Paul, 130
McKee, Arnold F., 151
McKeon, Richard, 149–51, 168, 243
McLaughlin, Vincent J., 108
McNabb, Vincent, 43, 77
Meany, George, 88–89, 176
medieval guild system, 21, 35–36, 45, 47, 92, 177, 199, 202, 204–6
Metzger, Sidney, 192

Mich, Marvin Krier, 7
Michel, Dom Virgil, O.S.B., 62, 143, 146–47
Monaghan, John P., 108
Morris, George, 116–17
Mounier, Emmanuel, 73
Muelder, Walter G., 180
Muench, Aloysius J., 193
Murray, John Courtney, 53, 207
Murray, Philip, 99–100, 210–14, 226, 228
Mussolini, Benito, 31–33, 36, 201–3
    and the American Catholic press, 203
myth, 3, 8–12, 14, 31, 37, 131, 145, 162, 175, 197, 199, 225, 238–39, 241, 244
    defined, 10
    and role in naturalizing ideology, 11
    and taxonomy, 10, 10 n. 19, 29, 238–39
    umbrella myth defined, 12

National Catholic Rural Life Conference (NCRLC), 15, 40, 43, 46, 48–71, 78–81, 83, 90, 115, 124, 131, 241, 243
National Catholic Welfare Conference, 83, 90, 160, 164, 214, 221
National Council of Churches, 180
National Association of Manufacturers (NAM), 15, 145, 157, 165, 170, 176, 178, 186
nativism, 48
National Industrial Recovery Act, 53, 166, 208
National Labor Relations Act. *See* Wagner Act
National Labor Relations Board (NLRB), 87–88, 188
National Recovery Administration (NRA), 208–9, 218, 233
natural law, 14–15, 17–18, 23, 23 n. 16, 30–31, 33–35, 37, 145, 155–56, 175–76, 182–83, 186, 195, 200, 227, 230–31, 238–41
Nell-Breuning, Oswald von, 200
Neoconservative Catholics, 6, 6 n. 9
Neo-Thomism, 74
Neuhaus, Richard John, 6 n. 9
New Deal, 13, 65, 91, 98, 101, 144–45, 164, 166, 208, 215, 228
New Society, 149
Nichols, William, 149
Non Abbiamo Bisogno, 202–03
Nostis et Nobiscum, 22, 96, 96–97 n. 30

Notre Dame University, 164, 171
Novak, Michael, 6, 6–7 n. 9, 243

O'Brien, David, 4–6, 5 n. 6, 36 n. 53
O'Hara, Edwin V., 48–49, 52–53, 90
On Atheistic Communism, 195

pacifism, 75
Papal States, 19, 22, 96, 202
Parsons, Wilfred, 205, 224, 227–28
Partito Popolare, 32, 203
Pastoral Life, 158
Paul VI, Pope, 240
personalism, 35, 73–74, 77, 221–22
Pesch, Heinrich, 47–48, 200–201
Piehl, Mel, 72, 78
Pius IX, Pope, 22
Pius X, Pope, 192
Pius XI, Pope, 13, 31–37, 48, 55, 58, 64–65, 76, 93, 104, 111, 120, 127, 134–35, 144, 154, 166, 169, 171–72, 182, 186, 192, 195, 199–205, 207, 209, 212, 218, 220–22, 227, 231, 233–35, 239
Pius XII, Pope, 50, 62, 120, 127–28, 134, 168–69, 169 n. 55, 184, 194, 229
Plato, 9
Pollard, John F., 19
Pope, Stephen J., 239
Popes and the Social Principles of Rural Life, The, 55
Popular Front, 86, 86 n. 8
Populism, 41
Populorum Progressio, 240
Powderly, Terrence V., 109
practical schools, 60
Priest, The, 182
Printing Pressmen's Union, 112
private property, 21–24, 23 n. 16, 34, 44–45, 49–51, 57–59, 81, 125, 133, 140, 148, 150–53, 166, 168, 175, 206, 241, 243
Program for the Family Farm, 51
Protestant Ethic and the Spirit of Capitalism, 45, 147
Protestantism, 41–42, 48, 98, 127, 147, 162, 180
    as origin of liberalism, 45, 96, 147
    and right-to-work laws, 180
    and rural life, 41–42, 48

Quadragesimo Anno, 3, 12, 14–46, 48, 50, 55, 58, 69, 74, 80, 82–83, 92–94, 102–3, 106, 110, 121, 125,

Quadragesimo Anno, (continued)
    131–32, 145, 148, 154, 156,
    166–69, 172, 175, 192, 199–205,
    208, 211–13, 220, 222, 225–26,
    229, 233–34, 238–41, 243
    and Church authority, 37
    and fascism, 36 n. 53
    and "just wages," 35
    and "neutral unions," 192
    and private property 34
    and social class, 34
    and socialism, 34
    and subsidiarity, 35
Quanta Cura, 96
Quod Apostolici Muneris, 20

Rawe, John C., 53, 207
Reece, Carrol, 164
Religion and the Rise of Capitalism, 45
Rerum Novarum, 1–3, 12, 14, 16–31, 34,
    43–44, 47–49, 55, 70, 80–81, 83,
    91, 99, 102, 106, 118, 121,
    125–26, 131–32, 145, 148, 156,
    163–64, 168–69, 175, 184, 199,
    225, 234, 238–41, 243
    and Church authority, 29–31
    and "just wages," 27–28
    and private property, 21–24, 26, 26 n. 27
    and social class, 23–26, 28
    and the state, 22, 24, 26–28
    and workers associations, 27–28
Reuther, Walter, 105, 212
Rice, Charles Owen, 116–17
right-to-work laws, 15, 139, 175–97, 199
"Roman Question, The," 19, 32, 96, 202–3
Roosevelt, Franklin D., 13, 87, 91, 98,
    144–45, 160, 164, 208, 210–11,
    215, 218, 234
Rosswurm, Steve, 100, 117, 122
Rural Life Bureau of the Social Action Department of the NCWC, 90
Rural Life in a Peaceful World, 59
Rural Life Prayerbook, 62
Rural Retreat Bureau of the NCRLC, 62
Rural Roads to Security, 53, 55, 207
Russian Catholics, 97
Russian Orthodox Church, 97
Ryan, John A., 5, 90–92, 101, 161,
    171–73, 181–82, 193, 204–5,
    208–9, 215, 229–30, 233
Ryan, William A., 122

Saint John's College (Cleveland, Ohio), 191
Saint John's University (Collegeville, Minn.), 161
Saint Louis University, 211
Saint Maria Della Cabeza, 63
Saint Martin's College (Washington), 181
Saint Mary of the Lake Seminary, 127
Saint Peter's College (New Jersey), 152, 195
Saint Thomas College (St. Paul, Minn.), 157
sanctification, 39
Saturday Evening Post, 145
Schackmann, J. H., 146
Schlarman, J. H., 63
Schmiesing, Kevin, 5–6, 5 n. 6
Schneider, Mary, 46
Schulder, Daniel J., 112, 124
Schuster, George, 72
Scully, Edward W., 102, 110
Seaton, Douglas P., 122
Sheen, Fulton, 98–99, 123
Sheen, John, 110
Sherman Antitrust Act, 166
Sign, The 151
Sillon movement, 71
Sisson, Elbert, 221–22
Smith, Jonathan Z., 16
Social Action Department (of the National Catholic Welfare Conference), 15,
    83, 89–95, 100–102, 104, 106,
    108, 140–41, 157–59, 182, 204,
    214–17, 221, 226, 230, 242–43
    and anti-communism, 95, 100–102
Social Gospel movement, 41, 162
Social Order 149, 151, 168
Social Principles and Economic Life, 104
Social Security, 143
    and farm workers, 67
socialism, 22–25, 33–34, 41, 53, 56 n. 61,
    71, 73, 76, 78, 86, 96, 96 n. 29,
    144, 165–69, 185, 201, 203, 229,
    238, 243
Sokolsky, George, 164
Southern Agrarians, 42–43, 46, 81
Soviet Union, 9, 33, 78, 88, 97–98, 118,
    144–46, 164, 176
Spalding, John Lancaster, 47
Spanish Civil War, 97–98
Spellman, Francis Cardinal, 98–99, 112
Stalin, Josef, 98
subsidiarity, principle of, 35–36, 46, 55,
    64, 69, 74, 80–81, 93–93, 123,

125, 129, 131, 134–35, 140, 151, 153–54, 170, 175–76, 182–83, 205–6, 211, 217, 234, 238, 241, 243
linkage with personalism, 74

Taft-Hartley Act, 88, 99–100, 135, 177–79, 186, 216
Tate, Allen, 42
Tawney, R. H., 45
tax policy, 65, 80, 169
Teamsters Union, 102, 179, 194
Time of Awakening, A, 136
"Tither's Creed," 58
Tocqueville, Alexis de, 84
Tolstoy, Leo, 75
Toner, Jerome, 181–82, 185–86, 190–91, 194–95
Trehey, Harold Francis, 205–9, 212, 233
Truth About Right-to-Work Laws: The Union Arguments, The People's Case, The, 176

umbrella myth, 12, 14, 17–18, 175
  defined, 12
Union-Management Production Committees. *See* labor-management committees
United Auto Workers, 109, 111, 179, 211
United Electrical Workers, 135
United Farm Workers, 56
United Mine Workers, 86, 99
United States Chamber of Commerce, 145
United Steelworkers, 100
U.S.A.: The Permanent Revolution, 149

Vatican II, 13, 137, 196, 237, 239–41
Vizzard, James, 68

vocational group order. *See* Industry Council Plan

Wage Earner, The (The Michigan Labor Leader), 109, 214
Wagner Act, 86, 88, 178, 216
Warner, Michael, 6–7, 6 n. 8
Warren, Robert Penn, 42
We Hold These Truths, 53, 207
Weber, Max, 45, 147
Weber, Orlando, 164
Weber, Paul, 109–10
Weber, Wilhelm, 36 n. 53
Weigel, George, 6 n. 9, 243
Wersing, Martin, 119
Wilson, Francis Graham, 155–57, 243
Wilson, Warren H., 41
women in Catholic ideology, 27, 35, 51–52, 60, 132
Work (magazine), 224
Worker's Educational Bureau of America, 107
World War I, 31, 90, 126, 210
World War II, 75, 87, 98, 108, 123, 127, 203, 210

Xavier Institute of Industrial Relations (Fordham University), 113

Yalta Conference, 98
Young Christian Students, 128
Young Christian Workers (YCW), 15, 83, 90, 125–41, 221, 242–43

Zotti, Mary, 136